英语专业实用翻译教材系列

廖益清 主编

English-Chinese Consecutive Interpreting

英汉交替传译

廖益清 高平 主编

中山大学出版社
· 广州 ·

版权所有　翻印必究

图书在版编目（CIP）数据

英汉交替传译/廖益清，高平主编. —广州：中山大学出版社，2019.9
（英语专业实用翻译教材系列/廖益清主编）
ISBN 978-7-306-06675-6

Ⅰ.①英…　Ⅱ.①廖…②高…　Ⅲ.①英语—口译—高等学校—教材　Ⅳ.①H315.9

中国版本图书馆 CIP 数据核字（2019）第 170051 号

Yinghan Jiaoti Chuanyi

出 版 人：	王天琪
策划编辑：	熊锡源
责任编辑：	熊锡源
封面设计：	林绵华
责任校对：	姜星宇
责任技编：	何雅涛
出版发行：	中山大学出版社
电　　话：	编辑部 020-84110771，84110283，84111997，84110779
	发行部 020-84111998，84111981，84111160
地　　址：	广州市新港西路 135 号
邮　　编：	510275　传　真：020-84036565
网　　址：	http://www.zsup.com.cn　E-mail：zdcbs@mail.sysu.edu.cn
印 刷 者：	广州市友盛彩印有限公司
规　　格：	787mm×1092mm　1/16　17 印张　362 千字
版次印次：	2019 年 9 月第 1 版　2019 年 9 月第 1 次印刷
定　　价：	45.00 元

如发现本书因印装质量影响阅读，请与出版社发行部联系调换

编写委员会

主　　编： 廖益清　高　平
副 主 编： 朱雪娇　欧衍伽　罗彩虹
编写人员： 桂　灵　刘家妠　鲁凯伦　陈悦笛　陈秋丽
　　　　　　梁昊文　黄越悦　姚　莹　肖岚心　龙　娟
　　　　　　周雪清

编写说明

随着中国经济持续、快速、健康地发展，中国与世界各国在各个领域的交流也更加密切，对口译的需求也越来越大。对于口译学习者而言，好的口译练习素材是提高口译能力的第一步。《英汉交替传译》借鉴了同类教材的优点，将口译理论与实践相结合，突出了自身口译素材的真实性、时代性特点，旨在为广大口译学习者提供最好的口译模拟实战体验。

教材特点

1. 科学性。教材吸收了口译最新理论研究成果，以深入浅出的方式讲解理论知识，并将理论与典型材料相结合，具有很强针对性。题材多样，均为真实口译场景中的常见主题。

2. 真实性。当前市面上的英汉口译教材所使用的材料基本都是经过修改和重新编排的，本教材则是编者在口译实战中的原版口译材料，讲话中会出现口误、模糊、停顿等现象，实操性更强，更能锻炼学生临场应变能力，让学生在使用教材时有身临其境之感。

3. 口音多样化。所使用的音频为口译现场的演讲录音，很多演讲嘉宾发音并不标准，会有各种英语口音，这在一定程度上增加了口译的难度，口译材料的真实感和实操性更强。

4. 时代性。所使用的实战材料均来自近年的口译实战，材料紧跟时代，如建设高科技园区和人工智能等，都是当前热门话题，教材实用性较强。

章节介绍

本书共包含3个部分、12个单元。第一部分为交传简介，共3个单元，每单元都包括交传简介、实战练习一和实战练习二。第二部分为交传技巧，共3个单元，每单元都包括交传技巧、实战练习一和实战练习二。第三部分为交传实战，共6个单元，每单元都包括实战练习一和实战练习二。所有的实战练习均为英译中，每篇演讲都由演讲背景、预习词汇、演讲文本3个部分组成。值得一提的是，本书以段落形式将演讲原文和译文对应起来，方便口译学习者在每一段的口译练习之后进行参考。各单元简介如下：

第一单元介绍了译员素养，包括深厚的语言功底、广博的知识、扎实的口译技能、良好的心理素质和良好的职业道德。实战练习一为西班牙工业技术发展中心（CDTI）的驻华代表在"建设世界一流高科技园区国际会议"上发表的主旨演讲。

实战练习二为新上任的以色列驻华大使在"创建世界一流高科技园区国际论坛"上发表的演讲。

第二单元介绍了译前准备,包括口译任务背景准备和主题内容准备。实战练习一为四季酒店 CEO 在召开广州四季酒店员工大会时对大会中提到的两个问题的回答。实战练习二为其对大会中提到的另外两个问题的回答。

第三单元介绍了公共演讲技巧,讲解如何从体态语言和口头语言两方面提高演讲技巧。实战练习一为广州南方国际学校的校长在"2017 必达亚洲春季峰会"上所做的主题为"户外教室的设施设计"的演讲。实战练习二为深圳贝赛思国际学校副总裁在同一会议上所做的主题为"从所有利益相关者的角度考虑来设计学校"的主旨演讲。

第四单元介绍了短期记忆,讲解了记忆机制和短期记忆的训练方法。实战练习一为英国驻广州总领事馆商务领事在"广交会(英国)国际市场论坛"上的开幕致辞。实战练习二为德国工商大会和德国联邦外贸与投资署的代表在"中欧企业投资合作峰会"上发表的主旨演讲。

第五单元介绍了口译笔记,讲解了口译笔记的必要性、特点、记录的内容、排版等。实战练习一为西澳大利亚州五大区之一的珀斯区旅游局 CEO 发表的演讲。实战练习二为"2012 西澳大利亚州旅游局中国旅游洽谈会"上 Esplanade 酒店集团的代表发表的演讲。

第六单元介绍了数字口译,讲解了数字口译的基本方法及对数字与信息结合的处理。实战练习一为全球前四大市场研究公司之一的 GfK 捷孚凯公司的家电部全球大客户副总裁在"2015 年广交会系列论坛——中国电子家电品牌与创新高峰论坛"上发表的主旨演讲。实战练习二为国际锰协 IMnI 市场分析师在"电解产品市场高峰论坛"上发表的主旨演讲。

在第七单元中,实战练习一为在线时尚潮流预测公司 Fashion Snoops 的亚太区总监在"广交会设计潮流趋势研讨会"上关于第一个主题内容"平静之心"的演讲。实战练习二为其在该会上关于第二个时尚潮流趋势"都市丽影"的演讲。

在第八单元中,实战练习一为皇家大律师 Jeremy 在由香港仲裁事务所举办的"国际仲裁峰会"上发表的主旨演讲。实战练习二为皇家大律师 Nicholas 在该会上发表的主旨演讲。

在第九单元中,实战练习一为中东 ASI(Amusement Services International)国际娱乐公司的代表在"全球室内游乐场商业运营模式高峰论坛"上发表的演讲。实战练习二为紫水鸟影视的制片主任在"东莞动漫展高峰会"上发表的主旨演讲。

在第十单元中,实战练习一为比利时 LTB 建筑事务所的建筑师在"比利时中国绿色建筑经验分享会"上发表的主旨演讲。实战练习二为奥雅纳董事在"敢创设·界亚太设计论坛"上发表的主旨演讲。

在第十一单元中,实战练习一为英国出版商协会代表在"广东版权保护大会"

上演讲的第一部分。实战练习二为英国出版商协会代表在"广东版权保护大会"上演讲的第二部分。

在第十二单元中，实战练习一为日本发明家、机器人大师高桥智隆在主题为"人工智能"的"腾讯智慧峰会"上发表的主旨演讲。实战练习二为尼尔森公司的代表在该会上发表的主旨演讲。

使用对象

本书是本科英语专业或翻译专业学生的英汉口译教材，也可作为选修、辅修英语专业或翻译专业学生的英汉口译教材，同时可以作为有志于提高英汉口译实践能力爱好者的自学教材。

结语

本书在理论编写过程中，参考了交替传译的最新研究成果，所参对象均在教材最后标明出处。如有不当之处，敬请原谅。本书使用的实战练习均为国际会议材料，音频为会议现场录音，非常感谢演讲嘉宾和会议主办方的支持。

由于编写时间有限，本书难免存在纰漏，请各位读者和专家指正。

编　者

2018 年 10 月

目　　录

第一部分　交传简介 ... 1
第一单元　研发合作 R&D Cooperation ... 2
- I. 译员素养 ... 2
- II. 实战练习一 ... 3
- III. 实战练习二 ... 18

第二单元　酒店管理 Hotel Management ... 24
- I. 译前准备 ... 24
- II. 实战练习一 ... 25
- III. 实战练习二 ... 29

第三单元　文化教育 Culture and Education ... 36
- I. 公共演讲技巧 ... 36
- II. 实战练习一 ... 37
- III. 实战练习二 ... 51

第二部分　交传技巧 ... 69
第四单元　经贸合作 Economic Cooperation ... 70
- I. 短期记忆 ... 70
- II. 实战练习一 ... 71
- III. 实战练习二 ... 79

第五单元　观光旅游 Tourism ... 88
- I. 口译笔记 ... 88
- II. 实战练习一 ... 90
- III. 实战练习二 ... 95

第六单元　行业介绍 Introduction to Industries ... 101
- I. 数字口译 ... 101
- II. 实战练习一 ... 102
- III. 实战练习二 ... 116

第三部分　交传实战 ... 133
第七单元　时尚潮流 Fashion Trend ... 134
- I. 实战练习一 ... 134

II. 实战练习二 ·· 141

第八单元　国际仲裁 International Arbitration ·················· 149
　　I. 实战练习一 ·· 149
　　II. 实战练习二 ·· 156

第九单元　动漫娱乐 Animation and Entertainment ·············· 163
　　I. 实战练习一 ·· 163
　　II. 实战练习二 ·· 186

第十单元　绿色建筑 Green Building ····························· 202
　　I. 实战练习一 ·· 202
　　II. 实战练习二 ·· 212

第十一单元　知识产权 Intellectual Property Rights ·············· 222
　　I. 实战练习一 ·· 222
　　II. 实战练习二 ·· 232

第十二单元　人工智能 Artificial Intelligence ···················· 241
　　I. 实战练习一 ·· 241
　　II. 实战练习二 ·· 252

参考文献 ·· 259

第一部分　交传简介

第一单元　研发合作
R&D Cooperation

I. 译员素养

口译涉及至少两种语言之间的文化交流，"是集知识与技能、脑力与体力为一体的工作"（雷天放、陈菁，2013：230），因此对口译员的综合素质要求很高。一名合格的口译员应具备深厚的语言功底、广博的知识、扎实的口译技能、良好的心理素质和职业道德。

1. 深厚的语言功底

一名合格的译员必须双语基本功扎实，能够规范地使用两种语言并流畅地进行双语转换。其次，译员应具有非常熟练的听解能力，不仅能听解发音标准的演讲，还要能听解具有浓重地方口音的演讲，比如南亚地区人讲的英语。此外，译员还要熟悉两种语言的文化背景知识。

2. 广博的知识

译员在口译实战中会遇到各种主题的讲话，包括计算机、医学、生物、法律等，不可避免会碰到较为专业的知识。如果译员平时了解某些主题，掌握较多的相关知识，在口译活动中碰到此类主题，翻译起来就会游刃有余。

3. 扎实的口译技能

在口译实践中，译员需要能够熟练运用口译技能，包括短期记忆、笔记、数字、公共演讲、译前准备等，这些技巧在前面的单元都有介绍和进行针对性的训练。

4. 良好的心理素质

口译是极具挑战性的工作，因此许多口译学习者在练习口译或者在初次接触口译任务时，通常会紧张胆怯。口译学习者需要通过大量的口译训练、自我情绪控制和不断积累实践经验来克服怯场紧张的情绪，做到镇定自若。

5. 良好的职业道德

目前许多口译机构都制定了各自的口译职业道德准则，《国际会议口译工作者

第一单元 研发合作 R&D Cooperation

协会关于职业道德准则的规定》是口译界普遍认同的准则。一名合格的口译员应当能够保证口译质量，能较为准确、清楚地表述发言人的信息；口译员应保持中立性，不对发言人和发言内容做任何评论；应认真负责，一旦承担了口译任务，就应全力以赴，以最饱满的精神状态完成口译任务。

II. 实战练习一

1. 演讲背景

西班牙工业技术发展中心（CDTI）的驻华代表应邀参加"建设世界一流高科技园区国际会议"并发表主旨演讲。他在演讲中介绍了西班牙的研发体系、领先的技术领域。此外，他还详细介绍了 CDTI 的使命是提高西班牙企业的技术水平，为他们提供资金、软贷款、补助金和补贴，并通过中西卡项目，为中国企业寻找合适、可靠的西班牙技术合作伙伴，最后还分享了两个中西卡项目的例子。

2. 预习词汇

Torch 火炬计划；火炬中心
Shenzhen High-tech Industrial Park 深圳高新技术产业园
CDTI 西班牙工业技术发展中心
CHINEKA 中西卡项目
R&D System 研发体系
SME（small-and-medium-sized enterprise）中小企业
Industry 4.0 工业 4.0
Barcelona 巴塞罗那
graphene 石墨烯
Ministry of Economy 经济部
Chinese entity 中国实体
biotechnology 生物技术
Smart City 智慧城市
spin-off 副产品；衍生品
health protocol 健康协议
medical care 医疗服务

3. 演讲文本

00:00—00:50
Good morning everyone. 对不起，我不会说中文，所以我说英语。对不起。

3

First of all, I would like to thank you, the organizers. I would like to thank you, Torch, the Shenzhen municipality, and of course Shenzhen High-tech Industrial Park, and the Shenzhen Science and Technology Business Platform for inviting me to be here. I'm going to talk to you about the Spanish R&D System and I'm going to talk to you about what we are doing here in China. So I hope you can find some fruitful information for the companies that are based in your high-end technology parks.

早上好，各位。Sorry, I can't speak Chinese, so I will use English, sorry. 首先，感谢主办方，感谢火炬计划，感谢深圳市，当然，还要感谢深圳高新技术产业园以及深圳科技商务平台，感谢你们的邀请。接下来我会讲讲西班牙的研发体系及我们在中国做的事情，希望能为高科技园区的公司提供一些有用的信息。

00:57—01:43

It's OK. It's OK. 没问题，谢谢。OK. So these are the lines of things I'm going to talk. First, I will be very brief, I don't want to bore you. I will speak about the Spanish R&D system, so in that way you can understand what is CDTI. CDTI is the Spanish innovation agency. It's the institution I work for. And then I will speak to you about what mechanisms for funding for our companies. We have to foster our companies to do international collaboration, especially with China. That's the reason I'm here for. You will find things that we are trying to do for helping the Spanish companies to do things with the Chinese companies, with the companies that are at your technology parks. And we will do this through our program CHINEKA.

没关系。没关系。It's OK, thank you. 好的，这是我要讲的内容。首先，我会尽量简洁，我不想让大家觉得厌烦。我会讲一讲西班牙的研发系统，这样你们能更好地了解什么是 CDTI。CDTI，西班牙工业技术发展中心，是西班牙的创新中心，我现在就在这个中心工作。接着我给你们介绍一下 CDTI 为西班牙企业提供的融资机制。我们鼓励西班牙企业进行国际合作，尤其是与中国合作。这也是我来这儿的原因。你们会发现我们中心一直致力于帮助西班牙企业与中国科技园区的企业开展合作。我们通过中西卡项目来做这件事。

01:45—03:08

So in the year 2011 and due to the economic crisis, the Spanish government decided to put all the Spanish R&D system under the Ministry of Economy. The idea to do this was trying to foster the Spanish technology companies to do bigger collaborations with the universities and the private R&D centers. So the idea was to have a system that at the end what we are trying to do is that, my Russian colleague once mentioned it before, was trying to, of course, starting doing a basic R&D, to apply R&D, but at the end what

第一单元　研发合作 R&D Cooperation

we have to try to look for in the long term is to develop technology products and to help the companies to access to the market with these technology products. Because if the companies do not access to the market, basic R&D is great, a private R&D is great, but at the end there is no utility for the society. This, the things that we develop has to reach the society. And to reach the society to help the companies to access to the market with the technology product, technology process or technology service to the market is a way of bringing back the society to the efforts they do, to develop R&D.

因此在2011年，由于经济危机，西班牙政府决定由经济部主管西班牙所有的研发体系。目的是为了促进西班牙的科技企业与高校、私人研发中心的合作。所以就像我的俄罗斯同行刚刚提到的那样，最开始我们试图进行基础研发，应用研发成果，但最终我们出于长远考虑，开发技术产品，帮助企业把产品推向市场。因为如果这些公司无法进入市场，基础研发再好，私人研发再好，最终这些研发对社会也起不了作用。我们认为开发出的产品应该流通到社会上去，帮助公司把技术产品、技术流程和技术服务推向市场，这也是利用社会能力助推科研发展的一种方式。

03:13—03:28

So, here you have some numbers, but at the basic what we are trying to do is having the science & technology park between the academia, universities and between the companies, so they are playing an important role in the Spanish system, I guess that also here in China.

这里你们可以看到一些数字，但我们做的最基本的事情就是促进科技园区实现产学研一体化，因此学术界、高校和企业在西班牙的研发体系中扮演着重要的角色，我想在中国也是如此。

03:29—04:54

But I want to talk to you also about three important things. They are the technology centers. I don't know if you have here in China something like this. I'm talking here about private technology centers. One thing that happens in Spain is that a lot of knowledge, a lot of technology is under the shadows in the hands of big and small and medium companies. I'm talking about companies that are 10 employees, 20 employees, 50 employees, companies like that. We have a lot of technology and a lot of knowledge, but the problem is that their size is small, so they don't, they cannot have big facilities. They cannot have big labs. They cannot have big clean rooms. And they cannot have dedicated teams to do technology measurements. So for that, that is the way that in Spain planned these technology centers that I was sent in lots of cases, they are private. That means that lots of companies, for example, I'm thinking about in the case of INIA, a biotechnology center in Valencia, the east of Spain. And they have like 700 SMEs that are associated with the fees they pay these technology centers. And these technology centers that are linked to the technology park do a lot of services and a lot of work for these technology companies. So in this way, the SMEs that are based in the technology parks share the burden of having these facilities.

但我还想和大家谈谈三件重要的事情。首先是技术中心。我不知道中国有没有类似的技术中心，我所说的是私人技术中心。在西班牙，大量的知识和技术掌握在中小企业手中。我说的中小企业是指有10名，20名，50名员工的企业。这些企业掌握大量的技术、知识，但问题是，这些企业规模小，因此他们没有，也无力购买大型设施，没有大型实验室，没有大的洁净室，也没有专门的团队做技术测量。因此，西班牙规划的这些技术中心就是这样的。我在很多情况下被派往这些技术中心，它们是私人的。例如，INIA是一个生物技术中心，位于西班牙东部的瓦伦西亚。他们大概有700个中小型企业，中小企业的数量与其支付给技术中心的费用紧密相关。这些技术中心与科技园区对接，为园区里的科技公司提供了大量的服务，做了大量的工作。位于科技园区的中小企业通过这种方式分担了设施的费用。

04:58—05:46

OK. This is about the facilities. This is another slide I want to focus a lot. What happens in Spain? Probably if I ask you, if I ask the audience about which are the technology countries in Europe? None of you would mention Spain. Probably you will mention Germany. Some of you will mention Sweden or Finland, maybe some of you will mention France or UK, but none of you will mention Spain. Because we are not in the top rank of the innovation list. I think we are about the 10th position or 12th position or something like that. But Spain is very well-positioned in some specific areas that I would like to mention to you, because some of them are very interesting for China and I want you to have this in mind. Because I think that's very important.

好的。下面讲一讲设施。这张PPT我也想重点讲一下。西班牙发生了什么？如果我问你，欧洲哪些国家是科技大国，你们不会提到西班牙。也许大家会提到德国，提到瑞典或芬兰，提到法国或英国，但谁也不会提到西班牙，因为我们不在创新名单的前列，我们大概排在第10位或者第12位。但是西班牙在一些特定的领域排名很前。我想告诉你们这些领域，因为中国对其中的某些领域很感兴趣，希望你们记住这一点，因为我认为这很重要。

05:46—07:13

For example, Spain is very strong in Industry 4.0 that I think it's something very important for China now. It is strongly linked with "Made in China 2025". And Spain is

第一单元　研发合作 R&D Cooperation

the second country in Europe behind Germany doing projects related with Industry 4.0. Spain is also very important, for example, in the Smart Cities. Barcelona is considered like the strongest Smart City in Europe, and one of the strongest Smart Cities in the world. Now we are doing a lot of projects regarding the Smart Cities. We are very strong, also for example, in the field of new material. New material is also a very interesting field for China, and you are doing a lot of things for example, developing new material like graphene. China is one of the countries with more research done in graphene and Spain is the country in Europe with most companies doing graphene research in Spain and with good quality of production of graphene. And apart from that, we can talk about biotechnology, we can talk about medicine, and we can talk something very important, that is agriculture and food safety, for example. Spain is the strongest country in Europe about food safety, for example. So when you think about technology, don't think about Germany or Sweden. Remember that in some fields, Spain could be very interesting for the companies that are based in your science and technology parks.

例如，西班牙的工业4.0非常强，我认为目前工业4.0对中国而言非常重要，它与"中国制造2025"紧密相连。在工业4.0项目方面，西班牙仅次于德国，居欧洲第二位。此外，西班牙在智慧城市方面也非常出色。巴塞罗那被认为是欧洲最强大的智慧城市，也是全球最强大的智慧城市之一。现在我们在做很多与智慧城市有关的项目。我们在新材料领域也很强大。中国非常关注新材料，在开发新材料方面，比如开发石墨烯，付出了巨大努力。中国是在石墨烯领域研究最多的国家之一，西班牙是拥有石墨烯研究公司最多的欧洲国家，西班牙产的石墨烯质量很好。此外，再说说生物技术、医学以及其他一些非常重要的领域，比如农业和食品安全。西班牙是欧洲食品安全技术最先进的国家。因此，提到技术时，不要只想到德国或瑞典。对于你们科技园区的公司而言，在某些领域，西班牙是更好的选择。

07:16—08:27

OK, CDTI. CDTI is an institution that belongs to the Ministry of Economy, as I said. And we have only one mandate from the government of Spain. Only one mandate, that's very simple. We have to do our best to try to increase the technology level of the Spanish company. OK. It's one mandate, but it's not a simple one. So we are working since the year 1977, so it's going to be 40 years now. Since the year 2011, we were designated as the Spanish innovation agency. But one thing very important. We are funding agency. We are an agency that provides funds to the companies. I think that is the essential difference with other innovation agency. Because that makes us the focal point of technology in Spain. What does that mean? That anything that is done in Spain related to technology goes to CDTI. Why? Because we have the funding. In Europe, it's, I don't know in China, but in Europe, the culture for R&D says that the companies that want to R&D normally ask for the financial support of the government.

好的,回到CDTI。我刚刚说过CDTI隶属于经济部。西班牙政府赋予我们一个使命,也是唯一的使命,就是我们要努力提高西班牙企业的技术水平。虽然只有这一个使命,但并不简单。CDTI从1977年创立以来,到现在已经40年了。自2011年以来,我们被认为是西班牙创新中心。有一点非常重要,那就是我们是一家资助机构,为公司提供资金。我认为这是我们与其他创新机构的本质区别,这也是为什么我们成为了西班牙技术的焦点。什么意思呢?西班牙任何与技术相关的事情都由CDTI负责。为什么?因为我们有资金。我不知道在中国是何种情况,但在欧洲,想要开展研发的公司通常会寻求政府的财政支持。

08:28—09:38

OK, this is our situation. We belong to the Ministry of Economy, and our Chairman is the Vice Minister of R&D in Spain. Funding. This meeting is about funding, so I would give you some, a couple of examples of what we do to do international collaboration with China that could be of interest of some of the companies that are at your science and technology park. This slide is very interesting. It gives you an idea of the level of activity of CDTI. But those for me, it's also very interesting because you know the economic crisis started in Europe in the year 2008 in Spain, but you can see that in spite of the economic crisis started in the year of 2008, the R&D activity remained very high through the years of the crisis. For me, that represents that technology companies, for the companies who have technologies, it's very important, because they can support better than companies that do not have technology from economic crisis.

我们的情况是这样的,我们隶属于经济部,中心主席是西班牙的研发部副部长。资金问题。这次会议主题是资金,所以我会举例子来说明我们如何与中国开展国际合作,可能你们科技园区的一些公司会对此感兴趣。这一页幻灯片很有趣。通过这些例子,相信你们会对CDTI的活动有初步了解。大家知道2008年欧洲爆发的经济危机始于西班牙,但是你们可以看到,尽管2008年开始有经济危机,西班牙随后这些年的研发仍然很活跃。我认为这表明科技公司至关重要,他们比无技术支持的公司更能从经济危机中挺过来。

09:38—10:36

This slide is also important, because here we can see that we are recovering from the economic crisis in Spain. We don't have the latest data but I can guarantee you that in the year 2016, we are around 1,600 projects, more or less the level that we were in

第一单元　研发合作 R&D Cooperation

2009, and we are going to provide more than 1,100 million Euros, that is more, about 8 billion RMB of funding this year. That's very important. In Spain the GDP now is growing at 3.2%. Compared to China, it's the middle, but compared to Europe, you must know that Spain now is the country in Europe that is growing faster. We are growing at the double of the average in Europe, and we are growing four times the speed that France or Italy are growing these days.

这一页幻灯片也很重要，因为大家可以看到，西班牙正从经济危机中复苏。虽然没有最新的相关数据，但我敢肯定2016年，我们有大约1,600个项目，基本上恢复到了2009年的水平。今年，我们将在这上面投入11亿多欧元，人民币约为80亿。资金投入很重要。西班牙GDP增速为3.2%。与中国相比，增速不算快，但与欧洲其他国家相比，西班牙的GDP增速非常快。我们的增速是欧洲平均水平的两倍，是目前法国和意大利增速的四倍。

10:39—12:07

This is the same data but we have also this red part. This red part represents the funding of CDTI in international organization. What does that mean? That means because CDTI is the Spanish innovation agency. And we work for the government, we represent the government of Spain in the international organization like for example, in Geneva, or like for example the European Aerospace Agency, or for example in Horizon 2020. I don't know if you know Horizon 2020. That is the biggest R&D program in Europe. It's the program that is done at the European level. But also very important for you, Horizon 2020 is open to third countries. It's open to the participation of Chinese companies. And since last year, the Chinese government agreed with European government to have a co-funding mechanism for the participation of Chinese entities in Horizon 2020. OK, so CDTI is the one that is representing Spain in that program. So if you have companies, or you have entities, or you have universities that are interested in working in Horizon 2020. And they don't know how to look for a consociation to present a bit in Horizon 2020. You get in contact with me, and I will get in contact with my headquarters, and we will try to find the most suitable consociation for your companies. OK?

这个数据是一样的，我们看一下红色的部分。这个红色部分是国际组织中CDTI投入的资金数额。这意味着什么？CDTI是西班牙的创新中心。我们为政府工作，我们是西班牙政府在国际组织上的代表，就像日内瓦的组织，像欧洲航空航天机构，像"地平线2020"项目。不知道大家是否知道"地平线2020"项目，这是欧洲最大的研发项目，是欧洲层面的一个项目。但对大家来说也很重要，"地平线2020"项目对第三国开放，对中国公司开放。去年，中国政府与欧洲政府达成协议，将为中国企业提供一个共同融资机制，参与"地平线2020"项目。因此CDTI

9

代表西班牙引入项目,所以如果有公司、实体、高校对"地平线2020"项目感兴趣,但不知道如何寻求合作,可以与我联系,我将与总部取得联系,努力为这些公司找到最合适的合作方式。好吗?

12:12—13:05

This is also another way of seeing our relevant activity. I will summarize these two main measures in this slide. What I was saying, a lot of companies, a lot of technology companies in Spain is small and medium enterprise companies. That is very important because those companies are the one that needs the support of the government and the support of the technology parks, because they don't have the strength by their own. And another important thing is the number of companies that work for CDTI every year. That means what I was telling you. This means that in the last 10 years, CDTI has been working with more than 12,000 companies in Spain. You know the way of talking. If there is a technology company in Spain, it works for CDTI or it's not a technology company. Simple as that. So if you're looking for a technology company, you can contact us.

这是另一种了解我们活动的方式。在这张幻灯片中我总结了两项最主要的措施。我想说的是,很多西班牙的科技公司都是中小企业,这些企业需要政府和技术园区的支持,因为他们自己没有相应的实力。另外,需要注意的是,每年为CDTI服务的公司数量,也就是说在过去10年里,CDTI与12,000多家西班牙公司合作。换句话说,凡是西班牙的科技公司,都为CDTI服务,就这么简单。所以,如果您在寻找西班牙科技公司,可以联系我。

13:09—14:13

So funding, what we do. I'll give you a couple of examples of what we do to promote Spanish companies, to foster Spanish companies to do technology and to promote them to work with China. This is one of the things that we have to do for funding and program with China, we provide soft loans for the companies. But the most important thing is that if these companies work with China, the Spanish companies of course I'm talking about, we give them a 30% of non-repayable part. What that means? That means that every 100 RMB that I give to the Spanish companies to do R&D with China, they only have to pay me back 70 RMB. 30 RMB of every 100 I give them, then to you, they don't have to pay me back for that. That is an incentive that we have for the Spanish companies to work for, with China. And these are very soft loans and all the example that what we are doing.

再说融资,这是我们致力做的事情。我举几个例子说明我们如何促进西班牙公司的发展，如何鼓励西班牙公司开发技术，如何促进他们与中国合作。这是我们为中国提供资金和项目所做的努力之一，我们为这些西班牙公司提供软贷款。最重要的是如果这些公司与中国合作，我指的是西班牙的公司，我们给他们提供的资金中30%免偿。这意味着什么呢？这意味着我们每借给这些与中国合作的西班牙公司100元，他们只需要还70元。我们每给他们的100元，因为与你们合作，他们就有30元不用偿还。这就是我们对西班牙企业与中国企业合作的一项激励措施。这就是我们现在提供的软贷款和我们现在做的事情。

14:19—15:27

Subsidy. This started last year. And also this is another tool that we have for the Spanish companies to work with China. What we provide here is grants, subsidies. The level of the grant that we provide depends on the level of the size of the company. If it's small company, we provide 50% of the project in the formal process of subsidy. If it's a large company, only 30% of course. And for the companies, the Spanish companies to have the opportunity to ask for this subsidy, they must do an international program. So if they do a project with China, then they have the opportunity to access to this subsidy. So this is the kind of things that we are giving the Spanish companies to encourage them to come to China and to work with the companies that you have in your technology park. The important things for your companies because you would say, OK, those are Spanish fund raising, the Chinese companies cannot access to them, of course. The Chinese companies, they want to access to fund. They must go to our nice spokesperson today Mr. Motan. And they will explain them what those can do with them.

再就是补贴。我们从去年开始做补贴，这也是我们为西班牙公司与中国合作提供的另一项支持。我们提供的是补助金，补贴。补助金的数额取决于公司的规模。对于小公司，我们通常提供50%的补贴。大公司，提供30%的补贴。西班牙公司必须有国际项目才有机会申请这种补贴。因此，如果他们与中国合作，那么他们就有机会申请这项补贴。这就是我们为鼓励西班牙公司到中国来，和中国科技园区公司合作所采取的举措。你们会认为这些是西班牙企业筹集的资金。当然，中国企业无法拿到这笔资金，但如果你们想要获得资金支持，可以联系一下我们的发言人Motan先生。他会解释这些措施能为中国公司带来什么。

15:27—16:14

But behind them, what CDTI offers to the Chinese companies, we offer to you three very important things. First, as I was telling you, all the Spanish technology companies work with us. So that means that if there is any technology company in one of your science and technology parks that is thinking to start working at international level, and they are thinking to start working with Europe, remember that there are some technology fields where Spain is very strong, biotechnology, new material, industry 4.0, Smart Cities. So maybe you can think. OK, maybe you can try with Spain, try something different, don't work with Germany. Don't go to UK. Go through with Spain because I heard that they are very strong in this field.

但在这背后，CDTI能为中国的公司提供什么？CDTI提供了三个非常重要的服务。首先，正如我刚刚所说，所有的西班牙科技公司都在和我们中心合作。这意味着如果你们的科技公司想要走出去，考虑与欧洲合作，那么请记住西班牙在一些技术领域居领先地位，比如生物技术、新材料、工业4.0、智慧城市。所以也许你们可以尝试和西班牙合作，尝试不同的东西。不要只和德国或英国合作。尝试和西班牙一起合作，因为我们在某些领域处于领先地位。

16:14—17:28

OK, so where do we start? I have to find a technology partner. OK, I will help you and I will help your companies to find a technology partner, the most suitable technology partner in Spain that matches better with your companies. I will try to help you to find the technology partner. And if we find the technology partner and we provide the funding. What does that means for the Chinese companies? That mean that CDTI will make a very deep and thorough evaluation of the Spanish company, so we will guarantee to your companies that the Spanish company that could collaborate with them will have a solid technology background and will have the financial capacity to do the project and to finalize the project. So I think that when we are talking about international collaboration, that I think that those are very good guarantees for your companies, because before starting the project when you are working without that kind of support, you would never know that your partner OK looks OK. I have visited the company. It looks nice. It has labs. But at the end, what's under there? OK, the Spanish government through this program we guarantee you that that is a serious company.

那么我们从何处着手呢？首先，找到技术合作伙伴。我们中心可以帮助你们，帮助你们找到最适合你们的西班牙技术合作伙伴，我们将竭尽全力。找到了技术合作伙伴后，我们会提供资金。这对中国公司意味着什么？这意味着CDTI会深入、全面地评估这个西班牙合作伙伴。因此，我们可以保证与你们合作的西班牙公司有坚实的技术背景，有开展和完成项目的经济实力。当我们谈论国际合作时，我认为这些措施对你们公司而言是非常好的保障，因为在开始项目之前，如果我们不提供这样的支持，你们永远不会知道你们的合作伙伴到底怎么样，是否只是看起来不错。你们会说我去过那家公司，看起来不错，因为它有实验室。但最后，最重要的是公司到底有什么能耐。通过这个项目，西班牙政府可以保证为你们寻求的合作伙

第一单元　研发合作 R&D Cooperation

伴是认真可靠的。

17:29—18:12

Let's focus in CHINEKA. CHINEKA is a bilateral program that we have with China. Of course, Spain works at European level, as I was mentioned. We have a good participation in Horizon 2020 that I mentioned to you before. Of course, we work because of historical reasons, we work a lot [of] in even America. For sure, Spain is very present over there. But we do recognize that Asia is very important nowadays. And on [in] Asia we recognized that China is monumental. If you are a European country, you want to do things in the world today that means that you have to do things with China.

我们重点看一下中西卡项目，这是我们在中国开展的一个双边项目。当然，正如我所提到的，西班牙在欧洲层面上开展活动。我们充分参与了我之前提到过的"地平线 2020"项目。由于历史原因，我们甚至在美国也开展了很多项目。西班牙在那里开展了很多活动。但我们现在认识到了亚洲的重要性。在亚洲，中国的地位举足轻重。欧洲国家若想在国际上有所作为，必须与中国合作。

18:14—19:41

So we came here in the year 2002. So we are not newcomers, and we opened our office in Shanghai, and we start working with our colleagues from Torch from the Ministry of Science and Technology of China. They are based in Beijing, but I fly quite often. I visit my friends in Beijing quite often. And as I was telling you, I'm here to act as a bridge between the Spanish companies, between the Chinese authorities, and between the Chinese companies and between you. I mean I am here to try to foster the collaboration with Spain and China at technology and innovation level. So you have any need regarding technology and innovation and it could involve Spain, that's my job to try to help you. So we started in 2002 and in the year 2006 we started with the CHINEKA project that I mentioned before. And I will show you the numbers later on. And also another kind of things that we do for trying to have the opportunity to the Chinese companies to have a better knowledge of the Spanish companies, from time to time, we organize technology forum between China and Spain, we do Torch-CDTI. Normally several years, every two years, no longer than two years. The last one was yesterday by the way. It was in Barcelona, and it was focused on Smart Cities. So I guess the new one, the next one will be in China. Maybe next year, we have to discuss about which would be the model.

我们 2002 年进驻中国。因此，我们不算新机构了，我们在上海有办事处，我

13

们与来自中国科技部火炬计划的同事们合作。火炬计划中心在北京，我经常飞北京，经常去拜访北京的朋友。正如我刚刚提到的，我在西班牙公司和中国政府，西班牙公司和中国公司之间起着桥梁作用。我的意思是，我致力于促进西班牙和中国在技术和创新方面的合作。所以如果你们有任何与西班牙有关的技术和创新需求，都可以联系我。我们2002年来到中国，2006年我们启动了中西卡项目，稍后我会给你们看些数据。此外，我们也在为中国公司创造机会去更好地了解西班牙公司。我们偶尔组织中国和西班牙技术论坛，比如火炬计划与CDTI联合举办的论坛。通常两年举办一次。顺便说一下，最近的一次论坛昨天开幕了，在巴塞罗那举行，这次论坛的主题是智慧城市。所以我想下一次论坛将在中国举行，也许是明年，我们到时候先讨论一下再决定。

19:44—21:13

So how does CHINEKA work? As I was telling you, CHINEKA, the basic idea was telling you the only opportunity for CDTI to increase the technology level for the Spanish company. OK. Very basic, very difficult. The only goal of CHINEKA is to have technology development, of course, but this, in this case between Spain and China, we should have one Spanish company and one Chinese entity, as simple as that. As we have one Spanish company and one Chinese entity that want to develop technology together, we have a potential CHINEKA. Of course as we are talking to develop technology by the companies, for the companies, we want the companies to develop new product, new process, new service. We want them to access to the market. We want them to develop something useful. We want to help the companies to increase their competitiveness. But when we talk the market, I'm not talking here about the Chinese market. We are not here just to take all the Chinese market. I'm talking here about the world market. I mean the Chinese companies and the Spanish companies can develop something to sell it here in China, but they can develop something to sell it in Europe, or they can develop something to sell it in Brazil, in Latin America. Why not? Nowadays, the world is very small, and it's only one market, so what we want them is to develop something for the market. We don't care about which market, but they want to, they have to develop something for the market.

那么中西卡是如何运作的呢？我刚刚提到，中西卡项目的基本设想是，中西卡是CDTI提高西班牙公司技术水平的唯一机会。很重要，但却很困难。中西卡的唯一目标是技术开发，当然，现在这种情况下，是西班牙和中国共同开发。要达到这个目的，我们需要一家西班牙公司和一家中国实体公司，就这么简单。这家西班牙公司和中国实体公司想要共同开发技术，那么这就是一个潜在的中西卡项目。当然，我们说的是公司开发技术，我们希望公司开发新产品、新流程，提供新服务。

我们希望公司进入市场，开发出有用的产品，希望帮助这些公司提高竞争力。这里提到的市场，不仅仅指中国市场。我们来这里不是为了拿下整个中国市场。这里指的是整个国际市场。我的意思是，中国公司和西班牙公司开发产品可以在中国市场销售，也可以开发产品在欧洲、巴西、拉丁美洲市场销售。为什么不呢？如今世界越来越小，全球只有一个市场，我们希望中国和西班牙公司可以开发在国际市场上销售的产品。我们不在乎具体是哪个市场，只希望能够开发出市场需要的产品。

21:13—22:13

As a technology program that is sought for the companies, we are open to the world here. We don't have cause. We don't ask the people, you have to develop this kind of technology in biotech, or in health or medicine or things like that. Because the companies know better than I what they need to develop to be competitive. The companies know better than I which are the strongest points of their competition and which are the weak points of themselves. So they know better than I what they have to develop, so that's why we don't tell the companies what they have to develop. They have to come to us with the most difficult part of this. That is the idea. The company must have the idea. So once they have the idea, we will be happy to fund their idea, but they must have the idea. And what I was saying, we provide the CHINEKA level. That is a way of supporting them and it's a way of guaranteeing them that the Chinese government and the Spanish government is supporting all of these. Of course the centralized funding, we can show you this here.

中西卡技术项目寻求合作公司，在中国开拓市场。我们没有其他要求，不会要求你们必须在生物技术、健康、医学或者其他特定领域开发某项技术。因为我们相信公司自身最清楚需要什么来提升自己的竞争力。公司自己最清楚竞争对手的强项是什么，自己的弱项又是什么。他们最清楚要开发什么，因此我们不要求公司必须开发什么产品。公司要带着最具挑战性的问题来找我们合作，也就是要有创意。一家公司必须有创意。一旦有了创意，我们会很乐意为他们提供资金。前提是他们必须有创意。我们提供中西卡项目支持这些公司，也能保证中国政府和西班牙政府也提供支持。这里就是集中性的资助。

22:14—23:06

This means that once they have their idea and the company comes with the idea, it doesn't mean, it doesn't matter if the original idea comes from Spain, or it doesn't matter if the original idea comes from China or from the both of them. The important thing is that we must gather the Spanish company and a Chinese entity, there must be an idea, and they must be willing to collaborate together. If they are willing to collaborate together, we have a potential CHINEKA, we do the international evaluation together between Torch and CDTI. And then the funding, CDTI will guarantee the Spanish funding. And Torch if the Chinese company wants, can ask for the financial support of Torch funding. And at the end, as I mentioned, because it is very important, they must access to the market. We are willing to increase the service of our companies because of the technology products. As easy as that.

公司得有自己的创意，有创意就行。不论是西班牙公司的创意，还是中国公司的创意，或者双方合作得来的创意，都不要紧。重要的是，我们必须把西班牙公司和中国实体公司聚集在一块儿，必须有创意，他们得愿意合作。如果他们愿意合作，那么我们有一个潜在的中西卡项目，我们在火炬中心和 CDTI 进行国际评估。然后是资金，CDTI 会保证西班牙的公司有充足的资金。至于火炬中心，中国公司可以申请获得火炬中心的资金支持。最后，正如我刚刚提到的，他们必须进入市场，这一点非常重要。我们愿意提供更多的服务给公司开发技术产品，就是这么简单。

23:07—23:54

This is an example of what we are doing. I like this example, because when we talk about our product, it's very easy to everyone to understand what we are talking about. For example, nowadays, we are doing a project with a Samsung company, and it's a very easy product to understand, it's very easy to understand. Because it's a camera, product camera to do profound television in 360 degrees. You put the camera in the middle of a sport field or in the middle of a scenario, and you can watch all the sport field or the scenario. And in that project, it's very simple to understand because all of the Samsung company is to develop the optics and electronics, and all of the Spanish company is to develop the software, and they are relevant, so the border there is quite easy to understand.

这是一个我们手头上正在做的事例。我很喜欢这个例子，因为谈论到我们的产品时，每个人都能理解我们在说什么。例如，现在我们正在和三星的一家公司做一个项目，生产的产品很容易理解，是做摄像头。生产的摄像头可以 360 度深度摄像。把摄像头安装在运动场的中间，或者在某个场景的中间，可以看到整个运动场或者整个场景。在这个项目中，很显然，三星公司要做的是开发光学和电子产品，而西班牙公司要做的是开发软件，这两项工作是相关的。所以这个边界很好理解。

23:54—25:16

But here is different. Here what we are talking about is the development of a service. The service is also, it's nontangible, so it's more difficult to understand. Here is something that is developed between this company. This company is a very small and medium enterprise company of the health sector in Spain. Remember I told you, health is the one of the strong sectors in Spain. This is a spin-off of the clinic hospital in Barcelona. The clinic hospital in Barcelona is one of the most advanced hospitals in Europe. And they have this spin-off, so they are working with the Beijing Academy of Science and Technology. I like this, because in China there is a lot of technology through the different municipalities and through the different science and technology parks, so this is a good example. And here the objective is to create a service, to create a health protocol based in collaborative care model. This means that all the participants contribute to the development of the protocol, but at the end, what we are trying to do is to provide medical care to people that is difficult for them to access to the medical care. In this case are the old population. We are trying to get closer the health care to the old population.

但是这里有点不同。这里我们谈谈服务的开发。服务是无形的，因此不容易理解。这是这家公司开发的产品，这家公司是西班牙卫生领域的一家中小型企业。我说过卫生领域是西班牙最先进的领域之一。这是一家巴塞罗那诊所医院开发的副产品。这家诊所医院是欧洲最先进的医院之一。他们开发了这个产品，和北京市科学技术研究院开展合作。我喜欢这样的合作，因为在中国，不同的城市、不同的科技园区开发不同的技术。因此，这个例子很贴切。我们的目标是创建一个基于协作护理模型的健康协议，这意味着所有的参与者都要为协议的发展做出贡献。最终，我们要做的是为那些难以获得医疗服务的人群提供医疗服务，这里特指老年人。我们努力让老年人都能获得医疗保健服务。

25:17—26:27

We are doing this in a pilot project in Beijing in 25 different neighborhoods with more than 25 patients. It will finish this year, and if the results are good, we'll try to, why not do this model in all the cities in China or in Europe. These are the total numbers of what we are talking about. Since we started in 2011, we have done more than 34 projects. It's not bad. It's another each of three projects per year. I hope we could have more and this year we are not doing bad. We have approved five projects so far now in November, I think we could have another project before the end of the year. So that means that in 2016, we would have 6 CHINEKA projects. That's important. But I want you to focus in [on] this. This means that the budget average of every CHINEKA project is like 1.5 million Euros that is more or less 12 million RMB. This project between Spain and China, both side. And here this is very important for me. I like it a lot. Because it's the places where we have the project.

我们在北京开展了一个试点项目，涵盖25个不同的社区，有超过25名患者。这个项目今年内可以完成。如果效果很好，我们将在中国或欧洲的其他城市推广。自2011年起，我们已经做了超过34个项目，效果还不错。这是另一项每年都做的项目。我希望可以做更多的项目，今年我们做得还不错。到11月为止，我们已经审批通过了5个项目，年底前还可以再做一个。这意味着2016年我们一共做了6个中西卡项目。这点很重要，我希望你们关注这一点。每个中西卡项目的预算平均是150万欧元，折合人民币约为1,200万元。这是中西之间的项目。中国对我来说很重要。我很喜欢中国，因为这里有中西卡项目。

26:27—27:11

You can see there is a lot in the north part of Spain. Here is a very important strong industrial area. A lot in Barcelona, here you have a lot of biotechnology, and new material, a lot in Madrid where you have a lot for IT. And in China, of course, you can see a lot in the east part, but some of them in the inner part of Chinese world distribution around China, and I think this gives you a good demonstration of how important of the municipalities are for fostering R&D technology in China. That's all. I hope it was interesting. Thank you and necessarily if you need anything from technology and Spain, please remember ring me. Goodbye. Thank you!

可以看到，西班牙北方地区很多中西卡项目，这里是西班牙非常重要的工业区。巴塞罗那有很多生物技术和新材料公司，在马德里你们可以找到很多IT公司。中国也有很多中西卡项目，主要分布在中国东部，也有一些分布在内陆地区。我认为这很好地展示了重要城市在促进技术发展方面的作用。我的演讲到此结束。希望你们对这个话题感兴趣，谢谢大家！如果你们需要技术支持或者任何西班牙方面的支持，请联系我。再见。谢谢大家！

III. 实战练习二

1. 演讲背景

新上任才3个月的以色列驻华大使应邀参加"创建世界一流高科技园区国际论坛"并发表演讲。他在演讲伊始首先高度赞扬中国改革开放30年来取得的辉煌成就，然后做了一个简短的自我介绍，还简单介绍了以色列的历史，发现中华民族与犹太民族的历史非常相似，这为两国开展合作打下了基础。最后，他还揭示了以色列能成为"创业的国度"的成功秘诀，那就是鼓励年轻人从小学会勤于思考、发问、创新。

第一单元 研发合作 R&D Cooperation

2. 预习词汇

cabinet 内阁
Ambassador of Israel 以色列大使
Minister of Science and Technology 科技部部长
Ministry of Defense 国防部
the Jewish people 犹太民族
before Christ 公元前
Abraham 亚伯拉罕（犹太民族的祖先）
Canaan 迦南地（古代地名，大致相当于今日以色列、西岸和加沙，加上临近的黎巴嫩和叙利亚的临海部分）
NASDAQ 纳斯达克

3. 演讲文本

00:00—00:22

Good morning. It is a great honor for me to be here and to give you some words about the experience of Israel, building the innovation and all the issues that you like to talk about.

早上好。很荣幸在此与大家分享以色列的经验，谈谈创新以及其它大家感兴趣的话题。

00:23—01:43

And I, first, I must say that China has undergone a dramatic change over the past three decades. You can see it here in Shenzhen. And now it is the second economic force in the world, second to the United States of America. It is a super power of the modern world. No one is in the position to tell you what to do or how to do, or to tell you what is good or what is wrong. You are so successful yourself that you are very pragmatic that you know how to work. And we only have to look at you, and to admire what you are doing, what you have achieved in the last three decades here in Shenzhen and all over China. It is very important to remember it, to understand it, because the changes that you have done in the last three decades are dramatic. And no nation in the world can do something like that, with a huge area, a huge population and what you have done. And it is very important to remember it. It is very important to remember it.

首先，我想说的是中国在过去30年间发生了翻天覆地的变化，从深圳就能看出来。中国现在是世界第二大经济体，仅次于美国，是当代世界的超级大国。没有人有资格告诉中国应该做什么、如何做，或者教育中国什么是对的、什么是错的。

19

你们已经非常成功,非常务实,非常了解应该怎么做。我们所能做的就是看着你们,佩服你们所做的一切,钦佩过去30年间深圳乃至全中国所取得的成就。记住并了解这些成就非常重要,因为你们在过去30年所发生的变化非常惊人。世界上没有其他任何国家能做到你们这样,你们幅员辽阔、人口众多,却能取得如此辉煌的成就。所以,请铭记你们取得的成就。

01:44—02:11

I would like only to share with you our experience and to tell you about Israel and about our history, only in order that we can work together and we can achieve growth, implement together achievements for the sake of China and, of course, for the sake of Israel.

我只想与你们分享一下我们的经验,介绍以色列及其历史,以便促进我们两国的合作,共同发展,实现中国和以色列的共同成功。

02:12—02:59

And I would like to say a few words, first of all, about myself and about history. I am here as the "大使", the Ambassador of Israel for three months. I am not a professional diplomat. I came after I served eight years as a Minister in several Israeli Cabinet. I was Minister of Science and Technology. I served for many years in the army and I am a General. And I served as the Minister in the Ministry of our Defense. So my experience is not from the diplomatic area, but from the ministerial and from the army.

首先,我想简单做一个自我介绍,谈谈以色列的历史。我担任以色列驻华"ambassador",已经上任3个月。外交官并非我的本行。我曾在以色列内阁担任过8年部长。我也担任过科技部部长。我还曾在军队服役多年,我是一名将军,担任过以色列国防部部长。所以,我以往的从政经验不是外交领域,而是担任部长和军职的经验。

02:59—04:14

And I found in the last months when I am here that the history of China and the history of the Jewish community, of the Jewish people, are very similar. You can't believe it. Both of us are going back 5,000 years in history. You are looking to the Yellow Emperor 3,000 years before Christ. In those days Abraham came to Canaan according to our tradition. And since then you are here in China. We were expelled from our country and we came back. And both of us, China and Israel, although is a very old civilization, we are the very new comers in the new global arena. You became a state, as you are now, a Communist state, in [on] the 1st of October, (19)49. And we

第一单元　研发合作 R&D Cooperation

became a state in [on] the 15th of May, (19) 48. And both of our states came to be states after a very bitter war against internal and outside enemies.

在我担任驻华大使的这几个月，我发现中国和犹太民族的历史非常相似。你们可能觉得难以置信。我们两国都有着五千年的悠久历史。你们的祖先是生活在公元前三千年的黄帝，而根据犹太历史记载，那个时期亚伯拉罕来到了迦南地。自那时起，你们就一直生活在中国这片土地上，而我们则被赶出了我们的国土，后来我们又回来了。尽管中国和以色列都是文明古国，但是在现代国际舞台上，我们都是新成员。1949年10月1日，你们成立了新中国，成为一个共产主义国家。1948年5月15日，以色列建国。我们都经历了艰苦卓绝的内外战争，最终才建立了国家。

04:14—04:41

So we are sharing the same experience. We are sharing the same history. And therefore, when we are talking to each other, we understand what we are talking about. We are not new comers in the global arena. We are very old, old civilization as I mentioned before. And therefore, it is interesting to speak about our experience.

所以我们两国有着相同的经历、相同的历史。因此，我们交流时，能够相互理解。从另一方面讲，我们又不算是国际舞台的新成员，因为我们都是历史悠久的文明古国，这个我刚才已经提到。因此，谈谈我们的经验是件很有趣的事儿。

04:41—05:18

And Israel has more companies on the NASDAQ than those from all of Europe, Korea, Japan, Singapore, China, and India combined. For years, Israel has been known for its innovation nature, innovative nature. As a global leader of technological and business innovation, Israel is recently named the Start-up Nation. According to the latest data from Israeli Venture Capital Association, Israel currently has around 5,000 technology start-ups in circulation.

纳斯达克上市的以色列公司数量超过欧洲、韩国、日本、新加坡、中国和印度的纳斯达克上市公司的总和。多年来，以色列都以创新而闻名。作为全球技术和商业创新的引领者，以色列最近被誉为"创业的国度"。以色列风险投资协会的最新数据表明，以色列目前大约有5,000家科技初创企业。

05:18—05:48

And you have to understand that Shenzhen is much bigger than Israel. We are speaking about 7 million. Some of them are Palestinians, aren't Israelis. So we are talking about 5.5 million Jews in Israel. This is the whole story. And there is… so we have to try to understand how it is going on, how it has happened.

21

你们要知道,深圳的人口数量可比以色列多多了。我们国家有 700 万人,这当中有些是巴勒斯坦人,不是以色列人。所以事实上以色列只有 550 万犹太人。情况就是这样。所以,我们需要了解这一切是如何做到,如何发生的。

05:49—07:28

And what I can tell you, there is no answer. There is no formula. There is no "Plus one, one will be two." Sometimes it will be two; sometimes it will be four. Sometimes it will be zero. There is no formula in this. And some speculate, because of the army education, that it is working in a very high-tech environment all the time, because our modern army is a very modern one, with a lot of technology, with a lot of innovation within the forces. Sometimes they speculate that it comes from the old Jewish tradition, because you know the old Jewish tradition and they were very smart people, smarter than us. I am sure about it. Nothing you can take for granted. Every time you have to ask questions. And as a student from kindergarten, you are educated to ask questions, why this, why that, you are wrong, you are to do it this way. And this is the formula. Nothing more than that. So you have to encourage the young people to create, to think, to ask questions. And you know God create the universe with much more questions and much less answers. This is the way. And you have to understand it. This is the way in order to innovate, in order to continue to advance all the time.

我能告诉你们的是:这一切没有标准答案,没有公式可循,没有所谓的"一加一等于二"。有时结果等于二,有时等于四,有时只是零。这里面没有公式可循。因为我们的军事教育一直是处于高科技的环境中,所以我们的军队非常现代化,享有许多高科技和技术创新。因此有人猜测这都得归功于古老的犹太传统。你们都知道古老的犹太传统,古代的犹太人非常聪明,比我们现在还要聪明,这一点我非常确信。没有什么事情是理所当然的,您得勤于提问。从幼儿园开始,小朋友就被教导要勤于提问:为什么是这样?为什么是那样?你那样不对,你应该这样做。这就是成功的公式。除此之外别无其它。所以,必须鼓励年轻人创新、思考、发问。上帝创造宇宙时,就设置了许多问题,却鲜少给出答案。这就是方法。您必须了解这一点。这就是创新和不断进步的方法。

07:28—07:56

And you did it, the tradition as I mentioned before, you did it very well. But you have to think about it all the time, and to try it, and to find the new high to encourage it all the time. When I served as the Minister of Science, I was responsible for this. You can encourage young people to go to new things. And you understand that someone, they will fail. And they are ready to fail and will try again.

你们做到了，做到了上述的传统，而且做得非常好。但你们需要不断思考、尝试，找到新动力，使得这种传统能延续下去。我任职科技部时，曾负责这方面的工作。你们可以鼓励年轻人尝试新事物。你们还要知道，尝试有可能会失败，年轻人要做好失败的准备，继续尝试。

07:56—08:25
As in the army, the same. You fight. Sometimes you win, sometimes you lose, but you have to remain on the battle, on the battlefield. The same in our experience. So you have to try. Entire era is part of innovation. And it is very important to understand it. This is very short. I am not going to tell you any more, because this is the main issue.

这跟打仗一样，胜败乃兵家常事，但是您必须坚持战斗，坚守阵地。我们的经验也是如此。所以您必须尝试。整个时代都是创新的一部分。明白这个道理很重要。我要讲的很短，就是这么多了，因为这就是最重要的内容。

08:25—09:13
And what I am sure that Israel… now I'm speaking as the Ambassador to Beijing, that Israel and China has [have] a lot in common. And we can work together and we are doing a lot. Never enough. We must do more. And Shenzhen and Guangzhou are wonderful examples for us. And we must cooperate and we must work together, not to teach each other, but to work together to find the right solution for your problems and our problems, for the sake of China and for the sake of Israel. Thank you very much!

作为以色列驻华大使，我认为以色列和中国有许多共同之处。我们通过合作取得了许多成果。但这还远远不够，我们之间还大有可为。深圳和广州都是值得我们学习的城市。我们两国必须合作，不是相互说教，而是携手合作，找到解决中国问题和以色列问题的正确途径，谋求两国的福祉。谢谢大家！

第二单元　酒店管理
Hotel Management

I. 译前准备

译前准备包括长期准备和短期准备。长期准备包括语言基础、专业知识储备、口译技巧等方面，这些需要经过长期系统训练和学习才能获得。短期准备指译员为了一次口译活动所做的准备，主要包括口译任务背景准备、口译主题内容准备和了解发言人和目的语听众。

1. 口译任务背景准备

在口译任务之前，译员需要尽可能多地了解关于口译任务的相关情况。

（1）了解口译任务的形式和基本情况。此次口译任务是同传还是交传？是正式口译还是非正式口译？演讲是什么主题？属于哪个行业？

（2）了解口译活动服务对象和日程安排。译员通常需要向翻译公司、主办方等口译活动联系人询问活动日程安排表，日程安排表上通常有活动主题、时间、地点、各个发言人、各环节安排等。

（3）索取或查找相关演讲资料。尽量向演讲嘉宾本人、翻译公司、主办方或者其他口译活动联系人索要演讲资料，可能是发言稿、提纲、PPT或者其他相关的准备资料，译员在条件允许的情况下，可以在活动开始前适当地跟演讲嘉宾面对面交流，了解讲话内容或重点。如果没能提前获得相应资料，译员可以自行在网上搜索、了解背景知识。

2. 主题内容准备

在对口译任务有了初步了解之后，译员接下来可以就口译主题知识进行准备。

（1）相关主题知识准备。无论译员是否能提前获得部分讲话内容的资料，都应当通过网络等渠道查找相关主题演讲。对相关领域知识了解得越多，准备得越充分，口译时表现往往就越好。

（2）术语准备。译员在获得相应的发言稿、PPT和口译相关主题资料后，应熟悉演讲资料内容，同时整理出一份术语表，列上重要词汇，并反复熟悉相关术语，翻译时可以将术语表放在手边。

3. 了解发言人

（1）了解口译服务对象的发音特点。中国演讲嘉宾普通话所带的地方口音对于译员来说听辨不会很难，但是英语的口音则较为多样，比如东南亚一些国家的人英语口音较重，语音分辨有很大难度。译员在译前可以多听听这些国家的人说的英语，熟悉其发音特点，这有利于提高口译准确度。

（2）了解口译服务对象的文化背景。尤其是在一些陪同口译的场合，口译员可能会负责口译之外的一些接待活动，了解口译服务对象的文化背景和习俗有利于更好地沟通协调。

II. 实战练习一

1. 演讲背景

四季酒店CEO在广州四季酒店成功开业后不久到访，召开员工大会，回答员工关切的问题。下文摘自她对大会中提到的两个问题的回答。第一个问题是"为何顾客的到达体验如此重要？"她引用了酒店高管的见解，顾客到达后希望尽快入住房间，因为他们希望重新掌控自己的时间和空间。第二个问题"四季酒店钦佩什么样的公司？"她认为四季酒店密切关注那些以客户为中心，有非常强的创新精神和能与时俱进的公司。

2. 预习词汇

Four Seasons 四季酒店
arrival experience 抵达体验；到达体验
guest experience 顾客体验
seamless 无缝的
vagary 出乎意料的变化；难以预料的转变
Senior Executive 高管
resort 度假村
inspiration 灵感
plethora 过多；过剩
word of mouth 口碑
harness 利用
Apple 苹果公司

3. 演讲文本

00:00—00:14

So the first thing I would like to do when I arrive at a hotel, and I think I am pretty typical when it comes to this, is I would like to get to my room as fast as I possibly can.

我到酒店后想做的第一件事，我觉得这方面我非常典型，就是我想尽快入住，到自己的房间。

00:14—00:54

A number of years ago, one of our Four Seasons colleagues explained why the arrival experience is so very important for our customers. If you look at the research you can see that the arrival experience ranks always in the top 2, 3, or 4 of the things that the guest experience depends on the most. It is an interesting thing to think about because you have to ask always why, not what, but why do customers want a seamless arrival experience more than anything else.

几年前，我们四季酒店的一位同事解释了为什么抵达体验对我们的客人那么重要。您看一下调查结果，就会发现抵达体验在众多决定客人体验的事物中，排名总是前二、前三、前四。这是个很有趣的问题，因为您会问"为什么"，而不是"是什么"，为什么客人最想的就是顺利、快速入住？

00:54—02:08

And one of our colleagues said it best when he said it was all about control. Busy travelers, business or leisure, leave their home wherever it is and get into a car. That car drives them to an airport. They are then subjected to all the vagaries of that airport screening process. Then he boards a plane. Somebody else is flying it. Then he gets off the plane and usually gets into another car, which somebody else is driving. Then he arrives at your hotel. So this person, typically a successful business person, typically someone who is used to exercising a high degree of control over their own life, has now been completely out of control for two hours, five hours, in some cases, traveling long distances, it could be 24 hours. So the need for that busy traveler to regain control over their own space, their own life, their own time, is very, very, very real.

我们其中一个同事说得好，他说这是因为"控制权"。日程忙碌的旅客，无论是出差还是旅游，无论住哪儿，离开家就上了车。车把他们送到机场，然后他们不得不接受机场安检过程中各种离奇的突发情况。然后他们登机，是别人开的飞机。然后他下了飞机，通常又上了另一辆车，也是别人开的车。然后他到了您的酒店。这个人，通常是一个成功的商人，一个习惯对自己生活拥有高度控制权的人，现在已经完全失去这种控制权长达 2 个小时、5 个小时，有时如果是长途旅行，可能是 24 小时。所以必须让这位忙碌的客人重新掌控自己的空间、生活、时间。这种需要是非常实在的。

02:08—02:50

And he believed, the Senior Executive at Four Seasons, that that was really one of the big emotional drivers to perfecting the arrival experience. It probably applies whether it is a busy business traveler in a city or leisure travelers in a resort. People really want to gain control of their own space and their own time, and then go on a tour, and then have a welcome drink, and then actually explore the hotel, the experience. But it is guest by guest. I am not saying it is all the guests. But it is for sure me, which means that I am probably like the majority of them.

这位四季酒店的高级主管相信，这确实是完善抵达体验的一大情感动力，这可能同时适用于城市的商务旅客或者度假村的休闲旅客。大家确实想要先掌控自己的空间、时间，然后再去观光、洗尘，再去深入参观酒店、去体验。当然这因人而异。我不是说所有客人都这样，但对我来说的确是如此，也就是说我和大多数人一样。

02:50—03:28

Which company would I wish that Four Seasons would be more like? I don't know if I can take one company, Natassia, that I would say let us be more like them. But when I look for inspiration relative to where we need to go in the future, I look at companies, probably mostly outside the hotel industry, mostly in other industries, and whether they are car companies, or electronic companies, service companies, in some cases, you know, big product marketing companies.

我希望四季酒店更像哪家公司？娜塔莎，我不知道我能否具体指出像哪一家公司。但是，当我寻找灵感，探究未来我们要走的路时，我会看各大公司，更多的可能是酒店业外的以及其他行业的公司，无论是汽车公司、电子公司或服务公司，在有些情况下，会是大型产品市场营销公司。

03:28—04:35

We really want to focus in watching companies that are all about the things that we aspire to. That includes excellence in everything we do, that includes an approach to people and leadership development, that core of our success. We are always going to be the kind of business that requires hundreds of thousands of people to get the job done in the future. We also want to focus on companies that really aspire to be evolutionary and innovative. So constantly being able to change, not necessarily with trends, being trendy, but making sure that we are aware of the trends in the marketplace, making sure that we are able to capture the thinking of young people, the thinking of old people, as everyone changes in the world, and make sure that our product offering is actually keeping with the times.

　　我们的确关注一些公司，它们拥有我们所期望的一切，包括做事力求完美、以人为本、发展领导才能，以及拥有成功的秘诀。我们想成为这样的公司：它要求成千上万人在未来完成要做的工作。我们也想关注一些真正渴望不断发展和创新的公司。因此，能够与时俱进，不一定要随波逐流、赶时髦，但是要确保我们意识到市场的趋势，确保我们能够捕捉到年轻人和老年人的想法，因为世界上的每个人都在变化，确保我们提供的产品能真正与时俱进。

04:35—05:19

　　This is a very hard thing to do, particularly today. Today, the taste of consumers, because of, I believe, the plethora of information that is available to all of us on the Internet, through friends, through recommendations, through word of mouth, through our social networks, through our on-line networks. We are all very aware of so many new things, so much faster. For companies, to be able to take the whole of that information and figure out what to do with it to serve the customer better, is something that we really need to stay focused on.

　　这非常不容易，尤其是在现在这种形势下。如今，我们了解消费者的品味，因为我相信我们可以在互联网上获取大量的信息，通过朋友、推荐、口碑、社交网站以及我们的在线网络等等都可以获得。我们清楚地意识到很多新事物，它们发展得也很快。对于公司而言，能够掌控所有信息并利用它们更好地服务客户，是我们真正需要专注的事情。

05:19—05:59

　　When I think about great companies for us to model, I look at companies that are actually harnessing the power of that consumer information very well and figuring out how to get out ahead of it and how to really be part of the stream that is going on. You know, companies like Apple easily come to mind, but there are dozens of others, where companies are taking new ideas, making them their own, making them better, and then creating better products. That is the kind of thing we have to continue to do as an organization.

　　当我想哪些公司可以作为我们的典范时，我想到的是这些公司：能够真正高效利用消费者信息，知道如何取得领先地位以及如何真正成为主流的一部分。很容易

第二单元　酒店管理 Hotel Management

想到像苹果这样的公司，但是也有其他几十家公司，这些公司吸收新想法，形成自己的想法，并不断地完善，然后创造出更好的产品。这就是我们作为一家公司一直在做的事情。

05:59—06:25
It is easy to say, all right, we set it up like this. It should stay like this. No, it shouldn't. It has to continue to evolve with the customer. So looking at companies that have a very strong customer focus, and a very strong innovation spirit, and a very strong capacity to change quickly, those are the kind of companies that I think we are watching.

我们往往会说："好，我们把公司建成这样，维持原状就好了。"不应该这样！公司必须随着客户的变化而不断发展。所以，看到很多公司以客户为中心，有非常强的创新精神和快速变化的能力，它们就是我们关注的公司。

III. 实战练习二

1. 演讲背景

四季酒店 CEO 在广州四季酒店成功开业后不久到访，召开员工大会，回答员工关切的问题。下文摘自她对大会中提到的两个问题的回答。第一个问题是"酒店最大的担忧什么？"她表示酒店一直以来最关注人才，培养足够的人才储备，确保新开业的酒店和已有的酒店一样成功。第二个问题是"要在四季酒店取得成功，需要具备哪些重要的素质？"她认为首先需要热爱本职工作，还需要具备团队合作精神和终身学习的能力。

2. 预习词汇

senior leadership 高层领导
property 房地产；酒店
assistant manager 副经理
Boston 波士顿
Bali 巴厘岛
Budapest 布达佩斯
bench strength 后备力量
taskforce 任务组
Roger Federer 罗杰·费德勒
positive energy 正能量
commute 通勤

29

food and beverage 餐饮部
banqueting 宴会部
spa 水疗（中心）
skimmed milk 脱脂牛奶
blueberry 蓝莓
pork steak 猪排
whole wheat toast 全麦吐司
bagel 百吉圈硬面包
hospitality industry 酒店业

3. 演讲文本

00:00—00:33

The biggest worry, the biggest worry for the hotel, for me, for the senior leadership teams of the company is always the same. I have been around for a long time, for almost 24 years now. I can tell you that the biggest worry, the thing that keeps us up at night, all the time, has never changed. It is always about people, our Four Seasons teams, on the ground in each hotel, making each property as successful as it can possibly be.

最担心的问题，无论是对于酒店，对于我，对于公司高层而言，最担心的问题始终如一。我在四季酒店任职快24年了，我可以告诉您我们一直以来最关心的问题，让我们夜不能寐的问题从来没变，那就是人，即我们四季酒店的各个团队，一线的员工，是他们创造了每家酒店的成功。

00:33—01:30

If you think about that for a moment, and you go back to the comment you made about all our hotels being successful, there is no doubt that the success of each property is largely, largely, almost exclusively dependent on the leadership in the hotel, and the top leadership of the hotel, the department heads, the assistant managers, all the employees, who everyday are personally responsible for delivering the guests experience. There is virtually nothing, in fact I would say nothing that I would do in my office in Toronto that will affect the guests experience in this hotel next week. It is all up to you. That is true in Boston, in Bali, in Budapest. It is true everywhere around the world.

您想想我所说的话，再回想您刚刚说我们酒店取得的成就。毫无疑问，每家酒店的成功在很大程度上，或者几乎完全依赖酒店的领导层、高层领导、各部门经理、副经理以及全体员工，是他们每天为顾客服务。事实上，我在多伦多办公，我几乎是无法影响到我们这家酒店下周入住顾客的体验的，全依仗各位的努力。无论是在波士顿、巴厘岛、布达佩斯，或其他地方，都是如此。

第二单元　酒店管理 Hotel Management

01:30—01:53

So as we grow as a company, when we think about adding these nine new hotels in China, having just added three this year, or anywhere else in the world for that matter, our big focus is on making sure that we have the bench strength, the depth of talents, the breadth of talents, the kind of people, the Four Seasons people.

因此，随着公司的发展，当我们考虑在中国新建 9 家酒店，今年已经开了 3 家，或在其他地方建设酒店时，我们的关注点是要保证我们有足够的后备力量、人才储备，也就是我们四季酒店的人才。

01:53—02:19

You all know what a Four Seasons person looks like. You are sitting in a room full of them, the kind of people who can go to the next destination, maybe permanently, maybe on taskforce, maybe just send your assistants to help that next hotel be as great as the last one. So our worry is always going to be about people, all of our employees in every hotel and the leadership that it takes to open all the new ones.

大家都了解四季酒店的人才是什么样的，在座各位都是四季酒店的人才。他们能够前往下个酒店，可能是永久性驻扎在那里，可能是以任务组形式前往，也可能只是派助理前往，目的是保证酒店的质量始终如一。因此我们担心的问题始终是人才，是各家酒店的全体员工和领导层，开办新四季酒店离不开他们。

02:19—03:14

So the most important quality for achieving success at Four Seasons, I think there are a few things about achieving success and achieving success at Four Seasons. There are probably many more that Mr. Sepahi, Mr. Hart and Mr. Mackay can share with you from their experiences and their careers. But on my list there is just a few things. The first thing I say to people about achieving success, and it applies not only to Four Seasons, but really to any job at all, is to make sure that you are doing a job that you love, that you are finding a career that you can be passionate about, that you are working with people that you respect and have fun with and succeed with.

至于在四季酒店获得成功最重要的素质，我认为有一些东西对取得成功以及对在四季酒店取得成功很重要。西帕伊先生、哈特先生、马凯先生就他们的经历和事业与你们分享的东西可能有很多，但是我的列表中只有几样东西最重要。我想和大家说的关于取得成功的第一点不仅适用于四季酒店，也适用于其他所有工作，那就是确保您喜欢自己的工作，您对自己的事业充满热忱，您和您敬重、玩得开的同事们一起工作，共同走向成功。

03:14—04:02

And I have a simple test for this. We all work about five days a week, sometimes six, depending on the weeks. If you don't jump out of bed in the morning, wanting to go to work, all of those days, except for one, I give everybody one, staying up too late, you know, having a fight with your friends, not getting enough sleep, whatever it was. But if in most days, you really aren't excited about the job you are in, then my view is you need to change it, because you need to find something in your life that drives your energy positively and makes you passionate about what you are doing.

我有个简单的测试。我们一周工作5天,有时6天,取决于每周的安排。如果您早上起不来,不想去上班,每天都是这样,只有一天除外。我给每个人一天例外,那天你们可以熬夜、和朋友吵架、睡眠不足,不管做什么。但是,在大多数时间里,如果您对自己的工作没有热情,那么我的看法就是:您需要改变,因为您需要在人生中找到一些东西,给您带来正能量,让您对自己做的事情更有热情。

04:02—04:23

My favorite example on this is a tennis player, Roger Federer. Now Roger Federer is one of those unbelievable tennis stories, right? But one thing is for sure that Roger Federer loves to play tennis. He would rather play tennis than do anything else. If it wasn't the case, he wouldn't be that good.

我最喜欢的例子就是网球运动员罗杰·费德勒。现在罗杰·费德勒是网球界的传奇人物,对吗?但是可以肯定的一点是,罗杰·费德勒热爱网球,他最爱的就是打网球。如果不是这样,他就不会成为如此成功的网球运动员。

04:23—05:19

So it is the same in our jobs. We need to find things to spend our time on that really generate positive energy in our brains and in our beings. Because we work hard, right? We work all day. The question before us is about hours of work. Yours are no different. We start early; we finish late; we work hard; we commute to and from, sometimes long, sometimes short. We get home; we talk to whoever we are living with, roommates, parents, friends, cats, dogs, whatever it is, talk about work. Then we go to sleep. We dream about work. Now it is about 18 hours' work. So it is better to be positive, 'cause if it is not, that's a lot of hours in the day to overcome with some other kind of positive energy. So loving what you do is very important.

工作上也一样。我们需要找到将时间花在真正能给我们大脑和身体带来正能量的地方。因为我们非常努力工作,对吗?我们一整天都在工作。我们每天长时间工作。你们也一样。我们起早贪黑,辛苦工作;我们要通勤,有时时间长,有时时间短；我们回到家，和住在一起的人聊天，如室友、父母、朋友、宠物，不管和谁，聊的都是工作。接着我们就睡觉了，梦到工作。所以现在是 18 小时都在工作。因此，最好积极乐观点，不然的话，每天都得找其他的正能量来维持长时间的工作。所以，热爱自己的工作非常重要。

05:19—05:56

The hotel industry is one of the great places for people to make sure they get this right. Because in every hotel, we have food and beverage; we have banqueting; we have spa; we have marketing; we have human resources; we have finance; we have technology; we have every job you can image. So there is no need to change companies, only to change roles. So just find in your way. Want to become a spa director, want to be in finance, these things can happen. Just find your passion and follow it.

酒店业是最好的行业之一，人们可以确保自己找到合适的工作。因为在每家酒店，我们都有餐饮部、宴会部、水疗中心、市场营销部、人力资源部、财务部、技术部，我们有您能想到的所有工作。所以没有必要换公司，只需要换岗位，找到自己的方向，比如您想成为水疗中心总监或者进财务部，这些都是可能的。只要找到自己的兴趣所在，听从自己的内心就行了。

05:56—06:31

So No.1 stay happy with what you are doing. I think the other things are about the Four Seasons in particular, but the hospitality business in general. Success in this business, you really do have to love being with the people you are working with. Because as I said before, we work hard. Bad things happen. Mistakes get made. We have to fill in for one another. We have to pick up for one another. We have to fill in for the folk that was late that day. We have to have them to fill in for us the next day when we are late. We are a team. We are all a team.

所以第一点就是喜欢自己的工作。其他的尤其适用于四季酒店，但总的来说也是关于酒店业的。想要在酒店业取得成功，您需要喜欢您的同事。就像我之前说的，我们努力工作，但是有时还是会发生不好的事情，会犯错，这时我们不得不临时找人顶替一下，选一个人代班，我们不得不临时顶替当天迟到的人，因为如果第二天我们迟到的话他们会帮我们临时替班。我们是一个团队，我们都是同一个团队。

06:31—07:33

So learning to work very closely with other people and respect the efforts of other people is a Four Seasons' trait. But it is really required in this business because it takes thousands of people to get it right. Well, you know, you think about something as simple as four people for breakfast in your restaurant in the morning. Somebody has to take the order; somebody has to communicate back, the kitchen has to get it ready. But it isn't a simple order. No body orders off the menu, right? This one is going to have porridge with skimmed milk and a few blueberries. This one wants pork steak, but on whole wheat toast with no butter. Over here we are going to have bagel with cream, cheese or somebody else is going to have Chinese breakfast. Somebody has to figure out how to get that all to the table, all hot, all of the same time. That takes a lot of communication, a lot of teamwork. That is just one and a half hour in a day of your hotel. You have got to do that hundreds of thousands of times every day, every week.

所以，学会与别人密切合作，尊重别人的努力，是四季酒店的特质。但也是这个行业所必须的，因为需要数千人通力合作才能把工作做好。想一下最简单的事情，如早上餐厅准备四个客人的早餐。必须有人接单，有人负责沟通，厨房要准备早餐。但这不是个简单的订单，没有人完全照菜单点菜的，对吧？这位客人要粥、脱脂牛奶和几个蓝莓；另一位想吃猪排、全麦吐司，不加黄油；那边那位想吃带奶油和奶酪的百吉圈硬面包；还有人想吃中式早餐。必须有人知道怎么把所有热气腾腾的早餐同时端到桌上。这需要大量的交流和团队协作。这只是酒店某天一个半小时的工作。你们每周、每天都要做很多同样的事情。

07:33—07:54

So it takes a village. It takes a village. Hilary Clinton used to say that about raising children. But getting it right in the hospitality industry takes a village. This is your village, but of course it is a much bigger village, 'cause a lot of folks didn't join us today. But learning to work cooperatively with other people, and lead, and follow and always be part of it.

所以这需要整个村庄的人共同努力，齐心协力。希拉里·克林顿曾说需要整个村庄的人共同努力才能把孩子培养好。但是，想在酒店业获得成功也需要整个村庄的努力。酒店就是你们的村庄，只是这个村庄大得多，今天很多同事没有参加会议，但是学会与他人合作，学会领导团队和听从安排。

07:54—09:00

The other thing that I think is very important. Then it goes back to the question about the kind of companies we need to follow. I will close on these final words is the need for continuous learning. So some of us grow up, we think, all right, I've graduated from school. I've finished my education. No. Life is an education. Every job we do and every place we go, and every hotel we work in, and every department we help serve, is some new learning. So keeping [keep] your mind open, the new things, always, every day, saying [say] I learned something today that I did not know yesterday. I am a better person for having learned that. Continuous passion, continuous curiosity, continuous desire to hear the views, to truly listen to the views of others' and learn from them. It is a very, very important, very important trait as well. I am sure there are many others. We can discuss over a cup of tea.

还有一件事情我认为也非常重要。那么回到我们该以什么样的公司为榜样这个问题上，我将答案总结为不断学习。有些人长大了，觉得自己从学校毕业就完成了教育。不是这样的，生活就是一种教育。我们做的每一份工作、去的每个地方、工作的每家酒店、服务的每个部门，都是崭新的学习过程。所以，思维放开阔点，每天都接受新事物，这样就可以说今天我又学到了一些我昨天不会的东西。学了这些后我又进步了一点点。保持热情、好奇心和渴望，真正去聆听他人的观点，向别人学习，这非常重要，也是非常重要的品质。我相信也有其他重要的品质，我们可以边喝茶边讨论。

第三单元 文化教育
Culture and Education

I. 公共演讲技巧

在交替传译中,译员是和演讲嘉宾一起出现在听众面前,因此译员在翻译时所传达出的信息一定程度上代表着演讲嘉宾。为了较好地传达出演讲嘉宾所要传达出的效果,一名合格的译员应具备良好的公共演讲技巧。口译学习者可以从体态语言和口头语言两方面提高演讲技巧。

1. 体态语言

仪表着装:听众可从译员的仪表着装中得到第一印象,如果第一印象不好,可能会直接影响听讲效果。译员仪表应整洁大方,不能过于招摇,这样会喧宾夺主,影响职业形象。着装应得体,如果是非常正式的场合,听众都穿正装,那么译员也应正式着装。

肢体动作:译员无论是坐、站、走,身体姿态都应当自然、大方。坐着的时候要坐正,不能萎靡不振。站着的时候应站稳,切忌摇晃身体,做出一些不合时宜的动作。译员作为演讲嘉宾和观众之间的纽带,在翻译中应当与听众有适当的眼神交流。有些译员在翻译中埋头于笔记,至始至终与听众无任何眼神交流,翻译则会稍显死板。优秀的译员应当在参看笔记的同时,适当地与观众进行眼神交流,这样既显示出对观众的尊重和关注,也能从观众的反应中收到一定的反馈,有利于演讲嘉宾和听众之间顺畅沟通。

2. 口头语言

音量:译员讲话时要声音洪亮,无论有没有麦克风,都要保证音量适中,观众能够清楚地听到译文。口译学习者经常出现的问题是因为紧张或者不自信,会不自觉地很小声,非常影响听众对译文的接收度。

音高:是指发言人声音的高低。一般人们在过于紧张时,声音会比较低,过于兴奋时,声音会比较高。译员在翻译时应当注意使用恰当的音高。

语速:是指讲话的速度。母语是英语的人讲话每分钟可达 120~150 个单词,对于译员而言,没有所谓既定语速。不能语速过快,这样听众容易跟不上讲话,继而走神;也不能语速过慢,让听众感觉到乏味。口译学习者通常会因为过于紧张而语速过快，因此在口译训练期间就应当多关注语速问题。

停顿：适当的停顿可以给观众一定的时间来理解讲话内容，也可以使一句话给听众留下深刻的印象。但许多口译学习者在练习时经常会习惯性地使用有声停顿，比如呃、啊等，这样的停顿容易干扰听众，留下不好的印象。

II. 实战练习一

1. 演讲背景

广州南方国际学校的校长应邀参加"2017必达亚洲春季峰会"，并就"户外教室的设施设计"发表主旨演讲。她在演讲中提到了户外活动有四大好处，第一，有助于孩子们的身体健康；第二，提高认知能力；第三，促进心理健康；第四，提升理解能力。此外，她还详细阐述了户外教室的选址要求和设计标准。

2. 预习词汇

whole child 全面发展的孩子
educate the whole child 培养孩子全面发展
renovate 翻新；修复
outdoor classroom 户外教室
accessibility 可达性
highly visible 能见度很高
usable 可用的；能用的
well-drained 排水良好的；排水性能好的
soccer 足球
tramp 践踏；踩踏
underutilized 未充分利用的
well-used 物尽其用；恰当运用；充分运用
elaborate 复杂的；精心制作的
functional 实用的
tight budget 预算有限
educator 教育家；教育工作者
learning space/area 学习空间/学习场所
fine motor skill 精细运动技能
gross motor skill 粗大运动技能
social emotion 社交情感
resilience 弹性；韧性；适应能力

37

creative expression 创意表达
palette 调色板
outdoor activity 户外活动
apartment 公寓
childhood 童年
backyard 后院；庭院
overprotective 过分保护的；过度保护的；过分溺爱的
responsible risk taker 负责任的冒险者
cause and effect 因果（关系）
interpersonal activity 人际交往活动
holistic development 全面发展
indoors 室内
outdoors 户外
children of early years 年幼儿童；幼童
outdoor curriculum 户外课程
rocket 火箭
obesity 肥胖症
diabetes 糖尿病
ADD/Attention Deficit Disorder 注意力缺陷障碍
ADHD/Attention Deficit Hyperactivity Disorder 多动症
cognitive 认知的
group activity 小组活动
self-initiation 自我促进
cognitive development 认知发展
self-esteem 自尊
stewardship 管理；照管；爱护
absenteeism 缺勤
innate 先天的；固有的；与生俱来的
memory channel 记忆渠道
concentration span 注意力集中时间
white board 白板
block 积木
Lego 乐高玩具
magnetic board 磁力板；磁性板
be engrossed in 全神贯注的；专心致志的
mud pie 泥饼

shovel 铲子；铁锹

toy car 玩具车

UOI/Unit of Inquiry 探究单元

team building 团队建设

biology lesson 生物课

shady 遮阴的

gazebo（花园内）凉亭

rug 地毯

snack 小吃；零食

drum circle/drumming circle 围坐击鼓

artwork 艺术作品

a sense of accomplishment 成就感

self-expression 自我表达；自我表现

stick 棍子；树枝

leaf 树叶；叶子

pebble 卵石；石子

reading circle 读书会

play time 游戏时间

3. 演讲文本

00:00—01:18

OK, good morning everyone. I think you probably find that my presentation is a little bit different to some of the others that you hear today because I am not an architect or designer. I am coming from the point of view of a head of a school, of an international school and thinking about teaching children and the learning of children with the experience of, you know, the whole child, educating the whole child. And so outdoor, the outdoor classroom is a very very important part of that. So I think whether you're planning to build a new school, whether you're renovating or planning to expand your school, why not plan for an outdoor classroom? I think it's really really important to think about this. You know, in the last presentation there were some wonderful spaces there for the type of learning that we want to go in our schools today and looking to the future of the sort of, you know, teaching and learning that goes on in the classrooms. But I also think that there's a very very important part of a child's education, is getting them outdoors as well.

大家早上好。你们可能会发现我今天的演讲跟你们听到的其他人的演讲有点不同，因为我既不是建筑师也不是设计师。我从国际学校校长的角度来发表我的看法。我一直在考虑如何教育孩子。关于孩子该如何学习,我有很多培养全面发展的孩子的经验。我的经验告诉我,户外课堂是一个非常非常重要的部分。所以我在想,不论你们是打算新建一所学校,还是翻新校舍,还是计划扩张学校,何不考虑建一个户外课堂?我觉得这非常非常重要。上一场演讲展示了一些非常精彩的空间,适合我们学校某种类型的学习,以及未来我们希望在教室里如何教导学生学习。但是,我认为孩子教育中非常重要的一部分是把他们带到户外去。

01:19—03:07

So think about is there suitable space in your school grounds, think of accessibility, some may close to the school that's highly visible that will make it very usable. The location. Make sure it's a well-drained area, not somewhere that's already well-used for a different purpose, 'cause if you start planning your outdoor classroom where, say, you know, students play soccer every day, you're going to find that they're gonna tramp all your space because they're out there playing soccer or if you take up somebody else's space where they used to, you know, doing a certain activity, then they're not going to be very happy either. So, you know, really, ideally, you should select, maybe an underutilized area of the school grounds, so you don't create conflict with others. And then the design. Choose the right design for your school and location. That will ensure it's well-used. I will start to get ideas from the students themselves. They often come up with wonderful ideas. Talk to the teachers, other people in the community to think about what's going to work best for you and your school. I think once you start talking to others, the creative ideas will start flowing. And you, you know, think of the very very good things especially for your students and your needs. And it doesn't have to be elaborate, to be valuable and functional. You know, you can do this on a very tight budget. I believe now you're very used to working on a very tight budget as my school.

请想一想你们学校是否有合适的位置,想一想这些场所的可达性。有一些场所就在学校附近,能见度高的,非常有用。注意选址。确保选取的位置排水良好,不要选已经被充分用于其他用途的地方。因为如果在规划户外教室时,比如说,将教室选在学生每天踢足球的地方,你们会发现他们会在你们选的这个区域到处踩踏。因为他们已经习惯在那里踢足球了。或者如果你们占用别人的地盘,别人已经习惯了在那里开展某种活动,那么他们会觉得不开心。所以,真正理想的地址是没被人占用的地方,选择学校里没有被占用的位置,这样你们就不会跟他人起冲突。然后就是设计。选择合理的设计,为你们的学校选择正确的设计、正确的位置。这有助于确保那里可以得到充分的利用。我会从学生们开始,从他们那里获得思路,因为他们常常能提出很棒的想法。跟老师们聊一聊、跟社区里的人聊一聊,想一想怎么做才能最好地满足学生和你们的需求。和别人交谈能给你带来创意,想到一些非常

第三单元 文化教育 Culture and Education

好的点子满足学生和你们自身的需求。不需要很详细、很有价值、功能性很强的点子。你们可以在预算非常紧张的情况下做到这一点。我相信,你们现在已经非常习惯像我们学校那样利用有限的预算工作了。

03:08—05:04

OK, so first of all, what does a researcher say? She supports the idea of an outdoor classroom. As I talked about the benefits of outdoor learning, look at my photos in this slide because I'll show you some of the different aspects of outdoor learning or part of the outdoor classroom idea. Modern child development research findings highlight the complexity of children. To nurture the whole child, which I think that we as educators, you know, think more and more of these days, we need to follow the principle that children are learning everywhere. I think we could saw [see] at the last presentation, all of those types of learning spaces where every part of their schools is an actual learning area. So they learn everywhere at any time. They need a broad variety of learning experiences to give them the opportunity to develop and grow their skills in four very very important areas. Two of these are "fine and gross motor skills". So you can see in my slide the equipment there that is planned especially to develop the multi-skills in children. We really really have to be very proactive in providing that so that they will be able to develop those skills. If they don't get to have the practice and the experience with that, those skills won't develop as they should. Also social emotional. Very important. So when kids are outside, if it's a whole different environment for them and they're going to develop more of the resilience that they really need these days as they're growing up.

首先,第一点,研究人员怎么说?她支持建户外教室的观点。刚刚我谈到户外课堂的好处,请看我这张幻灯片上的照片,我将向你们展示户外课堂有何不同,稍微展示一下户外课堂这个想法。现代儿童发展研究结果强调儿童的发展具有复杂性。如何培育一个健全的孩子,我认为这是我们作为教育者,思考越来越多的问题。我们需要遵循这么一个原则,即孩子们在任何地方都能学习。你们看,我们从上一场演讲中看到各种各样的可以学习的场所,实际上学校的每一个角落都是学习的场所。所以说孩子可以随时随地都在学习。他们需有各种各样的学习经历使他们能够有机会在四个非常重要的领域发现和发展他们的技能。其中两个非常重要的领域是:精细运动技能和粗大运动技能。所以,你们可以在我的幻灯片中看到,我们计划投入的设备尤其适合培养儿童的多种技能。我们真的必须非常主动地为他们提供这些设施,让他们能够发展这些技能。如果没有这些设施,那么他们将无法发展这些原本可以发展的技能。另外,社会情感也非常重要。当孩子们在户外时,如果这对于他们而言是一个完全不同的环境,他们就能够提高自己的适应能力,这在他们的成长过程中举足轻重。

05:05—06:00

OK, the other two areas are language. Say, we take children out of the classroom environment. They are outside. They have to use their language in a different way. They're interacting with each other in a different way and so their language does develop naturally as well. Creative expression. You know, give them a different palette, things to look at, and things to experience, see, hear, feel, touch when they're outside. That also helps with their creative expression and development. So the mastery of skills in all of these above areas are very critical to healthy development. And I think the outdoor classroom plays an important part in that.

另外两个重要的领域，一个是语言。当我们把孩子带出教室，他们在户外时不得不使用不同的交流方式。当他们以不同的方式相互交流，他们的语言自然能得到相应的发展。最后一个重要的领域是创造性表达。当他们在户外的时候，给他们一个不同的调色板，不同的东西，去体验、去看、去听、去感觉、去触摸。这也有助于他们的创造性表达和发展。所以说，掌握上述领域技能对健康发展至关重要，而我认为户外课堂在其中发挥着很重要的作用。

06:04—07:00

So you can see here the children have come [to] visit, early years' children in the top one and older children in the bottom slide and we've just taken their learning outside, and you really see a different set of kids. Don't restrict your thinking just to early years because I know traditionally we have a lot of indoor and outdoor play for the early years' children. But children of all ages benefit from this. You know, I really see a big difference in our school to the way that children concentrate and what they can do when you take the class outside. [It] doesn't even have to be necessarily special outdoor activity, that you just take a normal lesson outside and you will see a big difference in what they're doing.

你们可以从幻灯片上看到，来我们学校的学生各种年龄都有，上面这张幻灯片上是年龄小的学生，这张幻灯片的下面是年龄大一点的学生。我们只是带着他们到户外学习，你们可以看到培养出来的孩子完全不一样。不要将你们的想法局限在年龄小的孩子上，因为我知道，一般而言，我们会为他们设置很多室内和户外活动。但不同年龄段的小孩都能从这些活动中受益。我发现我们学校的户外课堂真的很有用，孩子们的注意力提高了，也能做更多的事情了。我们甚至不需要特别的户外活动，把普通的课堂搬到户外去，你们都能发现他能够做的事情已经跟以前有很大不同。

07:04—08:36

In China, with so many children living in apartments, the outdoor classroom is very very important, because it does help to restore some of those traditional benefits of childhood. You know, I think, probably from myself growing up with a big backyard, and you know, plenty of place to play and explore. You know, a lot of children these days have a very different experience where they don't get to have that same outdoors even a time where they are living. So, you know, we should really be thinking about providing that for them at school. So we can address some of these challenges by getting them outside and more active, involving them in hands-on, loose parts outdoor play, creating opportunities to learn how to handle outdoor risks safely. You know sometimes I think we tend to be too overprotective of our kids. They really need to experience certain things for themselves and learn how to be responsible risk taker. Bring children to nature in ways that encourage them [to] connect more deeply, teaching them about cause and effect through outdoor and interpersonal activities.

在中国,很多孩子在公寓里居住,所以户外课堂非常重要,这真的能让他们受益于传统童年的一些好处。我想,可能是因为我在一个大大的后院长大,在那里有很多地方可以玩耍和探索。现在很多孩子的童年体验和我的很不一样,他们住的地方没有这样的户外活动。所以,我们真的应该考虑在学校为他们提供这些户外活动的场所。我们接受这些挑战,让他们走出教室,活跃起来。让他们参与到实践中去,在户外玩耍,创造机会让他们学习如何安全地应对户外的风险。有时候我觉得我们太过于保护孩子了。他们真的需要自己经历一些事情,学会做一个负责任的冒险者。让孩子们接触大自然,鼓励他们更深入地交流,通过户外和人际交往活动教会他们因果关系。

08:36—09:18

Also, providing them with a wide range of activities that support their holistic development. We don't need elaborate or expensive equipment; just be very creative in what you are doing. You know you can see here our kids have designed their city in part of their garden area. And then we brought it. You know, they're experimenting different places, different colors, etc. So you know, bring it outside and they'll discover and explore themselves a lot more.

同时,为他们提供多种多样的活动有利于他们全面发展。我们不需要精密或昂贵的设施,只需要在所做的事情上加点创意就可以。你们可以看到,我学校的孩子们在他们的花园里设计了他们的城市,我们带他们到户外。他们设计了不同的城市,使用了不同的颜色等等。所以说,将课堂搬到户外,他们能发现更多,体会更多。

09:19—10:35

OK, so, what actually constitutes an outdoor classroom? What are the characteristics? Most activities that can be done indoors can be done outdoors. Some activities occur best outdoors. Some can only occur outdoors. So you really need to plan for children, particularly in the early years to be able to move freely from indoors to outdoors, very important aspect of your school design and designating the area for the early years. So our children spend a substantial part of their time outside. You must ensure that they can get in and out very very safely. So that's also a very important thing to keep in mind. There's such a huge range of activities for children to participate in, including many that you sort of traditionally think of as indoor ones. So, you know, just start thinking about what can you do, how can you get those kids outside more, what things can you do with them.

那么，户外教室由什么东西组成呢？它有什么特点？在室内可以做的大多数活动都可以在户外进行。有些活动在户外更好，还有些活动只能在户外。所以真的需要为孩子们规划，特别是为幼童们规划，让他们能够自由地从室内到户外，这是学校规划非常重要的一方面，为年幼的孩子设计户外活动区域。这样一来，我们的孩子大部分时间都在户外，所以必须确保他们安全进出。这是一个要特别注意的问题。有很多活动都适合让孩子们参与，其中包括很多传统上认为是室内的活动。所以，你们要开始思考你们能提供些什么活动，怎样才能让他们在户外呆更长时间，你们能和他们在户外做些什么活动。

10:41—11:55

So when you are designing your outdoor space, you need to make sure that you've got a balance of areas for the kids to be physically active and less active. Just because they are outside doesn't mean they have to be running around all the time and, you know, sort of racing off. They can still do some quiet play outside that is going to be beneficial. We need to give them the opportunity to initiate their own learning experiences and activities. Teachers are just there to support them. In that way, outdoor curriculum evolves and changes with children's changing needs and interests. We just need to ensure that children experience nature in as many ways as possible. So in the slide on the right hand side, the kids were actually designing rockets, and so they came outside to test their rockets and see how far they would fly.

所以，当您在设计户外活动的区域时，需要尽量取得平衡，既有奔跑打闹的地方，也有安静学习的地方。孩子们在户外，并不意味着他们必须一直在跑，甚至你追我赶。他们可以在外面做一些安静的游戏，这也非常有好处。我们需要给他们机会，让他们自己主动学习，积极参加活动。老师们只需稍加帮助。这样，户外课程会随着孩子们不断变化的需求和兴趣而改进、变化。我们只需要确保孩子们尽可能多地以不同的方式来体验大自然。在这张幻灯片的右边,孩子们实际上是在设计火箭,他们跑到户外测试他们的火箭,看看这些火箭能飞多远。

11:57—12:38

So I encourage you to look at what the research says when you are planning your designs. There're four basic benefits of the outdoor classroom. One is physical, so an increasing physical development, capability and activity, setting up patterns for active, healthy lifestyle. We have fewer children suffering from diseases such obesity, diabetes, ADD and ADHD, if they are getting outside and much more physically active. So think about what equipment that you need to meet this.

所以我鼓励你们先参考研究结果然后才开始设计。户外教室主要有四个好处。第一,有助于孩子的身体健康。有助于孩子的身体发展,能力提升和增加活动,为积极健康的生活方式打下基础。我们学校患有肥胖症、糖尿病、注意缺陷障碍、多动症等疾病的孩子数量更少,因为如果他们常常参加户外活动,会更活跃。所以想想你们需要什么设施满足这个需求。

12:39—13:20

OK, another benefit of the outdoor classroom is cognitive. Stronger language, problem solving and communication skills through projects and group activity. Developing an interest in science and math through connecting with nature. Fostering learning through self-initiation, control and personal responsibility. What basis or what area will help promote cognitive development?

户外教室的另一个好处是有助于提高孩子们的认知能力。孩子们能够提升自己的语言表达能力,解决问题的能力和沟通的能力,通过参与项目和小组活动。通过与自然的联系培养孩子们对科学和数学的兴趣。通过自我促进、控制和个人责任来促进孩子们的学习。什么方法或什么领域有助于促进认知发展?

13:20—14:00

Psychological is a third benefit of the outdoor classroom. You have happier, more positive children, better self-esteem. They've affected relationship building in a cooperative, non-competitive environment. Manifest classroom harmony and social emotional mastery. So if students are excited about the idea and involved in the planning, you are well underway to meeting this aspect.

促进孩子心理健康是户外教室的第三个好处。户外活动有助于培养更快乐、积极、自信的孩子。户外活动有助于在合作的、非竞争性的环境中建立良好的关系,有助于构建和谐的课堂和让孩子们在社交中学会控制情绪。因此，如果学生对这个想法感到兴奋，并参与到计划中来，那么你们就可以准备好迎接身心健康的孩子们了。

14:01—14:45

And the fourth benefit of having the outdoor classroom is understanding. So they get familiarity and appreciation of nature. They have a wide expansive view of how the globe works, and they build stewardship skills for the environment. So I think, you know, everybody can agree that all of these things are [a] very very important part of a child, of looking after the whole child and educating the whole child, planning for them and their future.

户外教室的第四个好处在于能够提升理解能力。孩子们熟悉、欣赏大自然，他们对地球的运作方式会有更广阔的视野，会建立自己的环境管理模式。没人会否认这些是孩子成长中非常重要的部分，这有助于培养更全面的孩子，为他们和他们的未来做计划。

14:45—15:40

So the outdoor classroom actually blurs the boundaries between academic learning and creative play. Kids love the outdoor classroom. So when the teacher asks who wants to go outside, every hand is raised. I think we often see that absenteeism goes down on the days when it's outdoor classroom day. So by preserving a child's innate sense of curiosity and wonder, we foster active and engaged life-long learners. Yes, learning can be fun. If you don't have a lot of space, you can still make this work. If you have a big space, but not the funds, add to your outdoor classroom in stages, several small components over a number of years.

因此，户外课堂实际上模糊了学术学习和创造性游戏之间的界限。孩子们喜欢户外课堂。当老师问谁想出去时，每个孩子都会举手。我们经常看到，在户外教学日，缺勤率会下降。通过呵护孩子们的好奇心和怀疑的天性，我们能培养积极主动的终身学习者。学习可以很有趣。即便没有足够的空间，你们仍然可以做到。如果你们有很大的空间，但没有足够多的资金，那你们可以分阶段添加户外课堂，每年添一点。

15:50—17:42

So when children are outside, you often see that they are very curious and want to explore. So you see they are more motivated, and their concentration increases. Several studies have found that learning outdoors actually increases memory because in natural environments, all senses are in use. That means more memory channels are active, leads to better retention and learning. Use of all senses supports our children's consciousness, to feel, to hear, taste, see, smell. That teaches our children a lot more than just looking at pictures in a book. Upon this slide, this one, this particular class, they're really really active kids. And when you see them indoors in the classroom, their concentration span is fairly limited, so the teacher has to keep moving, you know, from one different activity to another. You bring these kids outside to do a very similar activity and what they were doing here was patterns. So, you know, we just brought out the white boards and a lot of blocks and Lego, and numbers and letters, etc. that could go on the magnetic boards and then they are able to just look around them as well and decide how to work on patterns. For the whole hour, those kids were totally engrossed in what they were doing. Whereas if they had been inside the classroom, they would have been restless probably within about twenty minutes doing exactly the same activity. So you know, just taking them outdoors if you want to makes a huge difference to have the kids to look at their lessons.

当孩子们在户外时，你们会发现他们很好奇，想要探索。他们也会更有动力，注意力也更集中。几项研究发现，在户外学习能加强记忆，因为在自然环境中，我们会调动所有的感官。这意味着更多的记忆通道活跃起来了，有助于提升记忆力和学习能力。调动所有感官有助于提升孩子们的意识，让他们去感受、聆听、品尝、观察、闻气味。这教给孩子的东西远比只是盯着书上的图片看要多得多。请看这张幻灯片，这个班上的孩子们非常活跃。在教室里时，他们集中注意力的时间很有限，老师必须不停地开展一个又一个不同的活动。把这些孩子带到户外做类似的活动，我们这里是让他们学习形状。我们不过是把白板、一堆的积木、乐高玩具和一些数字、字母卡等等这些可以吸在磁力板上的东西拿到户外，学生们能够看着周围的东西，然后想办法自己拼出这些形状。整整一个小时，那些孩子完全沉浸在他们所做的事情中。如果他们在教室里，同样是学习形状，可能20分钟内他们就会不安分了。所以，如果想让孩子更有效地学习的话，把他们带到户外去吧。

17:43—19:45

So there's no standard design for an outdoor classroom. The key is to develop it in a way that would work best for you, for your school grounds and for the needs of your school. You don't have to limit yourself to just one area. Use what you have. Use the environment to support natural play. If you got a mud puddle somewhere in the school grounds, kids can make mud pies with a shovel in the play pool. If you got grass, they can grow flowers. Discovery is just waiting to be made by stepping outside. Any task could engage students to work together to achieve a common goal. But there is ensuring that the flowers are watered or building a bridge to support their toy cars, understanding which colors to mix to produce a desired hue. It encourages cooperative play, builds conversational skills through language and challenges students to come up with creative solutions. Look at the outdoor space that you've been a lot to play time and start getting creative. Make a garden for students to plan. Our students even use the garden area to build their cities. This is part of their unit of inquiry, so we made, you know, another use of the garden area. Then they brought their parents in to explain what that they've been doing.

户外教室没有设计标准。关键是要采用最适合的方案来设计，根据学校的场地和需求来设计。没必要把设计局限在一个区域内。充分利用已有的，利用环境来开展游戏活动。如果学校操场上有一个泥坑，孩子们可以在这个泥坑里用铲子做泥饼。如果学校有草地，那孩子们可以在上面种花。走到户外去发现。任何学习任务都可以派给学生，让他们共同努力，达成共同的目标。与此同时，学校也要给孩子种下的花浇水，给他们的玩具车建座小桥，了解哪些颜色搭配可以得到想要的效果。鼓励开展合作性游戏，通过语言提升会话技巧，并引导学生提出创造性的解决方案。看看户外空间，你们的空间足够多了，开始变得有创意吧。划出一块花园给学生自己规划。我们的学生甚至在花园上建了他们自己的城市。这是他们的探究单元的一部分，也是花园的另一个用途。然后带着他们的父母来看，向父母解释他们一直在做的事。

19:52—20:38

We put in a second playground that encourages motor skills and physical development and it's amazing when they first started, you know, learning to use this equipment they couldn't even hold on for more than a couple of seconds. Now they can actually hang on and move from place to, you know, sort of different one to, different one of this to the next, to the next, to the next and just shows how you are, you know, developing their physical development. They absolutely love going out using this place. We often use it in a particular way when we're going out there with them, not just in their play time but during the class to get them to do some team work, team building and some challenges.

我们还建了一个操场，用来鼓励孩子们发展自己的运动技能和体能。令人惊讶的是，他们刚开始使用这些设施时，最多只能坚持几秒。如今他们可以坚持更久了，可以从操场的一边走到另一边。这切切实实地向我们展示了这些设施是如何促进他们体能发展的。他们非常喜欢到这个操场来。当我们和孩子们一起出去的时候，我们经常用一种特殊的方式来利用这个操场，不仅仅是在他们的游戏时间，而是在课堂上让他们做一些团队活动、团队建设和接受一些挑战。

20:39—20:55

And then the sand underneath that playground, we actually provide a place for building and creating. So they can get out there and build things and then you just, you know, wipe it away and you can start again.

然后就是操场下面的沙子,这实际上为孩子们提供了一个建造和创造的区域。他们可以去沙子上建东西,然后推倒、重建。

20:56—22:32

Thinking how great it was to climb a tree when you were a child. So I think it's a really good idea if you got a few strong trees in your school grounds. Of course we have to make sure that the tree-climbing goes on under supervision. That… you know, so many kids just lack that opportunity these days. You can incorporate biology lesson, plants and animals found in the outdoor classroom, instead of just sitting in the lab and looking at slides or you know, doing the experiment that way. Take it outside, even if it is a shady and shelter place where children could sit in a circle or do table work. So these gazebos form a very cheap and easy solution. If flexible, we can have the kids doing their table work, we can move the tables away and just have chairs, we can have just kids sitting on rugs on the ground but they're sheltered in the shade. They really love getting outdoors and using this space. It also can be used in their play times if they want a sheltered and shady area to sit and eat their snacks. You can organize an outdoor drumming circle or create music based on the sounds of nature, the wind, birds' song, etc.

想想小时候,爬树多快乐呀。所以我觉得如果学校里有几棵大树的话,真的很棒。当然,我们必须确保孩子爬树时有人监督。现在很多孩子都没有爬树的机会。你们可以将生物课、户外教室里找到的植物和动物都用上,而不是坐在实验室里看幻灯片,或者在实验室做实验。把这些课堂搬到户外去,哪怕是遮阴的、遮蔽的地方,只要孩子们可以席地而坐,围在一起或者围坐在桌旁。这些凉亭既经济又方便,是很合适的地方。如果想要更灵活一点,我们可以让孩子们在桌子上做事,我们也可以把桌子搬走,只留椅子,我们可以让孩子们坐在地毯上,但是要让他们在阴凉处。他们真的很喜欢户外活动,喜欢在这个区域活动。还可以在游戏时间让他们坐在遮蔽的、遮阴的区域吃零食。可以组织孩子们在户外围坐击鼓,或者根据自然的声音、风、鸟的歌声等等来创作音乐。

22:33—23:05

You can use the local area around your school. We go further a field and take exploratory walks in the bush. And then we discuss history in context with the natural environment. We encourage cleaning up environment. The environment is not just in the school. So take the kids out to develop their social consciousness.

还可以利用学校周围的区域。走向更远的地方,在灌木丛中探索、散步。然后在自然环境中讨论历史。我们鼓励清洁环境。环境不仅仅指的是学校的环境。把孩子们带到户外,培养他们的社会意识。

23:06—24:12

For student work, students' art will go on display. There are so many art projects wanting to be explored outdoors. Students can use just about anything outside to enrich their creative side, key part in their early development. We just make sure that their artworks are appreciated, afterwards, upon display, so that it fosters a sense of accomplishment in the students, also leads to discussions about why they use certain colors or do certain things. Even discussing how it makes students feel is a great way to encourage self-expression and allow students to grow comfortable in sharing ideas. Why not use sticks, leaves and pebbles around the school for students to create natural works of art? You keep a natural work of art on display for a week then take it away and they can actually use the same materials to create something else the next week.

至于学生的作品,学生的艺术作品会展示出来。很多艺术项目都可以在户外探讨。学生们可以利用户外的一切来丰富他们的创造性思维,这是他们早期发展中很重要的一部分。我们只需确保他们的作品在展示时被人欣赏,这样带给学生成就感,激发他们讨论为什么他们会使用某些颜色或做某些事情。让学生分享自己的感觉是一种鼓励自我表达的好方法,让学生在分享想法时变得更自在。为什么不利用学校里的棍子、树叶和鹅卵石让学生们创作自然艺术作品呢?一件自然艺术作品展示一个星期,然后把它拿走,学生们实际上可以用同样的材料在下周创作出其他的作品。

24:13—25:17

Create a reading circle. Students can read anywhere and be transported as far as their minds are willing to go. But why not take the lessons that they love outside? Bringing reading time out of the classroom and into an outdoor environment is a great way to bring students closer. Use outdoor pillows to create reading circles and you can reach students at the same level as them rather than sitting high above them. Discussion on reading material can easily flow and it's open and encouraged. Dialogue circles are great ways to build collaboration, respect and positive behavior between students. But this goes on. I encourage you just to get creative and utilize what you have. Everybody can do that. There's a real place for the outdoor classroom I think in every school, no matter what setting it is and what age are the children. Thank you.

创建一个读书会。学生们可以在任何地方阅读，他们的想法可以把他们带到任何他们想去的地方。但是为什么不把他们喜欢的课程带到户外呢？把阅读时间从室内带到户外可以让学生们更亲近。可以带上户外枕头围坐在一起，老师可以和学生们坐在一起，不要坐在他们上面。关于阅读材料的讨论很容易会发散开来，这种讨论是开放的，是值得鼓励的。这种对话有助于促使学生相互协作、尊重，有助于鼓励正面的行为。建议你们去创造和利用学校已有的东西。每个人都能这样做。我认为每所学校都有这么一个真正的户外教室，不管这个学校背景如何，孩子们的年龄有多大。谢谢大家！

III. 实战练习二

1. 演讲背景

深圳贝赛思国际学校副总裁应邀参加"2017必达亚洲春季峰会"，并就"从所有利益相关者的角度考虑来设计学校"发表主旨演讲。他在演讲中指出，学校的利益相关者包括学生、老师、行政人员、学校领导、非教学人员、家长、课程、投资者等。学校需要既考虑校园设计的美观和课程设置，又要好好教育学生，才能使学生和家长都满意，并为学校盈利。他还分享了设计学校的时候需要注意的事情，包括走廊墙壁保洁、公共空间的花草、学生在校园攀爬追逐问题、储物空间、家长接送孩子、技术选择和采用等问题。

2. 预习词汇

analogy 类比；类推
single layer 单层
sprinkle 糖粒
fondant 软糖
cereal treat 燕麦零食
marshmallow 棉花糖
breaded cake 面包式蛋糕
wire 金属丝
plumbing 水管装置；水暖设备
building material 建筑材料
administrator 行政人员
non-teaching staff 非教学人员
parent 家长

positive reputation 良好声誉；好名声
continuation 延续；持续发展
for-profit education 营利性教育；以营利为目的的教育
curb appeal 房屋外观的吸引力
enroll 注册；登记；招收
curriculum 课程
bells and whistles 华而不实的东西
hallway 走廊
trample 践踏；踩踏
artificial turf 人造草
flower box 花盆
plan B 备用方案
bench 长凳
electrical box 电箱
storage box 存储箱；存储盒
millwork 木制品；磨坊
cabinetry 橱柜
passing period（课间）休息时间
drop-off and pick-up 往返接送
residential neighborhood 住宅区
industrial area 工业区
commercial area 商业区
turf 草皮
scrap 废纸；废料
misprint 印刷错误
printer 打印机
recycling plan 循环利用计划
printing room 文印室
STEM/Science, Technology, Engineering and Mathematics 科学、技术、工程、数学
specialty class 专业课
closet 壁橱；小储藏间
shelving 置物架
cabinet 橱柜
interactive whiteboard 互动式电子白板
dry-erase marker 可擦马克笔
in-thing 流行事物

must-have 必备的东西
skimp on 节省
wall-mounted 壁挂式的
projector 投影仪
computer lab 计算机实验室
AP school 预科学校
College Board 美国大学理事会
proper ventilation 通风良好
eyewash station 洗眼站
shower 淋浴室
entry-level grade 一年级
K12 school/K through twelve school 十二年一贯制学校
kindergarten 幼儿园
wait list 候补名单
UWC/United World Colleges 世界联合学院
UWC Changshu 世界联合学院常熟分校
school year 学年
cyclical 周期性的
back-to-school night 返校夜
musical 音乐剧
icing（糕饼的）糖霜

3. 演讲文本

00:00—00:42

OK. So before lunch, I am gonna go ahead and make you kind of hungry. I wanna share some of my experiences in building schools. My network basis is going very quickly in the United States. We went from one school in 1998. We had three in 2010, and next year, we will have over 30. We had our first international school in Shenzhen. And we've grown fast and we built a lot of schools. I also had the pleasure of visiting schools in Mexico, United States and China. I've seen a lot of schools and a lot of great designs. And I've seen a lot of not-so-great designs. So my purpose today is kind of give you a little bit of my experiences and some lessons I've learned.

午饭前，我要继续演讲，这会让你们有点饿。我想分享一些我在建设学校方面的经历。我们的学校在美国发展得很快。我们从1998年的1所学校起步。在2010年增加到3所。明年，我们会有超过30所学校。我们的第一所国际学校在深圳。我们发展得很快，我们创建了很多学校。我还有幸访问了墨西哥、美国和中国的学校。我看过很多学校和很多很棒的设计。我也见过很多不那么好的设计。所以我今天的目的是给你们分享一些我的经历和我学到的一些经验教训。

00:42—01:56

But first I wanna draw an analogy. Whenever I can draw an analogy, I will try to make it about food. And since it's just right before lunch, I think it's kind of fitting. So let's take cake for example. Let's assume right now that everyone loves cake. If you don't love cake, please bear with me and pretend that you do. (I went the wrong direction.) OK. So here's two cakes. The one on the left is very simple, single-layer chocolate cake. The one on the right is very elaborate, decorated, different angles, lots of colors. Here, the one on the left is, I think, very simple, single-layer cake. The one on the right got the cartoon character popping out of it. Some very bright colors. It's very eye-catching. It will definitely draw your attention. Another set of cakes. The one on the left: double-layer chocolate cake with some colorful sprinkles. The one on the right: a very scary-looking dragon which will definitely draw your attention. I think, well, that is an interesting cake. Another chocolate cake on the left, some candy pieces around it, the one on the right, yes, that's a cake in the design of a dress. That's very pretty. It's the one that's gonna get you talking. There's no doubt about that.

首先,我想做个类比。每次我做类比时,我总会将类比与食物搭上边。因为现在刚好是午饭前,我觉得这也很合适。所以,让我们拿蛋糕来做例子吧。假设在场的每个人都喜欢蛋糕。如果您不喜欢蛋糕,请原谅我,假装喜欢吧。好的,这里有两个蛋糕。左边的这个蛋糕很简单,单层巧克力蛋糕。右边的这个蛋糕非常精致,有很多装饰,有不同的角度和多彩的颜色。所以说,左边这个蛋糕是一个非常简单的单层蛋糕。右边的这个蛋糕上有卡通人物,有些非常鲜艳的颜色。它非常引人注目,一定会引起您的注意。来看另一组蛋糕,左边的这个,这是一个双层巧克力蛋糕,上面有五颜六色的糖粒。右边的这个蛋糕上有一只看起来很吓人的龙,一定会让你们注意到它。我觉得这个蛋糕很有意思。另一个是巧克力蛋糕,左边这个,上面有一些糖果。右边那个,是一个裙子形状的蛋糕,非常漂亮。看到这些蛋糕,你们肯定会有些想法,毫无疑问。

01:56—03:09

Let's talk about what's inside the cake. Because you want cake, you want to be able to cut it open and see cake. So first, on the left you have a pink and white frosted cake. And you cut it open and you see a pink and white cake. Around the left… I am sorry, on the right you see a fondant. You've already been familiar with fondant. It's frosted and kind of rubbery, and you can do all kinds of cool shapes with it. But it doesn't really taste that good. Over here, you got a red and white frosted cake. You cut it open and it's red and white. Over on the left... oh on the right you see a cereal treat... a white crispy, marshmallow cereal treat. This is how they get shapes. You can't do that with a breaded cake. So it's actually not cake. You kind of see the pattern here. Look at the right. Now you see wires and metal and wooden dowel rods inside your cake. Here you have plumbing. This is construction material inside your cake to make it look beautiful and make it look eye-catching. This one is more cereal treat than cake. It's got some sort of plastic platform. I'm sure there is some wood and some wires in it to hold it up and to make it look interesting.

我们来看看蛋糕里面是什么。因为想要吃蛋糕，就会想切开它，看到蛋糕。首先，左边这儿有一个粉白相间、裹了糖霜的蛋糕。右边你们看到的是一块软糖。想必你们很熟悉这种软糖。它上面裹着一层糖霜，有点像橡胶。这种软糖可以变成各种各样好玩的形状，但它的味道并不是那么好。这里，你们看到的是一个红白相间、裹了糖霜的蛋糕。把它切开，它是红色和白色的。右边你们看到的是美味的燕麦零食，白色的，脆脆的棉花糖燕麦。这就是这个蛋糕成形的原因，面包式蛋糕做不到这样。所以这实际上不是蛋糕。在这里可以看到这个图案。请看右边的这个蛋糕，可以看到金属丝和木棒在这个蛋糕里面。这里有管道。这是蛋糕里的建材，有了这些材料，这个蛋糕看起来才漂亮、引人注目。这是一种比蛋糕更美味的燕麦零食。它有个塑料平台，我相信里面还有木棒和一些丝线支撑整个蛋糕，让这个蛋糕看起来更有意思。

03:09—03:33

My point is it's not always cake. It looks beautiful from the outside. It brings people to it. It's interesting, but once you cut it open and get to the inside and you realize it's not what you had expected. So now let's jump. I will make the connection to the cake a little bit. But let's talk about who your stakeholders are, when you are building the school.

我想要说的是，这些看起来是蛋糕，但不一定真的是蛋糕。从表面看，这些蛋糕很漂亮、引人注目。有意思的是，一旦把它切开，看到里面的东西，你们会意识到它跟期望的不同。现在我们换个话题，等一会儿我会再和蛋糕联系起来。让我们看看你们的学校有哪些利益相关者和建设学校有关。

03:33—04:29

First of all, your students. That's obvious. You know. When you think of who is the main stakeholder of schools, it's the students. Next one, the easy one to think of, it's your teachers. That's the bare elements that you need of a school. You need students and teachers. Other stakeholders, you might guess, administrators, school leaders, non-teaching staff, these are also stakeholders in your school. Parents, obviously, are stakeholders in your school. The curriculum and your investors. Out of this list of stakeholders, the one that gets forgotten the most is the curriculum. It is what we do. It is what a school is for. When you see a school, you expect to see learning inside. You expect to go in and you expect to see students learning. It's what we do. The curriculum is what's forgotten often times in the very beginning in the stages of designing a school.

首先是学生。这显而易见。一提到谁是学校的主要利益相关者时，就会想到学生。另一个利益相关者，很容易想到的是老师。这是构成学校的基本要素。学校需要学生和老师。其他的利益相关者，你们可能会猜到，有行政人员、学校领导、非教学人员，这些也是学校的利益相关者。显而易见，家长也是学校的利益相关者。另外还有课程和学校的投资者。在所有的利益相关者中，最容易被忘记的是课程。然而，课程是我们在学校所学的，是学校存在的原因。看到一所学校时，你们希望看到的是在这所学校可以学到什么。你们会想进入这所学校，看看学生是怎么学习的。这个就是我们现在正在做的。开始设计一所学校时，以及学校设计的各个阶段，课程往往是最容易被遗忘的。

04:29—06:15

OK, let's talk about the purpose of the school. We know the purpose of a school is to teach kids. So if that's the case, oh, OK, if that's the case, you gonna invest in curriculum and this takes some thought. What are you going to teach? You invest in the curriculum. You teach the students properly. They learn. You get the student results that you want. This is gonna to lead to… (oh, there are some technical difficulties here.) This is gonna to lead to parents' satisfaction. So if you teach the kids properly, your parents will be happy. And if your parents are happy, your school is going to develop a positive reputation. Once your school develops that positive reputation, what are the patterns here? That positive reputation will create demand in the community. And that's going to ensure the continuation of your school. So having a good curriculum, developing the students, teaching them properly, making sure your parents are happy with the student results, and a good reputation. Now there's this growing market of for-profit education. It's your purpose of your school to profit. It's to make money. If that's the case, you might invest in facilities and marketing. You want that curb appeal. You wanna draw people to you. You want to get them feel, "Well, that's a beautiful school. I am gonna go [to] see that school." You wanna attract as many people as you can to come to your school. And of that group of people you wanna convince a percentage of them to enroll at your school. And if you keep the school looking beautiful and keep it interesting, a steady stream of interest, that's going to ensure the continuation of the school.

让我们谈谈建立学校的目的。我们知道学校的目的是教育孩子。如果是这样的话，你们会寄希望于一些课程，至于哪些课程，需要你们好好思考一下。你们打算教什么？你们会在课程上进行投入。你们好好地教学生，学生努力学习，得到期待的结果。这关乎家长的满意度。所以，如果好好地教育学生，家长就会很开心。如果学生家长开心满意，那学校就会有好名声。一旦学校有了好的名声，会怎样呢？好的名声会在社区中创造需求，有助于确保学校延续下去。所以设计一个好的课程，培养学生，好好地教育他们，确保学生家长对学生的成绩感到满意，为学校赢得良好的声誉。现在盈利性教育市场不断扩大。如果学校是盈利性质的，目的便是赚钱。如果是这样的话，你们要在设施和市场营销上投入资金。你们会想要学校看起来有吸引力，想引起他们的注意，想让他们觉得，"嗯，那学校很漂亮，想去看看"。你们会想尽可能多地吸引人来参观你们的学校。慕名而来的人，你想说服其中一部分人在你们学校报名注册。所以，如果学校看起来很漂亮、有趣，一直都很吸引人，这将有助于确保学校延续下去。

06:15—07:20

Now these seem like two different things. But it turns out they are not mutually exclusive. You can teach kids properly and the school can still make money. It's all that how you implement it. Designing a school with a curriculum with a good strong learning program but no thought towards aesthetics, it can be done. But it's tricky. Often the school that has no curb appeal, it's going to look bland and it's going to look boring, and not interesting. It's going to be hard to draw people to you. On the other hand, if you start to design a school without a curriculum in mind, and you are not thinking about what you are going to be doing academically, this is going to come off as superficial and hollow. You know, it's all bells and whistles. It's making a beautiful school just to make money. Designing a school with both of these things in mind, it makes it a lot easier. The sooner you can get the investment team and the education team together, to talk about the design of the school, the better it's gonna be for you!

现在这些看起来是两种不同的东西。但事实证明，它们并不是相互排斥的。学校可以很好地教育孩子，同时可以盈利。主要取决于你们怎么做。设计学校时，把课程集中在学习课程上，不要考虑美学，可以达到目的。但操作起来很棘手。通常，学校看起来很平淡、很无聊、没意思。很难把人吸引到你们学校。另一方面，如果开始设计学校时，没有事先考虑课程问题，没有考虑你们将在学术方面做些什么，会显得肤浅和空洞，华而不实。把学校变漂亮的唯一目的就是赚钱。设计学校时，同时考虑外观和课程这两件事，就会变得容易很多。越早让投资团队和教育团队聚在一起，探讨学校的设计，对你们就越有利！

07:20—08:07
So let's talk about some lessons that I've learned about developing schools and building schools in my experience. First of all, the hallways. About a meter up, depending on the grades that you serve, the walls of the hallways are gonna get disgusting. They are gonna get scratched and scraped from hundreds of backpacks scraping across them 180 days out of the year. Think about… these are kids and they are gonna lean on the walls and they are gonna drag themselves along the walls. There are some solutions to that. You can repaint it every year. You can buy materials aligned the walls with something that can sustain that type of abuse. But just know that's gonna happen. So take a few minutes… when you are thinking about your building materials, how are those materials gonna be affected by the students in the school?

接下来，我想谈谈我从经验中学到的关于学校发展和建设的经验。首先，关于过道。大约一米高，取决于学生的年级，走廊的墙壁会变得很脏很难看。走廊的墙壁会被学生的书包刮花，每年180天的上学日里，这些墙壁会被成百上千个书包刮来刮去。要知道，学生还只是孩子，他们会靠在墙上，在墙上蹭来蹭去。有些方法可以解决这个问题。每年重新粉刷，买一样的材料，每年重新刷墙可以解决这个问题。但是要知道，学生会刮蹭墙壁，这是肯定会发生的。所以花几分钟考虑一下，当你们思考要用什么建材时，学生们会对这些材料造成什么影响？

08:07—09:04
Flowers are going to get trampled. So what I've noticed in China, there is a lot of use of flowers in open spaces and kids get in there and they trample on them. They play on them. They pick them. They pull them up. And this is the area maybe could have very easily been developed into an area where they could have played, maybe it's just grass or artificial turf. But by adding the flower boxes, I guarantee you the kids are going to crawl in there. This also later on if you design that into your school, this is later on gonna cause a bit of discipline problem where now teachers and administrators have to come up with the rule you can't play in the flower boxes. But the kids are going to do that anyway. So if we just eliminate some of the unnecessary elements of the landscape and give them something to play on. In fact, I was very impressed with Mr. Wang's presentation. His use of outdoor space and giving them something to climb on is the solution. Just know if the kids are gonna go into the flowers, and the flowers are going to die.

校园里的花会被学生踩踏。我注意到在中国，学校公共空间里种了很多花，孩子们会去踩花，他们在花丛里玩，摘花，甚至连根拔起。这片区域很可能会变成学生玩耍的地方，也许只是草或人造草皮。但是如果放置花盆，我敢肯定孩子们会爬进花盆里去。此外，这个方法会带来一些纪律问题，现在老师和行政人员必须明确告诉学生不能在花盆里玩。但是，学生依然会我行我素。所以，不如取消这些不必要的景观元素，给孩子打造一片可以玩耍的区域。实话说，我对王老师的演讲印象深刻。他把这些景观改造成户外空间，孩子在这里可以攀爬，这就很好地解决了这个问题。要知道孩子们会去采花，这些花会因此死去。

09:04—10:01

Sharp corners are going to injure a child. It's inevitable. If you have sharp corners in your hallways, on your benches outside, whatever, at some point in time, a child is going to get hurt. So think about this, depending on the grades that you serve... round your corners. The kids are going to get hurt on them. It's inevitable. It will happen. Kids will climb on structures, even if they are not supposed to. Same with the trees. Again, I am very impressed with Mr. Wang's presentation. He knows they are gonna climb the trees, let's have a plan B in place, a nice soft place for them to fall to. Same thing with structures, whether it's a structure that's holding some electrical equipment or a structure that's holding some storage. The kids are gonna to climb on that. Think about these when you are designing your campuses. Where are you going to put the electrical boxes? Where are you going to put the storage boxes for outside? What about your benches? What about the walls? The ladders rigged along the walls? Think about the kids are going to climb on them.

尖角容易伤到孩子们，这也是不可避免的。如果过道里有尖角，或者户外的长椅上有尖角，或者其他地方有尖角，总会有某些孩子被这些尖角弄伤。所以，我们在设计时要把这一点考虑进来，要根据各个年级学生的不同情况来处理这些尖角。孩子们会被这些尖角磕碰到，这是不可避免的，会遇到这种情况。孩子们会爬上建筑物，即使他们不应该这样做。孩子们也会爬到树上。关于这一点，我再次发现王老师的演讲让人印象非常深刻。他知道孩子们会爬上树，所以准备了一个备用方案，在树下铺上软垫，这样孩子们即使从树上跳下来也不会受伤。对于建筑物也是一样的，不管是用来放置电气设备的建筑物，还是用来储藏的建筑物，孩子们肯定会爬这些建筑物。所以，在设计时将这些考虑进去。在哪里放置电箱？外面哪里适合存放存储箱？凳子放哪儿好？该怎么处理墙壁的尖角？梯子靠墙放吗？要注意，孩子们会爬梯子。

10:01—10:32

OK. No teacher or school administrator has ever said this school has too much storage. That's not something that we say. You have to have storage. When I say storage, it's not just big open rooms where you can put big bulky equipment. When I say storage, I also mean inside the classrooms, the millwork, the cabinetry… Your teachers need place to put these stacks of papers and all of their books. So the more storage, the better. Consider that when you are designing your schools.

没有老师或学校行政人员抱怨学校有太多的储物空间。我们从不会觉得储物空间太大。学校必须要有足够多的储物空间。我这里说的储物空间，不仅仅是大的可以在摆放笨重设备的开放式房间，还包括教室里的，木制品的，橱柜的储物空间。老师需要地方放置成堆的文件和书。所以储物空间越多越好。在设计学校时，请考虑这一点。

10:32—11:34

Consider the movements of your students from classroom to classroom, or to the cafeteria, or to the playground, or the office, or the nurses' station. A mini-school is built on a bell station where the halls are fairly empty for 50-60 minutes at a time. And then it is passing period and suddenly a thousand kids come out all at once. And all those kids are trying to get to their next destination. If you have various sizes of children, which I am sure every school is going to have, that little child who is trying to get to the bathroom in his five to six minutes passing period is going to get lost in the crowd. So think about how are we gonna move these masses of children in these small spaces of time that we have. Put that into your design plan as you're thinking about it early on. Mr. Wang also mentioned running. Students are going to run. There is nothing you can do to stop it. You can make rules, you can yell at them, you can put it in a student handbook, but they are still going to run. Rather than fighting it, embrace it. Just know that they are going to run, and have it built into your plan.

在设计学校的时候，还要考虑学生从教室到教室，或者到食堂，或者到操场，或者办公室，或者护士站的路线。设想一下，在车站建一所迷你学校，站台大厅每次有50～60分钟空无一人，到了课间休息的时候上千个孩子一下子出现。所有的孩子都想去往他们的下一个目的地。如果学校有各个年级的孩子，我相信每一所学校都有，那么这容易让那个在5～6分钟课间休息时间里想要上厕所的小孩在人群中迷路。所以想想要如何在这几分钟内快速有效地将这些孩子转移到各个地方去。设计学校的时候尽早考虑到设计中。王老师刚刚也提到了追逐。学生们喜欢跑来跑去，没有办法能阻止他们奔跑追逐。当然，可以制定规则，可以批评乱跑的学生，可以把不准乱跑写在学生手册里，但学生们还是会跑上跑下。与其想办法解决这个问题，不如想办法改善。知道学生会在校园跑来跑去，设计学校时把这点考虑进去。

11:36—12:50

Consider drop-off and pick-up. Consider this early on in your design process. When parents are coming in the morning to drop their kids off, and they are coming in the afternoon to pick them up, I can guarantee you a few things: The traffic will line up; your parents will queue up in their cars; some of the parents won't listen to your policies. They will turn right in the middle of the traffic. Someone will abandon their cars and run inside. Even if you say no parking on the curb, they are still going to do it. Think about this. And on that same note, consider the impact of your school on the neighborhood. Whether you are in a residential neighborhood, or maybe you are located in a more industrial area, or commercial area, architects and builders have only to deal with those angry parents or those angry neighbors for a period of time, for a few months while they are building the school. The school, the teachers, the leaders, the parents, they have to deal with that angry neighborhood forever. So the least impact on the surrounding neighborhood, the better. So consider this in your initial design. There is got to be a way to effectively and efficiently get your children into school in the morning, and then get them out of school and off to home in the afternoon.

考虑到家长往返接送孩子。在设计过程中尽早考虑这个问题。家长们早上来送孩子们，下午来接他们，有几点我敢说，接送时将会有一排长长的车队；孩子家长会在他们的车里排队；也有些家长不听指挥，在车流中右转。有人甚至会下车把孩子送到学校里面去。即使你们禁止在学校路边停车，有些家长还是会停在路边。考虑一下这个问题。同时考虑一下学校对周边地区有什么影响。无论你们的学校是在居民区，还是在工业区，或者是商业区，建筑师和建筑工人只需要在他们建学校的那几个月里跟那些愤怒的家长或愤怒的邻居沟通一段时间。而学校、老师、领导、家长，则永远得和那些怒气冲冲的邻居打交道。因此，学校对周围社区带来的影响越小越好。所以在最初设计时，要考虑这个问题。要找到一种方法，可以有效地让孩子们早上来学校上学，然后下午离开学校，放学回家。

12:50—13:32

Schools use a lot of paper. Technology is not going to solve this. Kids are gonna do worksheets. They are gonna color. They are gonna do art. There is a lot of paper that is gonna be used. Often times, we have stacks and stacks of paper, whether scrap paper or misprints, or old work, and it's just sitting around. And it's because often the stacks of paper are not conveniently located. The printers are put somewhere where is not convenient to the disposal of the paper. Have a recycling plan or at least a plan to get the paper out. Where are your printing rooms? Where are your workrooms gonna be located? Keep them conveniently easy to get rid of all that extra waste.

学校需要大量的纸张，技术也无法解决这个问题。孩子们做作业、上色、做艺术品，这些都需要用纸。通常，一堆纸张，不管是废纸还是印刷出错，还是旧的纸张，一堆杂乱地放在地上。这是因为成堆的纸张不太好处理，因为通常打印机放在不便于处理纸张的地方。制定一个纸张循环利用计划，或者至少解决废旧纸张的方案。文印室在哪里好？工作室呢？记得这些地方要方便处理掉所有多余的废纸。

13:32—14:05

Project-based learning, STEM (Science, Technology, Engineering and Mathematics) initiatives, art classes, music classes, for that matters, some very special classes, specialty classes… they all require storage. We don't just mean long term storage. But if you got an art class that needs every day for 50 minutes, that's not enough time for a child to finish his project. So often we have all these different projects in various phases of completion, they've got to be kept somewhere. And they can't be stacked on top of each other, and they can't just be put into a closet. So inside the classroom, we have to have a storage plan for this.

基于项目的学习，STEM（科学，技术，工程和数学）项目、艺术课程、音乐课，对于这些非常特殊的课程、专业课程，我们需要特别的存放空间。这里不只是指长期的存放空间。比如说，有一门艺术课，每天50分钟，这50分钟不够让孩子完成手上的艺术项目。所以我们经常需要把这些尚未完成的作品放置在某个地方。我们不能把这些作品堆在一起，或直接放进壁橱里。所以在教室里，我们必须预留一个空间来放置这些东西。

14:05—14:42

Shelving. Have a lot of shelving. And think about the shelving that you have. A lot of schools use cabins and cabins are OK, but make sure that cabins are big enough to uphold that A4 paper. That doesn't fit into a lot of places. So just be very careful when you're picking up the furniture and when you're designing shelving for your classrooms. And I don't know if I've mentioned this yet. But storage is a very important thing for schools. We can never have enough storage. And I think I've mentioned a few times, you kind of get that in your mind. Design storage into your classes or into your schools.

置物架，要准备很多置物架。学校有哪些可以放置东西的地方。很多学校用置物格子，可以，这没问题。但要确保置物格子能放下A4纸。很多置物格子并不合适。所以，挑选家具时，设计教室书架的时候要非常谨慎。我忘记我刚刚是否讲到储物对于学校而言非常重要。再多的储物空间都不嫌多。我想我提到了这么多次，你们应该记住了。设计教室或学校时记得设计储物空间。

14:42—16:13

All right. Some lessons on the use of technology. Technology changes. You got to be flexible. Now there is a lot of technology companies here that have a lot of great resources and great tools to use. Those folks in our industry just know that on the education side that we know that things change fast. And often times, that takes a lot of money to continue to upgrade and to continue to update that technology. An example of these is interactive whiteboard. When they first came out, there was a white space, you couldn't actually draw on them with dry-erase markers, otherwise you would ruin that board. And it just ended up becoming a big empty white square in the middle of the classrooms. That technology has now not moved on but a lot of schools initially invested a lot of money in that technology, and ended up just kind of being a waste of money. Now that technology has moved on and we progressed away from that, but we do know two, three, four years down the line, it's gonna change again. So school leaders are hesitant about technology. It's the in-thing. We know that we need it. We know that we want it. But we are also very aware that it's expensive and it changes quickly. And things get obsolete fast. Think about when you buy a new laptop or a new tablet, by the time you get it home and get it out of the box, there's already a new version. So schools are aware of this and they are very careful. So technology folks, be aware and try to adjust to this needs. How long is your product going to be relevant?

好的，接下来讲一下技术使用上的经验教训。技术会变化，所以必须要灵活。现在有很多科技公司都提供了大量的资源和很棒的工具。我们这个行业的人都知道，在教育方面，事情变化很快。通常需要花费大量的资金来升级更新技术。拿互动式电子白板来说，早期这种白板上有一个白色区域，不能在这个上面用可擦马克笔写字，否则会毁了白板。最终这个区域变成了一个空白的白色正方形，竖在教室中间。这项技术没有后续发展。当初很多学校在这上面投入了大量资金，结果到头来浪费钱。现在技术已经发展了，我们逐渐抛弃了互动式电子白板，但是我们知道，2年、3年、4年之后，这种技术会再次改变。因此，学校领导对技术投入犹豫不决。技术现在是个热门的话题，我们知道我们需要技术，我们知道我们也想要技术。但我们也很清楚，技术投入很花钱，而且技术变化很快。这些技术很快就会过时。就拿笔记本电脑或新平板电脑来说，当你们刚把它买回家，从盒子里拿出来时，市面上就已经有了一个新版本。所以学校要意识到这一点，要非常谨慎。技术人员也要意识到并努力适应这种需求。想想你们的技术产品可以使用多长时间？

16:13—16:57

Let's talk about some of the must-haves: Internet access. In this day and age, you have to have the Internet access in the classroom. And the faster, the better. This is one area where a lot of schools skimp on. They say, "OK, I only need a few access points per floor." Or whatever the plan is, but what actually happens is if the Internet is slow in the classroom, a good teacher is not gonna deal with that for very long. If they are gonna show a three-minute video in the beginning of class and develop a lesson around that, but it takes fifteen or twenty minutes for that video to load, a good teacher is gonna abandon that plan and not use the Internet. What a waste! We want them to use that very valuable resource. So please don't skimp on the Internet. It's gotta go fast.

再来聊聊不可或缺的东西：互联网。当今时代，教室里必须能够连上互联网，网速越快越好。这是很多学校都没太注意的。他们说，"好吧，每层只需要有几个接口就可以"。或者其他不管怎么安排都可以。但实际情况是，如果教室里的网速很慢，好的老师没办法长时间忍受这个情况。如果他们要在开课前播放一段3分钟的视频作为教学内容的导入部分，但是下载这个视频要花15~20分钟，老师就会放弃这个计划，不用互联网。太浪费了！我们希望他们利用这个非常有价值的资源。所以，请不要在互联网上省钱。网速一定要快。

16:57—17:17

Projectors are obviously a mainstay in classrooms. The projectors that are wall-mounted are much better than the ones that are hanging up in the middle of the classroom, because those will get hit by kids. But you gotta have a projector. That's gonna project the teacher's computer onto the whiteboard. If nothing else, it's for their PPTs or to show those videos.

投影仪显然是教室里的中流砥柱。壁挂式投影仪比挂在教室中间的投影仪要好，因为挂在教室中间的投影仪容易被孩子们撞到。教室里必须有投影仪，可以把老师的电脑投影到白板上。如果没有别的用处，那就用来投影老师的PPT或者播放视频。

17:17—18:12

Interactive whiteboards. I put them up there not because they are necessary. Not because you have to have them in the classroom, but they are very nice to have. So if you can have them, please get them. But on the other hand, like I just said, we know that that technology changes fast, so school leaders are very careful when they are choosing what technology to use. We don't want to spend a lot of money on something that is going to be obsolete in three or four years. Don't let IT fads drive your design; they should complement it. Don't design your school around IT. Design your school and then integrate IT. That is a big mistake that a lot of schools make. The computer lab is the center of the curriculum. But what happens on the day when the power goes down and the Internet is out? Don't let IT drive your school. IT is a tool. It is a resource. IT is not a curriculum.

互动式电子白板。我把它们放在这里不是因为它们必不可少，不是因为教室里必须有互动式电子白板。但教室里能有一块白板还是很棒的。所以如果你们教室有这种白板，请把它拿出来用。另一方面，就像我刚才说的，我们知道技术变化很快，所以学校领导在选择使用什么技术时要非常谨慎。我们不想花很多钱在三四年内就会过时的东西上。不要让互联网时尚驱动学校的设计，把这些时尚作为设计的补充。不要围着互联网设计学校，而是设计学校时把互联网整合进来。很多学校在这方面犯了大错误。计算机实验室是课程的中心。但是，停电和没有网络的时候怎么办？不要让互联网驱动学校。互联网只是一个工具、一种资源，不是一门课程。

18:12—19:15

OK. Curriculum is going to drive the design of your school, whether you like it or not. It's just inevitable. This could happen in the beginning with a well thought-out plan where the academic team sits down with the building team in designs [of] a school that takes into consideration. The academics... Or this is gonna happen later in the costly remodels and upgrades. For example, some of our schools are AP schools. Think of AP chemistry, the College Board has some very strict guidelines on what they want in a lab. If you don't design your lab with proper ventilation, or the eyewash station, or the shower, all of these things are required, if you don't plan that in, you can't have that curriculum. So if you gonna run an AP curriculum, you have to have these required elements. Design that in early. IB has the same thing. There are some requirements for your classroom. Think about the curriculum you are gonna have and design your school as early as you possibly can with the curriculum in mind.

课程将推动学校的设计，无论你们是否喜欢，这都是不可避免的。可能一开始就有一个深思熟虑的计划，在这个计划中，学术团队与建筑团队坐在一起设计学校，将这些因素考虑进去。这些会在后续昂贵的改造升级中出现。例如，我们的一些学校是预科学校。想到化学课，大学理事会对他们在实验室里想要的东西有非常严格的要求。如果你们设计的实验室通风不良，或者是没有洗眼站、淋浴室等等这些不可或缺的东西，如果没有把这些东西考虑进去，那么就不能开设那个课程。所以如果要开设预科课程，就必须要有这些元素。提早考虑这些。IB 课程也一样，对教室有一定要求。考虑一下你们即将开设的课程，并在设计中把课程设置考虑进去。

19:15—20:11

OK. A good curriculum is going to establish a supportive community over a period of time. What I've been talking about earlier is you teach kids properly and that's what we do. We are here to teach children. You teach them properly. The parents will be happy. And then this is gonna to lead to retention of students. It's so much easier to only enroll or to only recruit for entry-level grades. You know, if your school is K through twelve, it's so much easier to only have to recruit for kindergarten students. But if you have a lot of kids leaving you because they are unhappy, or parents are unhappy with the student results, and now you have to recruit kids in all grades levels. That's a much bigger task. If the kids are happy, the students are learning, the parents are happy, this is going to lead to them wanting to stay at your school. And it's gonna reduce the need to recruit more students. So curriculum is what keeps them there.

一个好的课程将在一段时间内赢得社区支持。我之前说好好教育孩子是我们该做的事。我们是来教育孩子们的,要好好地教育他们。家长们会很高兴,这也有助于留住学生。只招收一年级的学生要容易得多。如果学校是十二年一贯制的,如果只需要招幼儿园的学生,工作会轻松很多。如果很多学生转学,因为在你们学校他们不开心,或者学生家长对学生的学习成绩不满意,那么你们得想办法招收各个年级的学生,这个任务会繁重很多。如果孩子们快乐,学生们能学到东西,家长们开心,那么孩子们会继续在你们学校读下去。这将减少招生需求。所以课程就是用来留住学生的。

20:11—20:49

Although I admit, a good design is gonna attract parents' eyes and it's gonna create an interest pool of families. So you want to be that school that parents want to come [to] see. You want that interest list. You want a wait list. You want parents to want to come to you. So you have to have a bit of that aesthetics. You have to build in some curb appeal. When you have a nice fancy campus, it's a beautiful environment. This is gonna lead to happy teachers, happy students, happy parents, which also in turn leads to retention of the students. It's all about keeping the kids. The battle is not just on recruiting them. The hard part is keeping them there.

我承认,好的设计会吸引家长的眼球,会吸引家庭的注意。所以你们学校要成为家长想去的那所学校。你们要努力赢得家长欢心,想要候补名单,想让学生家长主动来学校,校园还必须漂亮一点,要使学校看起来不错。漂亮的校园提供美好的环境。美好的环境有助于让老师开心、学生开心、家长开心,反过来也有助于留住学生。所说的一切都是为了留住学生。招生不是最难的,难的是留住学生。

第三单元 文化教育 Culture and Education

20:50—22:17

OK. There is a great example of school design with aesthetics and curriculum in mind. I am not gonna sell my own school here. It's another school that I visited, the only school I am going to highlight. I don't know if anybody recognize this campus. This is UWC in Changshu, China. This is United World Colleges. It is a great example of an academic team that sat down with the architects and came up with what a good school design should look like. Famous architect, Mo Ping, says, "My main design concept is to envision the UWC Changshu Educational Complex as a living mother tree with sprouted leaves as students and the seasonal cycles as comings and goings." And that really rings truth. Think of a school year. It's very cyclical. It's gonna sit empty for a long time during the summer, and then all the kids show up at once and their parents are in the beginning. You will have back-to-school nights. We have to have large events. Eventually the fall comes down and you kind of hit the status quo where the kids are just doing a regular day-to-day school day. And then you are gonna hit your presentations where the musicals would have time to rehearse. You are going to do the holiday events. And then towards the end of the year, you are gonna have recruiting for kids to come and see your school. And it all starts again in summer. It is a cycle. And there are times where there are a lot of people from the outside coming to see your school. And there are times a lot of them… where it's kind of empty. Think about these cycles. When can you do the upgrades and what upgrades do you need to do?

有一所学校很好地将美学和课程结合在一起。在这里我不会自夸自己的学校。我要说的这个学校，我以前去过，是唯一我想强调的学校。我不知道是否有人注意到这个学校，中国常熟世界联合学院。这是一个很好的例子，学术团队和建筑师一起坐下来，商讨出一个好的学校设计应该是什么样的例子。著名的建筑师莫平说："我设计时把常熟世界联合学院的教育中心想象成一棵活着的大树，学生是树上的叶子，每年都有学生来来去去。"这是事实。每个学年都有非常强的周期性。暑假期间校园会空很长一段时间。暑假过后，学生返校，学生父母也会在学期开始时来到校园。我们会有返校夜等大型活动。终于，秋天来了，学校会进入这样的状态，学生们已经进入常规的学习。再后来，学生在外面排练音乐剧、筹备表演，节日即将来临。年底，学校开始招生，会请其他学生来参观学校。夏天一切又开始了。这是一个循环。有些时候，有很多人来参观学校。很多时候有很多人……然后校园再次没什么人。考虑一下学年周期。什么时候升级学校好，什么东西需要升级？

22:17—23:01

OK. So I went very fast, cause I want you to get back to lunch. But I want you to remember, the cake is the curriculum. The icing and the decorations, those are the aesthetics. These two things can work together to bring students to your school. So get the academic team together with the investment team and come up with a plan to not only make money for the school, but also to have a great curriculum and teach these kids properly. Because it can happen. That way, when the parents come to your beautifully designed, awesome school, once they get inside, they realize there is also a beautifully designed and awesome curriculum for the students to learn. Thank you!

  我讲得非常快,因为我希望你们能够快点去吃午饭。但是希望你们记住,蛋糕相当于课程。那些糖霜,装饰都是外在美。将课程和外在美结合起来,吸引学生到你们学校。把学术团队和投资团队召集在一起想办法,既为学校赚钱,又设置好的课程,好好地教育这些学生。这样,学生家长来到你们漂亮的校园,深入了解还将发现学校有很棒的课程供学生们学习。谢谢!

第二部分 交传技巧

第四单元　经贸合作
Economic Cooperation

I. 短期记忆

口译初学者对交替传译往往误认为在交替传译中译员可以记笔记，就几乎不需要依赖记忆。其实笔记只是记忆的延伸和补充，理解和记忆才占据了主导地位。因此对于口译学习者而言，记忆力训练非常有必要。

1. 记忆机制

"记忆指的是人脑对各种信息的储存、提取及加工，包括感官记忆、短期记忆和长期记忆"（任文，2011：55）。

感官记忆是人体的瞬时记忆，一般能保持 0.25～2 秒。如果听者在信息输入的那一刻没有获取信息，那么信息很快就会从瞬时记忆中消失，因此口译员一定要全身心专注，接收信息的能力一定要快。

短时记忆是口译的关键。短期记忆中的信息来自于两方面，一是译员获取的瞬时记忆，二是译员的长期记忆。译员从瞬时记忆中获取信息并将其暂时存储起来，形成短期记忆，同时将获取的短时记忆与长期记忆中的相关信息关联起来，激活长期记忆，再进行源语到目的语的转换。但是短期记忆信息存储空间较小，一般为 7 个信息单位左右，持续时间较短，因此短期记忆存储的信息要尽快使用，否则时间过长就会遗忘。

长期记忆可以永久的存储信息，存储空间较大。储存的是平时积累的生活常识、专业知识、各种经历等。译员可以提取长期记忆中的相关信息与正在听到的信息结合起来，以更好地理解和记忆信息。

在口译活动中，三种记忆相互配合，完成记忆工作。

2. 短期记忆的训练方法

（1）信息组织：在听取口译信息过程中，译员应迅速分析出信息组织方式和上下文的逻辑关系，以提高记忆效率。常用的逻辑关系有条件、让步、时间顺序、空间顺序、比较和对比等。

【例1】二十年前，移动电话和互联网都还没有诞生。时至今日，在座各位几乎每个人都拥有移动电话，可以跟远在地球另一方的人即时通话。

上面的例子信息组织方式既是时间顺序，也是对比，记忆起来比较容易。

（2）大脑重复：在听到第二点内容的同时可以在脑子里瞬时回忆下第一点内容，以增强对第一点的短期记忆。

（3）信息组块化：指的是把相关信息规整到一个信息单位，便于记忆。

（4）信息视觉化：指的是将信息以画面的形式呈现出来，这样记忆的内容会更加形象生动。

【例2】Hurricane Henry moved into northern Florida early yesterday morning. Nearly half a million people have had to be evacuated as the 200km per hour winds uprooted trees, tore roofs off some houses and completely demolished less sturdy ones. In coastal areas many boats were submerged by the 10 meter waves, while others were beached with their hulls ripped open.

听到这一段信息时，译员可以在脑海中描绘出这样一个画面：飓风亨利登陆佛罗里达州，人们被迫离开，狂风对树、房屋、船只造成一系列严重破坏的场景。再结合我们对相关灾害的常识性了解，记住这段信息并不难。

（5）信息联想：是指在听到某一信息的时候，可以联想到相同或者相关信息，这样回想起来会比较容易。比如信息中出现2008年的时候，可以将之与中国举办北京奥运会联系起来，这样就容易记住这个年份。

II. 实战练习一

1. 演讲背景

英国驻广州总领事馆商务领事应邀出席"广交会（英国）国际市场论坛"并发表开幕致辞。他在致辞中指出中英双边关系的发展已进入黄金时代，两国领导人重申将在诸多领域深化合作，中英两国在商业方面杰出的合作案例不胜枚举，涵盖领域甚广。

2. 预习词汇

Consul for Trade and Investment 商务领事
British Consulate General Guangzhou 英国驻广州总领事馆
G20 二十国峰会
offshore wind project 离岸风电项目
House of Fraser 福来德百货公司
Aston Villa Football Club 阿斯顿维拉足球俱乐部
Jaguar Land Rover 捷豹路虎（英国汽车公司）
Geely 吉利（中国汽车公司）

ARM　ARM 公司（英国移动端芯片巨头）
CGN/China General Nuclear Power Group 中广核集团
Hinkley Point C 欣克利角 C 核电项目
Huawei 华为
graphene 石墨烯
Bupa 保柏（英国医疗保健集团）
GP-based clinic 全科诊所
Asian Infrastructure Investment Bank/AIIB 亚洲基础设施投资银行；亚投行
The Belt and Road Initiative "一带一路"倡议
David Cameron 戴维·卡梅伦
Phillip Hammond 菲利普·哈蒙德
The Chancellor（英国的）财政大臣
The 13th Five-Year Plan "十三五"规划
drive train 传动系统
new energy vehicle 新能源汽车
Airbus 空中客车；空客
The Northern Powerhouse（英国）北部振兴计划
The Midlands Engine（英国）中部引擎战略
The National Infrastructure Plan（英国）国家基础设施规划
HS2/High Speed Two HS2 高铁项目

3. 演讲文本

00:00—00:17

尊敬的叶主任、黄局长，女士们、先生们，早上好！我叫梅隆，是英国驻广州总领事馆的商务领事。

Respected Director Ye, Director General Huang, ladies and gentlemen, good morning. I am Mellon, Consul for Trade and Investment at the British Consulate-General in Guangzhou.

00:18—00:42

Good morning, ladies and gentlemen. My name is Simon Mellon. I am Her Majesty's Consul for Trade and Investment at the British Consulate-General here in Guangzhou. I am delighted to be invited to speak at this Canton Fair (UK) International Market Forum. Let me thank Mr. Ye and Mr. Huang for their kind words so far.

女士们，先生们，大家早上好。我叫西蒙·梅隆，是英国驻广州总领事馆的商务领事。我很高兴能受邀来到广交会（英国）国际市场论坛发言。我想感谢叶主任

第四单元　经贸合作　Economic Cooperation

和黄局长刚刚做的精彩演讲。

00:43—01:18

My message today is simple. Never has China-UK relationship been as strong as it is today, never has it had such potential for growth, and never has it been so important to maintain. We've been talking about a golden era for UK-China relations recently since President Xi's state visit to the UK in October 2015. The state visit was symbolic of our relations entering a golden era particularly around trade. And since then, we have not looked back.

我今天要讲的很简单。中英关系目前的牢固程度是史无前例的,发展潜力之巨大前所未有,维护两国关系的重要性也达到了历史新高度。习近平主席2015年10月份对英国进行国事访问以来,我们就一直在谈论中英关系的黄金时代。那一次的国事访问标志着我们的关系进入了黄金时代,尤其是贸易关系。自那以后,中英双边关系一路向前,从未倒退。

01:19—02:03

At Prime Minister May and President Xi's meeting at the G20 in Hangzhou in September last year, where both leaders reaffirmed commitment on developing a genuine strategic partnership in this golden era of bilateral relations, and agreed to deepen cooperation in economy, trade, investment, infrastructure, finance and as well as emerging ideas such as urbanization, high technology and clean energy. Business has a huge role to play during this golden era. Because it is business that produces sustainable growth, business that creates long-term jobs and business that makes our economies as productive as they can be.

梅首相和习主席9月份在杭州G20峰会上会晤,两国领导人重申将致力于发展双边关系,发展黄金时代背景下真正的战略合作伙伴关系,同意加强双方在以下领域的合作,包括经济、贸易、投资、基础设施、金融以及一些新兴领域,例如城镇化、高科技和清洁能源。商业在这个黄金时期发挥了重要作用。因为商业能促进可持续增长,创造长期的就业岗位,提高我们经济体的生产力。

02:04—02:57

Trade has underpinned our bilateral relationship for hundreds of years. In the 18th century, our merchants exchanged wool and cotton for tea and porcelain on the docks of Guangzhou. Today, China is UK's third largest export market, with total exports growing by about 63% since 2010. And as we've heard already, our total bilateral trade reached nearly £60 billion last year. And the UK is also a leading destination in Europe

73

for Chinese investments. Chinese investment is boosting the UK economy from offshore wind projects in Scotland, to investments in retail such as House of Fraser and sports, including Aston Villa Football Club, even into biotechnology and the medicines of tomorrow.

贸易是我们数百年来双边关系的基石。18世纪，英国商人在广州的码头用羊毛和棉花与中国商人交换茶叶和瓷器。如今，中国是英国第三大出口市场，自2010年以来，出口总额增加了63%。大家也听说了，我们去年的双边贸易总额达到将近600亿英镑。同时，英国是中国在欧洲的首选投资目的地。中国的投资促进了英国经济的发展，包括苏格兰的离岸风电项目，以及零售业投资（例如福来德百货公司）和体育产业投资（包括阿斯顿维拉足球俱乐部），中国投资甚至进入了生物技术和未来医药领域。

02:58—03:51

There is an increasingly natural fit between our two economies. As we continue to implement our long term economic plan for the UK, China offers a huge new source of investment and export opportunities. Meanwhile, according to World Bank's estimation, China's GDP growth would still double the world average GDP growth in 2017. And as China rebalances and reforms its economy, UK companies, technology and services can complement your development and help you to achieve your ambitions. Doing more business together has already been a great benefit to both our countries. The UK has shown in recent years that we are perhaps uniquely open to China, its people, its business and the new dynamism that China brings to our country.

我们两国经济的天然互补性越来越明显。英国将继续实施其长期的经济计划，而中国为我们提供了大量的投资来源和巨大的出口机遇。同时，根据世界银行的估计，中国2017年的GDP增长仍然是世界平均水平的两倍。中国正在推动经济的再平衡和改革，而英国的企业、技术和服务能助力中国的发展，帮助中国实现抱负。加强商业合作已为两国带来极大好处。近年来，英国也专门向中国敞开怀抱，欢迎中国人民和中国企业为我们国家注入新的活力。

03:52—04:21

I can name quite a few remarkable UK-China commercial cooperations, which cover a wide range of sectors. China is now Jaguar Land Rover's largest market. And it has also opened its first ever overseas manufacturing facility in Changshu, creating jobs for Chinese workers. The Chinese car maker Geely is investing £250 million in a new factory, R&D center and assembly plant for the London Taxi Company.

中英两国在商业方面杰出的合作案例不胜枚举，涵盖领域甚广。捷豹路虎目前

第四单元　经贸合作 Economic Cooperation

最大的市场是中国,在常熟还设立了其首个海外制造厂,为中国劳动力创造就业岗位。中国的汽车制造商吉利正投资 2.5 亿英镑为伦敦出租车公司建设新工厂、研发中心和装配厂。

04:22—04:53

Ninety percent of the almost 400 million smartphones sold in China last year are powered by chips supplied by Britain's ARM. The prospect of over £25 billion into UK nuclear projects by CGN, starting with Hinkley Point C, represents one of China's biggest ever overseas investments. Hinkley Point C alone will generate a stable source of clean power to nearly 6 million homes and provide up to 25,000 job opportunities.

中国去年售出的约 4 亿台智能手机中,90% 都使用了英国 ARM 公司生产的芯片。以欣克利角 C 核电项目为开端,中广核集团将在英国的核电项目投资 250 亿英镑,这是中国最大的海外投资,仅仅欣克利角 C 核电站就能为 600 万户家庭稳定供应清洁电力,创造 25,000 个就业机会。

04:54—05:44

Huawei now employs 1,100 staff in the UK and the company is playing an active part in rolling out high-speed broadband across the UK. Huawei has three R&D centers across the country and they are partnering with leading UK universities to develop the next generation technology, including graphene, 5G and data management. And the UK-based international healthcare group, Bupa, just opened its first GP-based clinic here in Guangzhou in August 2017, providing high quality healthcare services to Guangdong residents. They plan to invest heavily in the coming 5 years to enhance their services. It's a great record of success. But what excites me most is a sense that this is still the beginning.

华为目前在英国雇佣了 1,100 名员工,且正积极将高速宽带推广至全英国。华为在英国有三个研发中心,正和英国顶尖高校合作,开发下一代技术,包括石墨烯、5G 和数据管理。保柏集团是英国本土的一家国际医疗保健集团,该集团 2017 年 8 月在广州开了第一家全科诊所,为当地居民提供高质量的医疗服务。该集团计划在未来 5 年加大投资,提升服务质量。我们的合作已经取得了巨大的成功,令我兴奋不已的是这仅仅只是开始。

05:45—06:40

The UK was the first European country to join the Asian Infrastructure Investment Bank and the UK is committed to work with China to strengthen economic growth across the region through the Belt and Road Initiative. At the 2015 state visit, the former UK

Prime Minister David Cameron and President Xi, as part of the global partnership between our countries, committed that both countries should have a strong interest in cooperating on each other's major initiatives, including the Belt and Road Initiative. As you've already heard, the first UK-to-China freight train reached Zhejiang Province at the end of April this year. That 7,500-mile journey is a modern echo of the ships that left the UK to trade with China. Its arrival was a first step in the creation of the Belt and Road, and I'm proud to see that the United Kingdom stands ready to help China in this endeavor.

英国是第一个加入亚洲基础设施投资银行的欧洲国家，英国也致力于和中国展开合作，通过"一带一路"倡议促进本地区的经济发展。2015年进行国事访问时，英国前首相戴维·卡梅伦和习近平主席都支持两国建立全球合作伙伴关系，并承诺我们应大力加强双方在各自重要倡议上的合作，包括中国的"一带一路"倡议。大家也已经听说了，首列从英国开往中国的货运列车于今年4月底抵达了浙江省。这条全程7,500英里的现代铁路与当年驶离英国前来与中国贸易的货轮遥相呼应。这是我们建设"一带一路"迈出的第一步，我也很自豪地看到英国已做好准备帮助中国实现这一倡议。

06:41—07:10

At the Belt and Road Forum in Beijing in May, the Chancellor, Phillip Hammond, stated that Britain was a natural partner for China in the Initiative, lying at the western end of the Belt and Road. And Mr. Huang has already said Chinese and British companies have very complementary skills and capabilities in finance, engineering and research that are required to realize this kind of infrastructure projects on such vast scale.

在5月份北京举办的"一带一路"高峰论坛上，英国的财政大臣菲利普·哈蒙德指出，英国天生是中国"一带一路"倡议的合作伙伴，因为英国位于"一带一路"路线的西端。黄局长刚刚也说了，中英两国企业在金融、工程和研究领域的技术和能力互补性强，而这些技能是实施大规模基础设施项目所必需的。

07:11—07:55

China has become a major financier of overseas infrastructure projects. Chinese contractors have developed a strong comparative advantage in delivering such projects. And UK companies can raise quality of project outcomes including evaluating and delivering wider economic and social benefits. UK banks can service a whole life cycle of a project from the planning phase to refinancing. They offer strong geographical coverage and experience of operating in a country along the route built up over many years. And the British government can also add value. We have development expertise and good relationships with many Belt and Road countries.

中国是海外基础设施项目的主要投资国。中国承包商在这些项目的交付方面也具有突出的比较优势。而英国的企业能提高项目成果的质量，包括项目评估和创造更大的经济和社会效益。英国的银行能够为项目提供从规划阶段到再融资的全生命周期服务，业务地理范围覆盖广泛，多年来积累了在"一带一路"沿线国家运营的丰富经验。英国政府也能提供附加价值。我们有专业的开发知识，与"一带一路"沿线国家保持着良好关系。

07:56—08:53

The province of Guangdong is of course an economic powerhouse in its own right, with a world's fifteenth-largest economy. It's a global leader in technological innovation, a major financial hub, and, with a population of nearly 110 million people, a major consumer economy. And the UK is the province's second-largest European trading partner. The UK retains a close commercial relationship with Guangdong. UK-Guangdong trade is generally on the rise and represents a fifth of China-UK trade volume. The UK invests more in Guangdong than any other EU countries. And Guangdong also brings high-value investment to the UK. As we've already heard, keen investors from Guangdong include from the ICT, medical devices and financial services sectors.

当然，广东省本身就是一个经济引擎，是世界第十五大经济体，也是全球技术创新的先锋和主要的金融中心，人口将近1.1亿，是巨大的消费经济体。而英国是广东在欧洲的第二大贸易伙伴。英国与广东经贸关系密切，双边贸易总体呈上升趋势，占中英贸易额的五分之一。英国在广东的投资额位列欧盟国家首位。广东同样也为英国带来了高价值的投资。大家都听说了，广东的投资者对信息通讯技术、医疗器械和金融服务等领域的投资兴致盎然。

08:54—09:40

When the Guangdong Provincial Party Secretary visited the UK in June this year, 26 cooperation agreements were signed, with a total value of £1.4 billion, which marked a significant progress on the bilateral economic and trade exchange between the UK and Guangdong. All of these achievements reflect the growing complementarity between the economies of our countries. Areas for expansion include advanced manufacturing, financial services, energy, research and development, logistics, automotive, healthcare, ICT, and other sectors where businesses share strong synergies.

今年六月份，广东省省委书记访问了英国，签署了26项合作协议，总价值达14亿英镑。这标志着英国与广东的双边经贸交流取得了长足进展。所有的这些成果

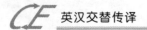

都表明了我们两国的互补性在逐渐增强。我们也将扩大以下领域的合作,包括先进制造业、金融服务、能源、研发、物流、汽车、医疗保健、信息通讯技术以及其他能产生强大协同效应的行业。

09:41—10:05

A strong government-to-government relationship provides an important foundation. But it is our people-to-people and business-to-business ties that give meaning and substance to the UK-China relationship. At a time when China is implementing the 13th Five-Year Plan and making a transition to a more market-based economy, trade and investment between the UK and China will benefit us both.

政府间坚实的关系为我们打下了牢固的基础。但正是人文交流和商业纽带的建立,中英关系才能取得实质性的显著进展。中国正在实施"十三五"规划,实现经济转型,提高市场化程度,中英两国开展贸易与投资将会带来互利共赢的结果。

10:06—10:46

And so we continue to welcome Chinese companies to the UK to compete on a level playing field with no barriers and with the same access to government-funded business support for growth and export as domestic British companies. We want you to be part of the renaissance of our rail industry. Through investing in R&D to develop better engines, drive trains and electronic control systems, we can work together to develop globally competitive cars and new energy vehicles. We want the UK supply chain that provides up to half the content of an Airbus to help China to develop its own aircraft build programs.

因此,我们继续欢迎中国企业到英国投资,在无贸易壁垒的环境中公平竞争,且享有与英国国内企业同等的政府资金支持,取得发展,扩大出口。我们期盼中国能帮助英国振兴铁路运输行业。通过加大研发投入,开发更优质的引擎、传动系统和电子控制系统,我们能够共同研发出具有全球竞争力的汽车和新能源汽车。每一架空客飞机有一半的组件都由英国的供应链提供,我们希望能帮助中国开展自己的飞机制造项目。

10:47—11:22

We want to increase the number of banks clearing RMB payments in London. And we want more British brands to tap into the dramatic growth in Chinese retail online and offline. We want more Chinese tech companies to do their R&D in the UK. We want our creative industries to take on the world together. We want to work with you to create better healthcare and help create the medicines of tomorrow. And we encourage Chinese

第四单元 经贸合作 Economic Cooperation

investment into the Northern Powerhouse, the Midlands Engine and the National Infrastructure Plan projects like the transport hubs around the HS2.

我们在伦敦希望越来越多的银行能够用人民币结算。我们也希望有更多英国品牌能够进军中国蓬勃发展的线上和线下零售业市场。我们希望中国有更多的高科技公司在英国开展研发工作,也希望我们的创意产业能共同走向世界。我们希望与中国合作,提供优质的医疗保健服务,共同研发未来的药物。我们鼓励中国投资英国的北部振兴计划、中部引擎战略和国家基础设施规划项目,如HS2高铁项目的交通枢纽。

11:23—11:57

In short, we want the UK to be China's number one business partner in the West. As we look to the future, I hope the UK and China will stand together on the global stage, championing the benefits of a global economic system that is free and fair. It is clear that we share the same belief in the ability of free trade to unleash the huge potential in our economies and raise the prosperity of millions around the world. It will be through trade that we ensure our Golden Era lasts for many years to come.

简而言之,我们期望英国成为中国在西方的第一大商业伙伴。展望未来,我希望英国和中国能并肩站上国际舞台,携手捍卫公平、自由的全球经济体系。显然,我们都坚信自由贸易能够释放巨大的经济潜力,为全世界多数人带来繁荣富强。贸易能使得我们两国的黄金时代走得更远。

11:58—12:22

And now as I finish my speech and before I hand over to my colleague, I would like to wish you every success in the Canton Fair and in this forum today, and say how much I look forward to working together across government and the private sector to deepen our trading partnerships. 谢谢大家!

我的演讲也快结束了,在我把麦克风交给我的同事之前,预祝广交会和本次论坛取得圆满成功。热切期盼我们的政府与企业能够通力合作,深化我们的贸易伙伴关系。Thank you!

III. 实战练习二

1. 演讲背景

德国工商大会和德国联邦外贸与投资署的代表应邀参加"中欧企业投资合作峰会"并发表主旨演讲。他在演讲中简要介绍了他所在的机构的职能、中欧经贸关系的进展、德国公司在中国投资的原因、首选投资地点，以及面临的十大挑战等。

2. 预习词汇

merger and acquisition 并购
entrepreneur 企业家
German Chamber of Commerce 德国工商大会
embassies and consulates general of Germany 德国大使馆和总领事馆
Germany Trade and Invest 德国联邦外贸与投资署
AHK 德国工商大会海外商会
Foreign Ministry of Germany 德国外交部
Ministry of Economics of Germany 德国联邦经济部
lobby 游说
first-tier 一线的
inbound 对内的
Greater Shanghai Area 大上海区
automotive 汽车的
regional diversification 地区多元化
Industry 4.0 德国工业 4.0
Made in China 2025 中国制造 2025
blockage of the Internet 网络屏蔽
hamper 阻碍
intellectual property rights 知识产权
turnover 营业额
value chain 价值链
mobile app 移动应用

3. 演讲文本

00:00—00:22

Good afternoon, ladies and gentlemen. Thank you for having me here. I'm very happy to hear that Germany is very popular for merger and acquisition. I feel actually a little bit displaced in between those entrepreneurs now because I kind of need to take a step back.

女士们，先生们，下午好！谢谢你们的邀请。我很高兴听到德国是并购的热门国家。身处各位优秀的企业家当中，事实上我感觉自己真是格格不入，因此我得后退一步来表示对他们的敬佩。

第四单元 经贸合作 Economic Cooperation

00:23—00:45

I wanna tell you a little bit about German and Chinese business relations from our point of view, how we see it, what the developments are, how German companies here in China do, so that you have an impression, and also where Germany and China can work together.

我想从我们的角度谈谈德国与中国的商务关系,我们如何看待这种关系,发展情况如何,德国企业在中国做得怎样,以便让大家有个印象。另外我还会谈一谈德国与中国在哪些领域可以开展合作。

00:46—01:32

So since we are running out of time, I try to make it short. Just a short introduction of the German Chamber of Commerce. We belong to one of the three pillars of German foreign trade promotion. That's the embassies and consulates general of Germany, the Germany Trade and Invest, and we as AHK as a German chamber. The Embassy belongs, of course, to the Foreign Ministry of Germany. And us [we] and Germany Trade and Invest are supported and partly financed by the Ministry of Economics of Germany.

因为时间有限,我尽量长话短说。首先简单介绍一下德国工商大会。德国工商大会是促进德国外贸的三大支柱之一。这三大支柱指的是德国各大使馆和总领事馆、德国联邦外贸与投资署和我们德国工商大会的海外商会。德国大使馆当然隶属于德国外交部,而我们德国工商大会和德国联邦外贸与投资署由德国联邦经济部支持和提供部分资助。

01:33—02:34

We basically have three functions here. We have 130 offices worldwide. Our headquarters is in Berlin. Here in China, we have five offices. Our main three function is political representation of German interests in the area, so doing lobbying with local and regional government. Then we have, as it was mentioned, in whole China, 2,500 German companies as member companies. There are in total about 5,200 German companies located in China. I will show you some more figures in a couple of seconds. And the third function is: basically we are a service provider for German, but also partly Chinese companies that do business between Germany and China.

我们有3个基本职能。我们在全世界有130个办事处,总部在柏林。我们在中国有5个办事处。我们3个主要职能包括代表德国在各地区的政治利益,游说当地和各地区的政府。刚才已经说过,我们德国工商大会在中国有2,500家德国会员公司。中国一共有5,200家德国公司。待会儿我会给大家看一些数据。我们的第三个职能是：基本上我们服务的是中德两国互相贸易的德国企业和部分中国企业。

02:35—03:27

As I said, we as the German Chamber have a couple of offices in China. Our main locations are Beijing, Shanghai, Guangzhou, and here in charge of Southwest China. We follow our German customers and member companies, so we also have opened offices in the yellow dots you see here. So we are not just present in the first-tier cities but also in second-tier cities. Here at the German Chamber in South and Southwest China, we have around 800 companies that are located here. Many focus, of course, in Guangdong.

刚才我提到过，我们德国工商大会在中国有几个办事处，主要位于北京、上海、广州，以及这里，负责中国西南地区。我们负责跟进德国客户和会员公司，所以你们可以看到在黄点标示的地方我们也开设了办事处。我们的驻点不仅在一线城市，二线城市也有。德国工商大会在华南和西南地区大约有800家成员公司，当然，很多集中在广东。

03:28—04:26

What do we do? As our services, we provide this, good, just give this really quickly, business partner search in both directions for German companies that are looking for suppliers and for business partners. We help them find them. But also for Chinese companies that are looking towards Germany to find suppliers or business partners there, we also help. We do investment support for German companies, we also together with Germany Trade and Invest, but also with the representatives of the federal states of Germany. Mr. Feng's here, for example, today. We support Chinese companies also with investment in Germany together with our partners.

我们主要做些什么呢？我们为德国和中国企业双向寻找商业伙伴，既帮助德国公司寻找中国的供应商和商业伙伴，也帮助中国公司在德国寻找供应商和商业伙伴。我们为德国公司招商引资。我们也与德国联邦外贸与投资署和德国各联邦州的代表合作，比如今天在场的冯先生就是我们的合作伙伴。我们与合作伙伴一道支持中国公司在德国进行投资。

04:27—04:57

We have a lot of inbound delegations we took care of as the German Chamber. We have also outbound delegations where we cooperate with Chinese companies but also Chinese governments here in South China for un-special topics whenever they need to go to Germany.

第四单元　经贸合作　Economic Cooperation

我们有许多国外的代表团，由我们德国工商大会负责接待。我们也有对外代表团与华南地区的中国公司企业和政府合作，解决他们需要去德国时容易遇到的问题。

04:58—05:29
So for the German-Chinese relations, it was mentioned before. Germany is the most important partner within Europe for China. More than 30% of the European-Chinese trade activities are German-Chinese business. And China has government consultations with Germany which is an important means of exchanging policy views.
　　关于德中关系，此前已经提过。德国是中国在欧洲最重要的贸易伙伴。欧中贸易活动30%是德中贸易。并且中国与德国展开政府磋商，这是双方交流政策观点的重要方式。

05:30—06:30
For Chinese-German exports, we have a total trade volume of 140 billion Euros from Germany to China. For this year, we expect a slowdown of exports. Or let's say, for last year, the final numbers are not out yet. We expect that the German exports to China have decreased by 3%. But if you look at China's percentage of Germany's imports and exports, you will see that here around 7% of the Germany's exports go to China and about 9% of German imports come from China. So the business relationship is very much developed.
　　中德外贸方面，德国对中国的出口总额为1,400亿欧元。今年，德国对中国的出口预计会放缓。其实，德国去年对中国的出口最终数据尚未统计出来。预计今年德国对中国的出口将下降3%。但如果您看看中国在德国进出口贸易中所占的比重，您会发现德国约7%的出口是面向中国，约9%的进口是来自中国。因此两国的贸易关系非常密切。

06:31—06:56
China, we've heard about it just now, it's one of the biggest investors in Germany, not in terms of volume actually yet, but in terms of numbers of projects. And last year, I think this is an old number, Chinese companies had the most investment projects including merger and acquisitions in Germany.
　　刚才我们已经听到了，中国是德国的最大投资国，不是指投资额方面，而是指项目数量方面最多。我想这个数据还没有更新，去年中国公司在德国投资项目，包括并购项目，数量最多。

06:57—07:44

As for the 5,200 German companies in China, they are mainly distributed in the Greater Shanghai Area, where we have around 40% of them. And here in the South and Southwest China, we have around 17% of the German companies located here. For industrial focus, not very surprising, mechanical, engineering and automotive lead. So the majority of German companies is from this area and is specially industry-driven.

在华的 5,200 家德国公司主要分布在大上海区，占了近 40%；17% 分布在华南和西南地区。产业重点方面，当然是机械、工程和汽车行业占主导地位。所以大部分德国公司都是这些行业的，非常工业化。

07:45—08:40

Since we are here on an investment forum, we every year ask our German companies, "What are the reasons for investing in China?" And then that's basically the answer. As you know, low cost is no longer a reason for German companies to establish companies here, but it's more following key customer. What is meant here by regional diversification is... Regional diversification just means they are expanding into the Chinese market and invest there and cost reductions only being in the second place.

因为这是一个投资论坛，每年我们都会问我们德国公司："为什么在中国投资？"答案基本都是这样：众所周知，低成本不再是德国公司在中国设立公司的主要原因，更重要的原因是这里有关键客户。地区多元化指的是德国公司在开拓中国市场，在中国投资。降低成本只是次要原因。

08:41—09:37

In terms of top investment locations, we asked, last year, so the companies that are already in China, the German ones, "Where are you planning to invest in the next couple of years?" The ranking is basically Shanghai area leads, then followed by Guangzhou, which is quite interesting. So that means, you've seen the figures, the majority of German companies is located in Shanghai and Beijing and they are looking southward to also invest more to develop the southern Chinese market. And the third interesting market, there we also have an office that belongs to the Guangzhou office, it's Chengdu. So Western China will become more and more interesting for German companies.

关于首选投资地点，去年我们问过在中国的德国公司："在未来几年内，你们打算在什么地方投资？"基本上首选是上海地区，其次是广州。这个很有意思。你们都看了数据，目前大部分德国公司位于上海和北京。所以，这个回答意味着他们在逐渐南移，将更多地投资开发华南市场。至于第三个潜在市场，我们也有办事处

第四单元 经贸合作 Economic Cooperation

在成都，它隶属于我们的广州代表处。所以中国西部成为德国公司越来越感兴趣的投资地区。

09:38—10:30

Since we are also an investment forum and we talk about a lot of opportunities, let's also talk about some challenges companies are facing. That's our top ten list of the challenges German companies face. Here in China, the No. 1 to 3 challenges are HR-related. That's also not surprising. There is a shortage of qualified labor. We know that the Chinese government is already working hard on this topic, but especially on the blue collar level, finding qualified labor is a big challenge for German companies since they are very much industrial and manufacturing driven.

既然这是一个投资论坛，关于机遇我们已经说了很多了，那么让我们来谈谈公司面临的挑战。这是德国公司面临的十大挑战。在中国，前三大挑战都是与人力资源有关的，这一点也不奇怪，因为合格劳动力短缺。我们知道中国政府已经在努力解决这个问题，但是寻找合格的蓝领工人对于德国公司而言仍是个很大的挑战，因为德国公司以工业和制造业为主。

10:31—11:37

So for the other challenges, I think if we look in the future and talk about cooperation in terms of Industry 4.0 and China Manufacture 2025 (*Made in China 2025*) and also making China a very innovative country, I think, this point here, slow Internet speed and blockage of Internet, is really hampering development of German companies, but not only of German companies, but also Chinese companies in the market. We know that there are a lot of German companies that are considering not developing research and development here because the Internet is just too slow and exchanging data with their mother company is a problem. So also here in Guangdong and in other areas, I think this is a topic and local government and also the central government should work on this topic.

至于其它挑战，如果我们讨论"德国工业4.0"计划和《中国制造2025》未来的合作以及致力于将中国打造成创新型国家，那么网速太慢和网络屏蔽确实阻碍了德国公司和中国公司的发展。我们了解到很多德国公司之所以不在这里进行研发，原因就是网速太慢了，影响了他们与母公司进行数据传输。在广东和其它地区，我认为也存在这方面的问题。地方政府和中央政府应该解决这个问题。

11:38—12:03

For protection of intellectual property rights, it's still an issue but it has been

85

removed down the list of top challenges. But it's still a valid issue. And we also know that the government is taking a lot of steps to improve that. We see it. But there are still a lot of open issues.

知识产权保护仍然是个问题，但已不再是主要挑战之一了，但这仍是切实存在的问题。我们也知道政府采取了许多措施来改善这个问题，我们看到了政府的努力，但仍有很多问题亟待解决。

12:04—13:10

Just closing, I think in Germany, there is a lot of concern among German companies about the situation of Chinese economy. I think in China or in Germany, companies are rather pessimistic. If you ask German companies here in China, they are much more optimistic about it. But if you look at the figures here… At the end of last year, we asked companies in Germany, "What is basically your… What about your dependency on the Chinese market?" For 12%, in terms of turnover and profit, China is the top one market, which is pretty much. So you can see that the connection between China and Germany is pretty big and the dependency on the Chinese market for German companies is also rather high.

最后，许多德国公司担心中国的经济形势。我觉得无论在中国还是德国，很多公司都相当悲观。如果你们去问在中国的德国公司，他们会乐观得多。但是请大家看看这里的数据。去年年底，我们调查了在德国的公司："你们对于中国市场的依赖度如何？"其中，就营业额和利润而言，有12%的德国公司说，中国是首选市场，这个比例相当大了。所以您可以看到中德之间的联系非常密切，德国公司对于中国市场的依赖程度也非常高。

13:11—14:02

So I think Germany is very much interested in also helping China restructuring its economy. I think there are chances for German companies, especially when Chinese companies move up the value chain, so providing new equipment and machinery for them, but also Industry 4.0 in health sector and environmental sector. I think this is where the future trend in the next couple of years will go. I am not sure if German companies can step up with the speed of the development of Internet and mobile apps here in China, but that's a topic we should discuss somewhere else.

所以，我认为德国非常乐于帮助中国调整经济结构。对于德国公司来说机会很多，尤其是中国公司在价值链中不断上升，所以德国公司可以为他们提供新设备和机械，还可以为中国的医疗领域和环保领域提供德国工业4.0方案。我想这是未来几年的趋势。虽然我不确定德国公司能否跟得上中国互联网和移动应用的发展速度，但这个话题还是留到别的场合再讨论吧。

14:03—14:05
OK. That's it. Thank you very much.
我的发言完毕。谢谢大家！

第五单元　观光旅游
Tourism

I. 口译笔记

1. 为什么要记口译笔记？

"短时记忆容量有限，通常只能容下六个意义毫不相干的单词组成的词群，或七位无意义的数字"（王燕，2009：142）。尤其当演讲嘉宾讲话时间较长、信息量较大时，译员的短时记忆负担较大，这样就容易丢失信息，影响译文质量。因此，交替传译中，译员可借助笔记来补充短期记忆的不足，提高译文质量。

2. 口译笔记是不是听写？

口译笔记不同于听写。口译学习者在初学口译笔记时通常会过度依赖笔记，想记下听到的所有信息，误认为记在笔记上的内容才能记得住。结果往往适得其反，造成口译笔记难以辨认、丢掉许多重点信息、理不清信息内部逻辑关系等问题。因此口译学习者需要认清口译笔记和记忆之间的关系。

3. 口译笔记有什么特点？

（1）时效性。一般来说，讲话人讲话速度都要比书写速度快，因此译员记口译笔记记起来要快。

（2）精简化。前面提到过度依赖笔记会导致译员顾此失彼，影响译文质量，且口译笔记具有时效性，因此笔记需要简洁。

（3）个性化。口译笔记可以有译员自己的特点，比如使用自己创造的符号等。

4. 口译笔记记什么？

（1）关键词。能够帮助译员想起发言人讲话信息的词，主要为实词。

（2）逻辑关系词。帮助译员理清讲话上下文逻辑关系。

（3）数字和专有名词。

（4）列举。

基本原则：口译笔记记下的应当是能够表达源语内容的提示，而不是无意义的词。

5. 口译笔记怎么排版?

(1) 纵向记笔记,阶梯式缩进。
(2) 多分行,结构尽量宽松。
(3) 结尾标识明显,可用横线或者其他标识。

【例1】On behalf of all the members of my delegation and in my own name, I express my heartfelt thanks to our host, Mr. Zhang for giving this grand banquet.

▲　　Mb
个
　　　　　　Tk　zha
　　　　　　　　　Baq　　//

【例2】目前青岛已经开通至北京、上海、广州等主要城市的82条航线,至东京、首尔、巴黎等城市的12条国际地区航线。

青,
北
上　　　　82 线
广

东　　　　　I
首　　　12　　线
巴　　　　　R　　　　//

6. 口译笔记怎么记?

(1) 使用文字。英文可以选择单词前几个字母,如 y = year, gov = government, comp = computer;英文可以提取其中的几个辅音,如 bk = book, gvt = government, prp = preparation;中文可以用一个字表达一个词语的意思,如被 = 被子,楼 = 楼房,挑 = 挑战。
(2) 使用符号和图像。如:
下降↘
上升↗
正确、肯定√

大约≈
不同≠
合作∞
代表▲
疑问?
重要!

II. 实战练习一

1. 演讲背景

2012年,西澳大利亚州旅游局在广州举办"西澳大利亚州旅游局中国旅游洽谈会",来自西澳大利亚州的20家当地旅游供应商和多家中国旅行社深入交流,积极探讨如何进一步展开合作,共同推广西澳大利亚州丰富的旅游资源。下文为西澳大利亚州五大区之一的珀斯区的旅游局CEO的演讲,她在演讲中介绍了珀斯市中心和周边小岛、小镇的旖旎风光,呼吁中国旅行社把中国游客带到珀斯去观光游乐。

2. 预习词汇

Perth 珀斯
wine region 葡萄酒产区
wildlife 野生动物
Swan River 天鹅河
cruise 游轮
King's Park 英皇公园
Central Park(纽约的)中央公园
Tree Top Walk 树顶栈道
Fremantle 弗里曼特尔
Fishing Boat Harbor 渔船港口
motor scooter 小型摩托车
jet boat 喷射艇
Indian Ocean 印度洋
marinist 喜欢大海的人
Rottnest Island 罗特尼斯岛
ferryboat 渡轮
snorkeling 浮浅

kayaking 划皮艇
Rockingham 罗丁汉姆
cruise operator 游轮运营商
Seal Island 海豹岛
Penguin Island 企鹅岛
Mandurah 曼都拉
canal 运河
Swan Valley 天鹅谷
winery 酒庄
bushwalking 丛林徒步旅行
Avon Valley 埃文河谷
Holiday Planner《旅游指南》

3. 演讲文本

00:00—00:39

Thank you. I'm from Perth city. And I'm here today to tell you all of the best reasons for visiting the city of Perth and the surrounding countryside. The best thing about Perth is that there are many things to see and do, very close to the city center. So from wine regions to wildlife, beautiful beaches, everything is available within only twenty minutes' distance or up to half an hour distance of the city center.

谢谢! 我来自珀斯。我今天来到这里是为了跟大家分享一下为什么珀斯以及周边乡村最值得大家去游玩。珀斯的美妙之处就在于在市中心附近就有很多值得观赏的美景和游玩的项目。因此,不论是去葡萄酒产区还是去看野生动物,还是到海滩玩,从市区出发到这些地方只需 20 分钟,顶多半个小时。

00:39—01:16

So Perth is a small city, owning a population of 1.5 million people, so compared to China's cities, very small. But it is a very relaxing city and a great city for a holiday. So we hope that you will send all your customers to our beautiful city, which is located on the river called the Swan River. Perth has great shopping, good night life, and many things to see and do in the city center itself. A very popular activity is to take a river cruise.

所以,珀斯是一个小城市,只有 150 万人口,跟中国的城市相比非常之小。但却是一个非常休闲的城市,也是度假的好去处。因此我们希望你们能把所有的客户都推荐到我们这座美丽的城市来,她坐落在河畔,这个河畔叫天鹅河畔。珀斯是购物天堂,也是一个夜生活丰富的地方,在我们的市中心有很多值得观赏游玩的地方。其中，天鹅河游轮这个项目就大受游客欢迎。

01:16—01:48

Right beside the city center is a beautiful park. This is called King's Park. King's Park is larger than Central Park in New York. It's also the most visited attraction in Western Australia. So all of your customers or when you come to Perth, send them up to King's Park. Because it is very beautiful. It has a Tree Top Walk. It has many beautiful flowers. It is a very relaxing place to visit.

在市中心旁边有一座风景如画的公园，叫做英皇公园。该公园比纽约中央公园还要大一些。那是西澳大利亚州最受游客欢迎的景区。因此，不论是你们亲临珀斯，还是你们的客户来珀斯，都请到英皇公园来。因为那里风景秀丽，有树顶栈道，还有鲜艳的花卉。那是一个非常适合放松身心的好去处。

01:48—02:49

Now the city of Perth, the city center is located twenty minutes inland from the coast. But if you want to come down to the coast, you can come down by river to a place called Fremantle. Fremantle is a beautiful, old, historical town. It's only, as I say, thirty minutes from the city and it has many beautiful historical buildings. It's also famous for its coffee shops and its Fishing Boat Harbor. This is a harbor that has many seafood restaurants and it is famous for its fish and chips. Fremantle has a lot of attractions, very good markets and many things to see and do. You can hire a motor scooter or a little car, or take a high speed jet boat ride. So definitely for your customers, recommend them come to Fremantle for the day.

珀斯市中心距离海滩有20分钟的路程。但如果您想到海岸去，您可以顺着天鹅河而下，来到一个叫做弗里曼特尔的地方。那是一个风景秀丽、历史悠久的小镇。刚刚我提到，那里距离市区仅仅是30分钟，而且还有很多漂亮的历史建筑。那里的咖啡馆和渔船港口也让小镇芳名远扬。港口那里有着很多海鲜餐厅——餐厅的炸鱼和炸薯条非常有名。弗里曼特尔有很多名胜，还有商品琳琅满目的市场，此外还有很多值得大家观赏游玩的地方。您可以租用当地的小型摩托车或者小汽车，也可以试一试速度飞快的喷射艇。此外，给你们的客户推介一下弗里曼特尔，去那里绝对不虚此行。

02:49—03:24

What Perth does have is a beautiful coastline. We are on the Indian Ocean. And we have pure white sand and beautiful sunset in the afternoon. The water is crystal clear and our summer is very long, dry and hot. So for people who enjoy swimming, surfing and anything to do with the ocean, so definitely Perth is your place to visit. Marinist visits along the coast, many things to see and do.

珀斯有一条风光无限的海岸线。这个城市坐落在印度洋边。在珀斯可以看到纯白的沙滩和傍晚时分的落日景致。海水如水晶般透亮,这里的夏天绵长、干燥而炎热。因此,对游泳爱好者而言,可以在那里冲浪,也可以在海上做其他的水上活动。因此,来珀斯绝对是来对地方了。喜欢大海的人可以到我们的海边走走,会有很多有趣的事儿在等着您。

03:24—04:05

Thirty minutes off the coast, this is a little island called Rottnest Island. This is another, a very good day trip. You come out here by high speed ferryboat. And then on the island you can have some very nice scenery to enjoy. There's tool you can take. You can hire everything for snorkeling, swimming, diving and kayaking. And the most popular activity is to hire a bike. Because there are no cars on the island. So you hire a bike and you can ride around. It only takes two hours to ride around the whole island if you are feeling energetic for the day.

从海滩出发,30分钟便可以来到罗特尼斯岛。这是另一个值得玩上一天的景点。您可以坐高速渡轮到岛上来。上岛之后,您可以饱览迷人景色。您可以使用岛上的设备,可以租借各种水上运动设备,去浮潜、游泳、潜水和划皮艇等等。岛上最受欢迎的活动是租借自行车——因为岛上没有汽车。所以您可以租一辆自行车,然后环岛骑行。如果您觉得精力充沛,可以环岛骑行,一次环岛的时间只需要两个小时。

04:05—04:44

With another day trip from the city, this is Rockingham, south of the city. It only takes 45 minutes. But it is the popular destination for marine life and nature. So come down to Rockingham for the day. There is a very good cruise operator and you can take a cruise that will take you seeing dolphins, then out to a little island called the Seal Island, where you will see seals. Get right across the Seal and then the same little cruise will take you out to the Penguin Island, where you can see many many penguins.

从市区出发,还有另一个一日游的好去处,那就是市区南边的罗丁汉姆。那里离市区只有45分钟路程。那里以海洋生物和自然景观著称。那里有一家游轮运营商,您可以乘坐游轮去看海豚,然后再到外面的海豹岛上去看海豹。过了海豹岛后,坐上小游轮,就可以到企鹅岛去。在岛上,您可以看到很多很多的企鹅。

04:44—05:13

South of Rockingham and only one hour from the city is a place called Mandurah. Mandurah has very nice beaches. It has a lot of canals, a little like Florida. But what you can do on the canals is to take the canal cruise. There are hundreds of dolphins in the canals and they will follow the canals. And the canal cruise boat is such an enjoyable way to spend the day. Mandurah is also quite famous for golf.

在罗丁汉姆的南边，有一个地方叫做曼都拉，距离市区仅一个小时路程。那里有非常迷人的海滩。曼都拉有点像美国的佛罗里达州，有很多运河。游客只能坐运河游轮观光。运河里生活着数百只海豚，在运河中游弋。坐游船观光是一种非常惬意的事情。曼都拉还以高尔夫球闻名于世。

05:13—05:43

Then for an entirely different experience, 30 minutes inland we call this is Swan Valley. So it is the closest wine region to a city center in the world. The Swan Valley is famous for its wineries, with over 80 wineries out here, many places to taste wine, enjoy lunch, even ride down to a chocolate factory, you can taste cheese, you can buy fish, produce and all of these within 30 minutes from the city center.

接下来讲讲跟上述景点不同的观光体验，从市区往内陆走30分钟，就可以来到天鹅谷。这也是世界上最靠近市中心的葡萄酒产区。天鹅谷以酒庄著称。这里有80多家酒庄，大家可以去不同的酒庄品鉴葡萄酒，享用午餐。此外可以到巧克力厂品尝奶酪。您可以在那里购买鱼肉和农产品。那个地方离市中心只有30分钟的路程。

05:43—06:18

Then the things as you go, this is when you are going to start enjoy our national parks. So it would only be 45 minutes from Perth and you are going to see this type of scenery. So you can go bushwalking, bird watching, all of these things right on the door of the city, including little Australian towns, very unusual little historical towns. We call this Avon Valley. We can also ride a hot air balloon. So you got a great deal of things to see and do, all within a very short distance of the city center.

接下来您可以到我们的国家公园观光。我们的国家公园仅距离珀斯45分钟的路程，然后您在那里可以看到这类景观。您可以丛林徒步，可以观赏鸟类。这一切的一切就在城市的家门口，包括澳洲小镇，与众不同的历史小镇。这个小镇叫做埃文河谷。此外，我们还可以搭乘热气球。因此，你们可以在距离市中心不远之处饱览旖旎风光，参加各种活动。

06:18—06:48

So we hope that you will all encourage your customers to come to Perth and come yourself for a holiday. Because I can guarantee you that we will give you a very good holiday. You can build a wonderful itinerary and everything you can see and do within a very short distance of Perth. Please visit our website. When you leave this afternoon, our *Holiday Planner* is out on the table outside. Please take one. And thank you! Welcome to Perth!

因此，我们希望你们能够大力推介你们的客户到珀斯来，也欢迎你们到珀斯来度假。因为我保证，我们会给你们一个绝佳的假期。你们可以制定丰富的行程，就在珀斯附近，你们可以将各种美景一览无余，还能够参加各种旅游项目。请浏览我们的网站。今天散会的时候，您可以取阅外面咨询台的《旅游指南》。谢谢大家！欢迎到珀斯来！

III. 实战练习二

1. 演讲背景

下文同样摘自"2012 西澳大利亚州旅游局中国旅游洽谈会"。演讲嘉宾是 Esplanade 酒店集团的代表。该酒店集团旗下有两家酒店——位于弗里曼特尔的滨海酒店和珀斯南部的埃斯普勒纳河套房酒店。演讲嘉宾首先详细介绍了两家酒店所处城市的知名景点和迷人风光，然后才具体讲解酒店的配套设施。

2. 预习词汇

Esplanade Hotels Group Esplanade 酒店集团
Esplanade Hotel Fremantle 弗里曼特尔滨海酒店
Esplanade River Suites 埃斯普勒纳河套房酒店
CBD/central business district 中央商务区
Captain Cook Cruise 库克船长游轮
Cappuccino Strip 咖啡大道
café 小餐厅
Fremantle Jail 弗里曼特尔监狱
carnival 嘉年华
Cat Bus 猫巴
tram 电车
Maritime Museum 海事博物馆
Rottnest Express 罗特尼斯岛快艇

Best Superior Accommodation 澳大利亚最佳优越住宿奖
apartment hotel 公寓酒店

3. 演讲文本

00:00—00:29

你们好，谢谢光临！I am learning mandarin. Thank you. Thank you for coming here today. As Alan said, my name is Karen. And I represent the Esplanade Hotels Group. We have two hotels in Perth. One is called the Esplanade Hotel in a lovely place called Fremantle and the second one is called Esplanade River Suites which is in South Perth.

Hello, thank you for coming. 我正在学习中文。谢谢！谢谢你们今天来到这里。Alan 刚刚已经介绍了，我叫 Karen，是 Esplanade 酒店集团的代表。我们在珀斯有两家酒店。一家是坐落于美丽的弗里曼特尔的滨海酒店，另一家是位于珀斯南部的埃斯普勒纳河套房酒店。

00:29—00:53

So just showing you on the picture here, you can see the Perth central business district and we have the beautiful Swan River. You can take a lovely Captain Cook Cruise down to Fremantle. And Fremantle is very much a port city. It's very relaxed. It's a wonderful place to send your leisure and business visitors, where they can enjoy the lovely laid-back lifestyle.

正如图片所示，您可以看到珀斯中央商务区，那里有美丽的天鹅河。您可以乘坐漂亮的库克船长游轮来到弗里曼特尔。弗里曼特尔是一个港口城市，非常休闲。这是一个适合度假旅客和商务旅客的好地方，人们可以在这里享受非常悠闲的生活方式。

00:53—01:38

When you are in Fremantle, it's very easy to get around. You can go from Perth also by train at about 30 minutes from the international airport. Our hotel is across the road from the Fishing Boat Harbor, which you can see here. We are very famous for our fish and chips, lovely fresh seafood, and also we make our own beer there. We have a chocolate company. We have a famous street called the Cappuccino Strip which has a lot of outdoor cafes and coffee shops. Because we have such wonderful weather, we have blue sky and lots of sunshine, we do tend to eat out in the lovely cafes and sidewalk or pavement cafes.

当您置身于福利曼特尔，您会发现那里的交通非常便利。从珀斯国际机场出发，乘火车大约30分钟就可以到达弗里曼特尔。我们的酒店位于渔船港口的对面，看看，就在这个位置。我们的炸鱼炸薯条、鲜活海鲜都非常有名，我们还自己酿造啤酒。我们有一家巧克力公司。有一条名为咖啡大道的大街，那里有很多室外餐厅和咖啡馆。我们那里天气非常好，总是晴空万里、阳光普照。我们常常在典雅的小餐厅或者露天茶座用餐。

01:38—02:13

The buildings there and the city is very different from Perth. Perth is, of course, very beautiful as well. But Fremantle has more colonial style buildings, lots of heritage buildings and lots of culture. It has got a very cosmopolitan feel. Very famous also for the Fremantle markets, we have fantastic fresh Western Australian produce and we also have about a hundred stores that have fantastic souvenirs. Many of those are made in Fremantle so that it's good to take something from there back for your family and friends.

弗里曼特尔的建筑和市容市貌与珀斯大不相同。珀斯当然也非常漂亮。但弗里曼特尔拥有更多殖民时期风格的建筑，有许多文物建筑以及丰富的文化底蕴，给人一种非常国际化的感觉。弗里曼特尔的市场也非常有名，那里有新鲜的西澳大利亚农产品，还有大约一百家卖精美纪念品的商店。其中有很多都是弗里曼特尔本地产的，非常适合带给亲朋好友。

02:13—02:34

We have lots of old buildings. This is the old Fremantle Jail, which is now a tourist attraction. You can do an underground tunnel tour, an adventure type tour that you see here. And you can also do a daytime and a night-time tour which is a little bit of a spooky ghost tour. It is quite fun.

这里有很多古建筑。这是古老的弗里曼特尔监狱，现在是一个旅游景点。您可以体验地下隧道之旅，就是这张图展现的冒险之旅。您可以选择白天或者晚上过来，这有点像幽灵之旅，非常刺激。

02:34—03:13

We are known for many carnivals and festivals. And even as local people, when we want to go out at the weekend, we all go to Fremantle. Because there is a lot to see and do. When you are there, getting around is very easy. You can do a wonderful walking tour. And we can provide mandarin speaking guides if you need us. There is a free bus. The orange bus that you see up there is called the Cat Bus. And we have free buses in Perth and Fremantle. You can hire a scooter or enjoy a guided tram tour on the Fremantle tram that you see.

我们以众多嘉年华和节假日而闻名。哪怕是当地人周末想出游都会去到弗里曼特尔。因为那里有很多观赏游玩的地方。在那里出行很方便，您可以来一场美妙的徒步旅行。如果有需要，我们可以提供中文导游。那里还提供免费的巴士。您在PPT上看到的橙色巴士叫做猫巴。我们在珀斯和弗里曼特尔都有免费巴士。您可以租小型摩托车或者是乘坐PPT上展示的弗里曼特尔导览电车观光旅游。

03:13—03:35

I mentioned earlier the Captain Cook Cruise boat from Perth to Fremantle which is a great way to enjoy the city. We have Maritime Museum, telling the history of Fremantle. And we also have some fabulous golf courses, not just in Fremantle. But I am sure the others have told you we got some great golf courses throughout Western Australia.

我早些时候提到了从珀斯到弗里曼特尔的库克船长游轮，这是游览城市的好方法。我们有展示弗里曼特尔历史的海事博物馆。我们还有一些高大上的高尔夫球场，不仅仅是在弗里曼特尔。但我敢肯定刚才有演讲嘉宾曾经告诉过你们，澳大利亚西部还有很多很棒的高尔夫球场。

03:35—03:55

A wonderful place to go, especially for a day trip, it is the Rottnest Island. It's about 25 minutes by fast ferry in Rottnest Express from Fremantle. There are no vehicles on the island. You can take a small bus tour or hire a bicycle and cycle around.

罗特尼斯岛是一个好地方，尤其适合一日游。从弗里曼特尔乘坐罗特尼斯岛快艇25分钟就可到达。岛上没有机动车。您可以乘坐小巴士游览或租用自行车环岛骑行。

03:55—04:21

We have a cute little animal on the island. I bet you have seen this one in some of the presentations, but his name is quokka. He is a very small animal. He is very harmless. He is just very curious. He likes to come and have a look and see what you are doing. We have dolphin watching and we also have whale watching in seasons through various parks, very easily accessible from our hotels.

岛上有一种可爱的小动物。我敢打赌你们在某些嘉宾的演讲中看到过它，它是短尾矮袋鼠。它非常小而且没有攻击性，好奇心很重，喜欢看看您在做什么。很多公园一年四季都可以观赏海豚和鲸鱼，我们酒店去这些公园很方便。

第五单元 观光旅游 Tourism

04:21—04:56

So our hotel in Fremantle is 300 rooms. We are a four-and-a-half star hotel. And as you can see, we won the Best Superior Accommodation in 2011. We catered for FITs to large groups and we have all of the modern facilities that you expect from a large hotel, many restaurants, bars. And we have many cafes and restaurants that you can walk to as well, very many different styles of rooms and lots of suites as well with fabulous views across the water.

我们在弗里曼特尔的酒店有300间客房,是一家4.5星级酒店。正如您所看到的,我们在2011年荣获澳大利亚最佳优越住宿奖。我们可以接待背包客和大型的旅行团,拥有您期望大型酒店所能提供的所有现代化设施,有许多餐厅、酒吧。我们还有很多只有一步之遥的咖啡馆和餐馆。酒店有不同风格的客房和大量的江景套房。

04:56—05:20

Onto our second hotel which is called Esplanade River Suites, this one is closer to the city. We are about 10 minutes to Perth itself and about 20 minutes from the international airport. You can drive to the city in about 10 minutes and you also can take a ferry which takes about 8 minutes across the Swan River. So it's very easy to get there.

我们的第二家酒店是埃斯普勒纳河套房酒店。这家酒店距离市区更近。距珀斯约10分钟车程,距国际机场约20分钟车程。您开车大约10分钟就能去到市区,您还可以搭乘渡轮,穿过天鹅河,大约8分钟就能到,非常方便。

05:20—05:45

So just show you a picture in the Perth central business district. We are on this side of the water. It's very relaxed area. We have lots of little shops and cafes and more boutique shopping, lots of walkways. We have two very good golf courses. And we are very close to Perth Zoo. So families really enjoy it.

给大家看一张珀斯中央商务区的图片。我们在天鹅河的这一边。这是个非常休闲的地方。我们有很多小商店和餐厅,还有许多精品店和人行道。我们有两个非常好的高尔夫球场。我们离珀斯动物园也非常近,所以很多家庭都很喜欢去那里玩。

05:45—06:11

And this hotel is... we have this hotel for about four years, and it's only very new for the Chinese market. But recently we had fairly good sized family groups come and stay with us, all ages from very young to their grandparents. And everybody really loved this hotel we have because it is an apartment style accommodation and it's close to all of these things that you see.

这家酒店已经有四年的历史了，但对中国市场来说却是非常新的。但最近我们有相当大规模的家庭团来到这里，从小孩子到老年人，所有年龄段的客人都有。大家都非常喜欢我们这家酒店，因为它是一种公寓式的住宿，离您看到的所有这些设施都很近。

06:11—07:01

You can see it's quite oriental in style, which is the Pagoda, the restaurant of the front of the hotel. We have 101 rooms and this won also an award last year for the Best Apartment Hotel in Western Australia. So it's got the kitchen. It has the washing machine and dryer. It has all the facilities you need. We also have 24 hours reception and room service, swimming pool, lovely restaurants and bars. Every single room has a spa and many of the rooms, as you can see, do have river views. We have the suites for honeymoon and we also have the choice of one and two bedrooms. The two bedrooms are very popular with the smaller groups traveling together because they have two bedrooms, two bathrooms and a shared kitchen and a lounge area.

您可以看到这个叫做"宝塔"的餐厅颇具东方风格，它位于酒店前面。我们有101间客房，去年酒店荣获了"西澳最佳公寓酒店奖"。它配有厨房，洗衣机和烘干机，有您需要的所有设施。我们还有24小时接待和客房服务、游泳池、精美的餐厅和酒吧。每间客房都配有按摩浴缸，如PPT展示的那样，许多房间都可以看到河景。我们有蜜月套房，也可以选择有一个或两个卧室的套房。两间卧室的套房非常受小型旅行团欢迎，因为那种套房有两间卧室、两间浴室、一间共用厨房和客厅。

07:01—07:38

So that is all from me. 谢谢！Thank you very much for listening! And there is an information tag that I think you have of my hotel and an important thing I just must say before I close. Sorry. It's most important that I forgot to tell you is that we have at the hotel in Fremantle, 20 mandarin speaking staff. So we have lots of Chinese people working with us. At the Perth hotel about 5 mandarin speaking staff and all of our collections and brochures are developed in mandarin. So anything you need, might call us in the tags. Thank you very much.

我的演讲到此结束。Thank you！非常感谢您的聆听！我想你们都有一个我们酒店的信息标签，在结束之前我必须说明一件重要的事情。抱歉！我忘记告诉你们最重要的是我们在弗里曼特尔的酒店有20名会讲中文的员工。我们有很多中国同事。在珀斯的酒店约有5名会讲中文的员工，我们所有的宣传单和小册子都有中文版本。您有任何需要都可以通过标签上的电话联系我们。非常感谢！

第六单元　行业介绍
Introduction to Industries

I. 数字口译

不论是对于口译初学者还是有经验的译员而言，数字口译都是难点。原因在于两个方面，一是英汉两种语言数字的表达方式不同，即分段方式不同；二是译员需要在很短的时间内记录下正确的数字信息，且在翻译时需要迅速的把数字在两种语言之间转换。

1. 数字翻译的基本方法

（1）点线法。"点线法"是针对英汉两种语言数字分段方式不同而专门设计的。英文数字是三位一段，记录方式为从右向左每三位一个逗点；中文数字是四位一段，记录方式是从右向左每四位一条斜线。这样数字在两种语言中的记录和转换就比较清晰。如下例所示：

【例1】英文：1,000,000,000,000

译文：1/0000/0000/0000

上面的例子中中英文数字同样都为1兆，数字在英文表达方式下三位一段，共隔了四段，从右向左每个分段处的单位分别是 thousand, million, billion 和 trillion，每一段起始位为"百"位。而中文表达方式下四位一段，共隔了三段，从右向左每个分段处的单位分别是万、亿和兆，每一段起始位为"千"位。

（2）小数点移位法。对于一些以 thousand, million, billion, trillion 以及万、亿和兆为单位的大位整数，采用小数点移位法，转换起来更快，如下例所示：

【例2】637 million

末位数字7后面单位为百万，可转换成中文的单位亿，则小数点向左移动两位，中文数字为6.37亿。

【例3】78万

末位数字8后面单位为万，可转换成英文的单位 thousand，则小数点向右移动一位，英文数字为780 thousand；或者转换成英文的单位 million，则小数点向左移动两位，英文数字为0.78 million。

2. 数字与信息结合

在进行数字口译的时候，不能忽略数字通常是出现在上下文当中的。如果数字有加上单位，例如美元、千克等，一定要连同单位一起译出。另外一些与数字有关的常用表达法，如趋势、数值等，也应为口译学习者所熟知。

（1）表示向上的趋势。

增加 increase, rise, grow, go up

爬升 climb

飙升 skyrocket, soar, surge, shoot up

（2）表示向下的趋势。

下降 decrease, fall, drop, go down

稍降 slip

暴跌 plunge, plummet

（3）数值。

总数达 reach, be up to, stand at, amount to, total, add up to

占百分比 account for, occupy

大约 about, around, approximately, roughly

多于 more than, over, above

少于 less than, under, below

II. 实战练习一

1. 演讲背景

全球前四大市场研究公司之一的 GfK 捷孚凯公司家电部全球大客户副总裁应邀出席"2015年广交会系列论坛——中国电子家电品牌与创新高峰论坛"并发表主旨演讲。他在演讲中谈到了全球两大对家电业利好的趋势：家庭人口规模的缩小和中等收入国家的增长，并分析了大小家电市场持续增长的根本原因：创新和互联互通。在演讲结束前他还展望了未来，认为这场"联网家居"和"完全联网个体"的竞赛已经开始。

2. 预习词汇

Canton Fair 广交会

CCCME/China Chamber of Commerce for Import and Export of Machinery and Electronic Products 中国机电产品进出口商会

home/household appliance 家电

connectivity 互联互通；联网

household composition 家庭组成；家庭结构

household size 家庭人数

第六单元 行业介绍 Introduction to Industries

precondition 先决条件；前提条件
emerging country 新兴国家
per capita income 人均收入
major (household) appliance 大家电
refrigerator 电冰箱
washing machine 洗衣机
microwave oven 微波炉
cooking appliance 厨具
dish washer 洗碗机
middle class 中产阶级
small (household) appliance 小家电
global economic downturn 全球经济下行
Brown Goods 黑色家电
geopolitical 地缘政治的
Southern Europe 南欧
slow juicer 慢速榨汁机
hand/hand-held vacuum cleaner 手持式真空吸尘器
liquidizer 带刀片的榨汁机
kitchen machine 厨房用具
blade 刀片
low oil deep fryer 低油量炸炉
Dyson 戴森
Philips 飞利浦
suction 吸力；抽吸
hand-stick rechargeable vacuum cleaner 立式可充电吸尘器
robotic vacuum cleaner 机器人吸尘器
electrical cooking pot 电煮锅
multi-cooker 多功能电饭煲
food preparation with cooking function 带有烹饪功能的厨具
traditional filter coffee machine with grinder 带研磨功能的传统过滤式咖啡机
electronic personal scales with mobile connectivity 具有联网功能的电子体重秤
long tail 长尾效应
shelf life 货架期；保质期
market segment 细分市场
tumble dryer 滚筒式烘干机
full-sized dish washer 全尺寸洗碗机

mobile platform 移动平台
drone 无人机
health and fitness tracker 健康追踪仪
blood pressure monitor 血压监测仪
digital thermometer 电子体温计
glucose monitor 血糖仪
mobile connected scale 联网的体重秤
window cleaning robot 清洁玻璃窗机器人
lawnmower robot 除草机器人
solar cleaning robot 太阳能清洁机器人
pool cleaning 清洁泳池
pet feeding robot 给宠物喂食的机器人
massage robot 按摩机器人
prototype 原型

3. 演讲文本

00:00—00:41

Hello, 你好。I'd like to start by thanking the Canton Fair organizers and the members of CCCME for inviting GfK to participate. We are quite pleased to be here today. Also, I should say that I am not trying to make a new fashion statement with my sneakers for those of you who've noticed. I had a knee surgery just a few weeks ago. It is impossible for me to walk right now in anything but sneakers. So please forgive the casual attire. OK. Let me see if I can make this work.

你好！Hello！首先，我想感谢广交会主办方和中国机电产品进出口商会的各位会员，感谢他们邀请捷孚凯参会。我们很乐意亲临现场。同时，我必须说明：我今天穿着这双引人注目的帆布鞋并不是为了标新立异。数周之前，我做了膝关节手术。因此，除了帆布鞋之外，我没办法穿别的鞋子。因此，请原谅我穿着休闲服装到会。好了，接下来我将开始我的演讲。

00:45—01:02

OK. My presentation today will really focus primarily on two parts: home appliance growth and the role of innovation and connectivity in the marketplace today as well as in the future.

我今天的展示将会把焦点放在两个主要的部分：家电的增长，以及创新和互联互通在当今和未来市场中的角色。

01:02—02:27

But before I get into the details of this sort of core topic, I would like to speak a little bit about household appliances. It's difficult to speak about household appliances without first acknowledging the word "households". I think everyone here is well aware; you don't need me to tell you that, as we look around the globe, household composition is very very different from country to country. That makes sense. But there is a trend and one trend which is consistent across many many countries is that household sizes are becoming smaller. So if we look back to the 1900s, early 1900s, it would not be uncommon to find an average household size of five or six individuals living in a single home. Of course, today, again in many many countries, what we are really seeing are average household sizes of two or three. So when we look to the future, with China as just one example, you can see that we would expect this trend to continue and there will actually be many more one-and-two-person households than three-or-more-person households over time. This holds not just for China but for many of the world's population centers.

但是，在我详细讨论核心话题之前，让我先稍稍讲讲家电。但如果不首先谈谈家庭，就很难讲家电，所以我先谈家庭。我想在座的各位都应该有很清楚的认识。相信大家应该不需要我赘言了：放眼环球，不同国家的家庭组成大相径庭。这点的确如此。但是还有一个多个国家都面临的趋势：很多国家的家庭规模越变越小。因此，如果我们回望20世纪初，一般家庭有5～6个成员并非罕见。当然，今天，在很多国家，我们看到的家庭的规模一般为2～3人。因此，当我们放眼未来，仅以中国为例，您将会看到，这种趋势将会继续下去，随着时间流逝，这种只有一两个人的家庭将会比3人乃至更多人的家庭要多。这种事不仅仅会在中国发生，还会在很多的人口大国出现。

02:27—03:22

So it is a very consistent trend. Of course, it is an important trend for all of us here for two reasons. One it sets a precondition of household growth, which is good for our industry. The more households, the more appliances. It is very simple. The other nice thing about this is that as a precondition of household growth, not only will we sell more appliances, presumably, but we will sell different types of appliances. I think this is important to keep in mind, particularly when you look at how drastic the trend is in China. So a household today in China may look or the composition of households today in China may look very different five or ten years from now. As it does, we, of course, as an industry, need to adjust to this.

因此，这是一个全球性的趋势。当然，这种趋势对在座各位而言非常重要，原因有二：首先，这将会是家庭数量增加的前提，这对我们行业而言是一件好事：家庭越多，家电就越多。这显而易见。其次，作为家庭数量增长的前提，我们不仅可以售卖更多的电器，应该还能出售不同品类的电器。我认为记住这些非常重要，尤其是当我们着眼去看这种趋势在中国何其明显的时候。因此，从今天开始，五到十年之内，中国的家庭或者是家庭的构成将会发生极大的变化。中国的家庭在变，我们作为一个行业，自然需要适应这一趋势。

03:22—03:43

The second precondition, if you will, is the middle-income market is growing. It is growing in developing nations. It is growing in emerging countries. It is growing throughout the world. This, again, is also good for us.

第二个前提条件，可以这样说，是中等收入国家的增长。增长集中在发展中国家、新兴国家。几乎全球都在发展。这对于我们而言同样有好处。

03:43—04:33

So the chart perhaps is a little busy, but if you look on the bottom of the chart, you will see that we range per capita income from zero to about 60,000 dollars per person. Then on our vertical axis, what we are seeing are the purchases of major appliances per household. What we find is that there is really a very high correlation between the two. So as an example, when we look at markets that have a very high per capita income, like Great Britain or Germany or the USA, we see that a wide variety of nine sort of available major appliance products are purchased per household.

给大家看的这个表格有点复杂，但如果您看一下表格的底部，您会发现我们的人均收入在0～6万美元这个范围之内。然后请看看纵轴，纵轴代表的是每个家庭大家电的平均购买量。我们发现上述两者之间有很高的关联性。举个例子，当我们把目光投向人均收入很高的市场，如英国、德国或者美国的时候，我们会发现平均每个家庭会购买九大类大家电。

04:33—05:18

When we look at developing and emerging markets, if we look at India, if we look at China, you can see that the first two appliances that a typical household is going to buy are a refrigerator and then a washing machine. But you can also see if you look closely particularly at India and China, is some early developments in microwave ovens, some early developments in cooking appliances and some early developments in dish washers. So we will expect this trend to continue. As Africa comes on line and more people in Africa into the middle class, it almost looks like a bundle of opportunity for our industry. To me, two very positive and important sort of overarching preconditions.

当我们放眼发展中国家、新兴国家等市场，比如印度、中国，就不难发现，一般家庭要买的前两类电器首先包括电冰箱，然后是洗衣机。但您还可以发现，如果再仔细地研究这些国家，尤其是印度和中国，您会看到微波炉、厨具、洗碗机的初步发展。我们希望这种趋势得以继续。随着非洲也加入到新兴市场行列中来，非洲越来越多的人跻身为中产阶级，这对我们行业而言，意味着一连串的机会。对我而言，这是两个非常积极的、重要的前提条件。

05:18—06:21

So let's look at the appliance market and see how things are going. So on this chart, you are looking at 2009 forward for major appliances as well as small appliances. When we look at this data you can see that since the global economic downturn in 2009, both of these market sectors have done very well, particularly. By the way, if we compare this to our cousins or colleagues in Brown Goods, they do not have this type of consistent growth from year to year since 2009. It is much more dragging; there is a lot more red on the chart. So we were in a good place. If you look at 2012, there is a little bit of softening in the marketplace. This is primarily due to geopolitical change as well as Southern Europe still being deeply in crisis during this period of time. But otherness, it is a nice picture and again a good condition for our industry.

让我们一起看看家电市场，看看情况是怎么变化的。在这张图上，您看到的是2009年以来大小家电的情况。当我们研读这些数据，可以看到，自2009年全球经济下行以来，大小家电两个市场的表现都令人非常满意。顺便说一下，如果我们把这些数据和我们的黑色家电同行进行比较，就会发现黑色家电自2009年以来并没有经历同样的持续增长。它的增长有所放缓，在图表上有更多的红色。由此可见，我们行业前景光明。如果我们再看看2012年，就会发现市场有所疲软。这主要是因为地缘政治的变动，以及南欧仍深陷危机当中。但从其他国家和地区来看，这都是一张数据很好的图表，我们的行业发展势头良好。

06:21—06:52

So what is driving this growth? So we will start with small appliances. You can see that there are nice mix of products up here. For each growth segment, I try to provide the percent growth, so you can see for slow juicers, remarkable growth, 141%, hand vacuum cleaners which I'll come back to in a minute, 109%. Those are the two leading categories.

是什么促进了增长？我们首先从小家电开始。你们可以看到这里有很好的产品组合。每一个增长领域我们都用百分比来衡量。慢速榨汁机增长很快，达141%。

手持式真空吸尘器增长高达109%，我待会还要谈到这个。这两个是领先的品类。

06:52—07:32

So truthfully, we could spend 30 to 60 minutes to get into each and every one of these categories. Unfortunately, we do not have time for this. Maybe I'll bore you a little bit if we did. But in any case, there is a few things to be thinking about when you look at this chart. One is there is an overarching demographic or a lifestyle trend here which is that people are enjoying healthy living; they are enjoying a more healthy lifestyle and they are enjoying a sense of personal well-being. Most of these categories really fit into those overarching demographic trends, of the living, of the lifestyle, personal well-being.

老实说，我们要花30~60分钟来介绍每一个品类。遗憾的是我们没时间，如果这么做的话你们也许会无聊。不管怎样，看这幅图的时候要考虑几个问题。一个是非常重要的人口和生活趋势，人人都享受健康生活，追求更健康的生活方式和个人幸福感。大多数的品类符合这种人口和生活趋势，符合他们的生活方式，能带来个人幸福感。

07:32—08:03

In addition to this, when you look at these categories, there are maybe two core groups. Core group No. 1, a brand new category, like slow juicer, which just wasn't here five years ago. The other is, there are sort of older or maybe a better term would be heritage categories like a liquidizer or a kitchen machine. These are very traditional categories. They are not new by any standard. But they are doing exceptionally well.

除此之外，我们来看看分类，大致可以分成两大组。第一组是全新的品类，像慢速榨汁机，5年前还不存在。另外一种比较老，或者换个词说，很传统的品类，像是带刀片的榨汁机和厨房用具。这些是传统的品类，用任何标准来衡量都不是全新品类，但是增长得特别快。

08:03—09:04

So how and what innovations have revitalized these sectors? Let's say in the case of liquidizers, it is high-powered, better blades for chopping, improved design as an innovation for kitchen machines, improved functionality through attachments. Some kitchen machines now, what's helping to drive some growth in kitchen machine now is a cooking function. So we can work with relatively mature categories and improve upon those categories. Let's look at low oil deep fryer. Deep frying was nothing new. But now low oil deep frying is a nice innovation. It is a nice product extension. As an

第六单元　行业介绍 Introduction to Industries

industry, this is what we need to be thinking about. Where can innovation come from? What types of product extensions or new initiatives can continue our successful growth?

　　有哪些措施以及什么样的产品创新可以重振这些传统品类呢？例如带刀片的榨汁机，其创新措施包括功率增大，刀片更耐用，对于厨房用具来说改善设计，通过附加装置改善功能。一些厨房用具现在有烹饪功能，促进了增长。因此，我们可以专注于一些相对成熟的品类，改善它们。让我们来看看低油量炸炉。油炸不是什么新鲜事了。但是低油量油炸是个不错的创新，也是不错的产品延伸。作为一个行业，这是我们需要思考的。创新来自哪里？什么样的产品延伸和新的做法可以有持续的增长？

09:04—10:09

So I'll just focus on one more, which is hand-held vacuum cleaners as an example. Some of you may be aware of this, perhaps some not. But when I saw 109%, I said wow, "What is this?" I really have to look a few months ago because I had no idea. But Dyson, Philips, LG have all been engaged and developing a hand-held vacuum cleaner that is specific to bed cleaning. Yes, these products use ultraviolet light. These products have a high degree of suction. They have a vibration or maybe a pounding motion which helps to lift the dust out of your bed, kill the germs or pull the germs into the product, remove them from your household. 109%, unless you think this is not relevant in your market. By the way, it is very big in Japan, for sure. Philips has launched new models in China as recently as August of this year. So there is a lot of momentum behind this category.

　　我还想拿手持式真空吸尘器做个例子。有些人意识到了，有些人没有，当我看到增长率达109%时，我很惊讶，我要看一下几个月以来的发展情况，否则我完全没有头绪。但是戴森、飞利浦和LG都参与研发手持式真空吸尘器，专用于床单清洁。这些产品使用紫外线，吸力很强，有震动和拍打模式，可帮助除灰尘和尘螨，将它们从家居环境中清理出去。增长率109%！务必要把握好商机！在日本，商机很多，毫无疑问。飞利浦最近在中国推出了新款式，就是今年8月推出的。这种品类还有很大增长动力。

10:12—10:58

So we think about innovation. I want to drill in a little bit further. This is really one of my favorite charts. It is so interesting to watch this chart change over a period of time. But if you look on the left, you can see that in 2009 the measurable market for GfK, in a consistent basis, was about 20 billion in small appliance sales. In 2014, five years later, 11 billion, so 31 billion, excuse me, an increase of 11 billion. At that time,

109

none of the products on the right hand side of the screen, none of the products in color, short of vacuum cleaners, were available in the market, just five years ago.

来看看创新,我想深入谈一下。这是我最喜欢的图表之一。看着这张图随着时间的变化而改变很有趣。但是您看左边,2009 年 GfK 持续追踪的小家电市场的销售额达到了 200 亿美元。过了 5 年,到 2014 年,增长了 110 亿美元。那时候,右边那些标有颜色的产品一个也还没诞生。除了真空清洁器之外,一个都没出现,那只是 5 年前啊。

10:58—11:51

So in a five-year period of time, we see about 2.7, 2.8 billion or 25% of the market growth coming from these new innovations. So what are they? The three biggies, hand-stick rechargeable vacuum cleaners, robotic vacuum cleaners and electrical cooking pots which some people know as multi-cookers. So these three products, they essentially didn't exist just five years ago, are now a two-billion-dollar industry. Significant. Behind this, there is wave two. Wave two has lots of interesting products like slow juicers and deep fryer with low oil, food preparation with cooking function, traditional filter coffee machines with grinders. It might not be such a huge generation but coming on strong now.

5 年内,我们见证了 27 亿,28 亿,高达 25% 的市场增长,出现了新的创新。有哪些创新呢?有三大类。立式可充电吸尘器、机器人吸尘器、电煮锅——人们也称之为多功能电饭煲。这三种产品 5 年前还没出现,现在成为 20 亿美元的产业了。此后,还有浪潮二。这其中也有很多有趣的产品,比如慢速榨汁机、低油量炸炉、带有烹饪功能的厨具、带研磨功能的传统过滤式咖啡机。这一代产品的市场也许不大,但发展势头越来越强劲。

11:51—12:14

Then I point out the last one, which is one of the reasons why I think we are here is that for the first time, we see at a very top electronic personal scales with mobile connectivity. This is coming to our industry. Connectivity is going to drive growth for sure in the future. We will come to this a little bit more in a few minutes.

最后一点,也是我们来到这里的原因之一,我们有史以来第一次看到具有联网功能的高级电子体重秤。未来互联互通肯定会促进增长,待会儿我们会继续谈到这一点。

12:14—13:26

So let's talk about major appliances. I will give you some insights into what's happening in the small appliances marketplace. If you go back to 2004, the far left hand side of the screens, you can see that new model activities and new models launched in all of broader Europe in 2004 were about 25,000 models to serve the broader Europe marketplace for major appliances. So in 2014 we see pretty consistently that this number is now 30,000 to 35,000 models. So clearly, new product developments, new initiatives, new model offerings are helping to drive growth in major appliances as well. Very interesting thing to know, to take note of here is a very long tail associated with major appliances. Yes, the household products that were launched in 2004 have a very very long shelf life. I do not think this is the same in small appliances. I didn't think to make the comparison until last night when it was too late. But I think I will for my next presentation because I think you will see a very very different picture.

接下来谈谈大家电。在此之后，我会跟大家分享一下我对小家电市场的看法。2004年，也就是屏幕最左边的数据，可以看到新款产品在全欧洲上线，大约有2.5万个新款大家电。直至2014年，款式还在持续更新，现在已约有3万至3.5万个款式了。因此，新产品的发展，策划和款式都可以促进大家电市场的发展。还有一点需要注意的是，大家电市场出现了一种长尾效应。2004年推出的家电产品的货架期都很长，但对小家电来说并非如此。我一直没想到要做个对比，昨晚突然想到，不过已经来不及了。下一次演讲的时候我应该就会讲到了，届时将和大家分享一些不同的想法。

13:26—14:01

So what are the developments in the major appliances industry? I am sorry that this chart may be a little hard to read. Perhaps it is a little technical. But there are essentially eight or nine market segments that make up a huge amount of growth. Essentially one in every six appliances sold in Europe come from one of those eight or nine segments on the left hand side of the screen. That's it. All you need to do is be a player in one of those eight or nine segments and be good at it and price your products well, and then you will have a good chance at growth.

那么大家电行业的发展如何呢？不好意思，这个表格可能不太清晰。看上去可能过于专业了。但简单来说，8个或9个细分市场带来了巨大的增长。每6件在欧洲售出的家电产品中就有1件就是来自这些细分市场的，大家可以看屏幕的左边。情况就是这样。各位需要做的就是，参与到这八九个细分市场中去，做大做强，并且进行合理定价，那么就会有很好的发展前景。

14:01—14:33

So what are those? OK. I am simplifying a little bit. What are those? Washing machines that are greater than or equal to eight kilogram that are energy efficient, tumble dryers that you see on technology and of course are also very energy efficient, full-sized dish washers that are less than or equal to 10 litters, low water capacity, low water usage, refrigerators, a traditional sort of combined model which is a two-door freezer, bottom no frost and energy efficient model.

那么这些又是什么呢？我简单说明一下。洗衣机的容量更大，大于或等于8公斤，更节能高效。滚筒式烘干机的技术改进了，也更加节能。全尺寸洗碗机的容量不多于10公升，而且水容量小的话，也会更加节水。冰箱一般是双门冷冻柜，是法式无霜节能的款式。

14:33—14:54

So you know when it comes to major appliances, I don't want to take these up as a subject, I think you do not have to be necessarily a leader. You can be a fast follower and find great opportunity to catch the innovations at the right moment and ride the wave with major appliances.

所以谈到大家电的时候，我就不再赘述了。我认为您不一定要成为一名领导者，您可以跟随这一潮流，寻找创新的机遇，抓住大家电的浪潮。

14:57—16:22

OK. So these are the growth drivers. Let's talk a little bit about connectivity and the innovation that we are seeing through essentially the mobile platform. So this is a little staggering to me, a little bit. In 2014, close to 2 billion. Just one year, close to 2 billion core Internet devices will be sold. But added to those 2 billion, 1.2 billion are smartphones. So 1.2 billion smartphones sold in one year. This is like one smartphone for every person in China, or one smartphone for every person in India. It is staggering. It is, of course, changing the way we behave. If you think that the typical smartphone, perhaps last two to three years, now you are talking about 2.2 billion maybe even close to 3 billion smartphones that are entering into the marketplace in many cases to these middle income households that I was talking about before at the very first screen. It is empowering. It changes shopping behavior which is a separate subject not for today. But it also changes the opportunities for our industry.

这些是增长动力。让我谈一谈互联互通和创新是如何在移动平台上体现出来的。这有点令我震惊。2014年，在一年之内，接近20亿的核心网络设备被销售。其中12亿为智能手机。所以一年内手机的销量为12亿。这就好比每个中国人一台手机，每个印度人一台手机。这很令人震惊。这正在改变我们的行为方式。您可能觉得智能手机，在过去的两到三年，这种情况很正常。现在我们说的是22亿到30

亿的智能手机正进入我们的市场,在很多情况下这种手机是被中等收入家庭所购买,就像刚刚第一页 PPT 中所提到的,它的影响深远,改变着消费模式,这是另外一个主题了,也改变着我们行业的机遇。

16:22—17:41

So how connected are we to our smartphones? Some research indicates that the average users check their smartphones 40 times per day. Forty. I am way more than that. I am sure many of you in the room are as well. 66% will wake up with their smartphones, first thing that I do every morning, for sure. 75% of us remarkably in this survey admitted to using their phones even while on the toilet. This I won't talk about. Normally I sure am. OK. So we are highly connected to these devices. The reality is, as the platforms, as the hardware becomes more mature any day, very mature at this age, we see more and more creative applications written and users who are already extremely relying on, checking their phones right when they wake up and checking their phones 40 times a day are going to come to expect the same interactivity that they have with their phones to help control other aspects of their lives. That's for sure. This is our future.

我们有多依赖我们的智能手机呢?一份研究表明手机用户一天平均看手机 40 次。40 次,我都不止这个数了。我深信在座很多人也和我一样。66% 的人起床后就是看手机,我每天早上起床后当然也是看手机。我们当中有 75% 的受访者承认就连上洗手间也玩手机。我就不再讲这个话题了。通常情况下我也是一样的,我们高度依赖这些设备。现在,随着各种平台、硬件越来越成熟,它们已经很成熟了,我们看到越来越多的创新应用诞生,那些已经高度依赖手机的用户一起床就看手机,一天看 40 次,他们也会变得离不开这些应用,就像对待手机一样,借此来掌控自己的生活。这是毋庸置疑的,这就是我们的未来。

17:41—18:49

We see two degrees, connectivity in consumer electronic products, 33% of TVs are of some level of connectivity. You can see the other sectors. You either sort of join this vision or you don't. Me, I am all in. I see this and I say, mobile technology is going to change our world, mobile platform is going to change our world. In doing so, we as an industry need to adapt. Because when I wake up in the morning, I want my phone not just to wake me with an alarm, but to turn on my coffee machine and brew my coffee. If a drone can bring my coffee to me in my room, even better, a robot maybe. But in any case, I definitely want the coffee brewed. I want it hot. So I do not want to set at 7am if I happen to sleep until 8am. I want it when the alarm goes off or when I wake up I push a button, done.

我们看到两类产品，一类是消费电子产品的可联网特性。33%的电视是可以联网的。您可以看到其他的品类。您可以自由选择是否支持这种趋势。我是完全支持这种想法的。我看到这个趋势，我认为，移动技术即将改变我们的世界，移动平台即将改变我们的世界。所以，我们行业要适应这种变化。我早上起床的时候，我希望我的手机不仅是一个闹钟，而且能够命令咖啡机帮我煮咖啡。如果还有无人机帮我把煮好的咖啡送到我的房间，那就更好了。又或者是机器人帮我送咖啡。但我需要的是已经煮好了的热咖啡。我不想固定7点的时候来喝咖啡，因为我可能会睡到8点。喝咖啡的时间要在我睡醒后闹钟停了，或者我醒后按一下按钮就能喝到咖啡。

18:49—20:29

OK. So where are we seeing this today? Because I am now going way out there to the future. So there are many personal diagnostics categories or reading about these categories, health and fitness trackers, blood pressure monitors, digital thermometers, scales as I mentioned on a few slides ago, and glucose monitors. So the question is, when manufacturer, let's say, a personal scale really thinking about connectivity three, four, five years ago, I am not sure, maybe they were, some of them were for sure. But when we look, let's say, at the sales of personal scales over just the last couple of years, you can see an enormous growth in these categories, just one example, and there are many enormous growth of connectivity for personal scales. Truthfully, a lot of these companies, if we look at the leading brands, they are not the heritage brands, they are not the traditional brands. They are upstart companies. You know, the advantage and the reality is when you sell a mobile connected scale, you sell it at a price point that's much much higher than when you sell a regular scale. When you sell a mobile connected scale you have a cool factor or a wild factor. So if I give my wife a mobile connected scale for her birthday, she is probably going to throw me out of the house. But after she starts using it, maybe, maybe she will let me in. If I just give her a plain old scale, I am kicked out of the house forever.

所以，我们今天应该关注什么？因为我们是着眼于未来的。现在有很多个人诊断仪器，这些都是健康追踪仪，比如血压监测仪、电子体温计、之前提到的体重秤、血糖仪等等。问题是，有些制造商在三五年前可能就会想做联网的体重秤，不知道有没有，但我可以肯定是会有的。但我们看看体重秤在过去几年的销量，您可以发现联网的体重秤的销量大幅度增长。事实上，我们看到这些领先的品牌，他们都不是传统的品牌。他们只是一些新兴的企业。他们的优势是，当您卖出一个联网的体重秤，它的价格比普通体重秤的价格要高很多。您卖联网的体重秤，就有一个很好的卖点。如果我送一个联网的体重秤给我的妻子作为生日礼物，她可能会把我赶出家门。当她用了一段时间后，可能又会让我回来。如果我送她普通的体重秤，那她肯定永远都不会让我回家了。

20:29—21:01

OK. So where else? If we look at major domestic appliances and smart connected major domestic appliances, this is still relatively small numbers compared to overall sales. But look at what happened in December of 2014 and January of 2015, just huge, huge growth. Again, small markets today, but indicative of the high growth that we will see for sure in the future.

别的还有什么呢？如果我们看看大家电和智能联网的大家电，这和总体的销售额相比，还只是小数目。但看看发生了什么吧，在2014年12月和2015年1月，它们有了非常巨大的增长。今天的市场很小，但却预示着高增长，我们一定会在将来看到的。

21:01—22:57

So one last point. There is another category. Not all products are connected. Robots. But many of them are. We see more and more of them. Whether they are connected or not, I think this is a category to keep your eye on as well. Whether it is inside the home with robotic vacuum cleaners which everyone is familiar with, window cleaning robots and now lawnmower robots which are available on the marketplace, we also see solar cleaning robots, pool cleaning of course. But perhaps newer products like pet feeding robots and a massage robot. I happen to be in an industry event where a cooking robot was literally launched. It is prototyping and maybe years from being done. But it is a product that is really set to prepare an entire meal based on a manual and some ingredients you choose throwing into the machine prior to leaving the house in the morning. In talking to a number of our manufacturing clients, we even here talk of an ironing robots, which would be great but the reality as we understand it this is just not commercially viable today. So the race for the "connected homes" and "fully connected individuals" is on. Again, I've bought into this concept wholeheartedly. Pleased to talk afterwards with anybody about sort of my personal vision and where GfK comes from and how GfK can support these interests. Thank you very much!

最后一点。还有一类。并不是所有的产品都联网。机器人不是。但是许多机器人是联网的。我们可以看到越来越多这样的机器人。不管它们是否联网，我认为这是一类你们需要关注的。不管是大家都很熟悉的家居使用的机器人真空吸尘器，还是已经上市了的清洁玻璃窗的机器人以及除草机器人，我们还看到了太阳能清洁机器人，当然还有清洁泳池的机器人。但或许更新颖的产品，比如给宠物喂食的机器人和按摩机器人。我碰巧参加了一个行业活动，那里发布了烹饪机器人。它还只是原型而已，可能还要几年才能完成。但这个机器人真的可以根据指南准备完整的一顿饭，可以把您放进机器的食材变成菜肴，您早上离开家之前要准备好这些即可。在和大量制造业的客户交谈时，我们甚至听说了熨斗机器人，这很棒，但现实正如我们所理解的一样，它还没有成为商品。所以这场"联网家居"和"完全联网个体"的竞赛已经开始。我打心底里相信这个理念。我很乐意接下来和任何人交谈，谈谈我的个人看法，捷孚凯公司以及捷孚凯如何支持大家的业务发展。非常感谢！

III. 实战练习二

1. 演讲背景

国际锰协 IMnI 市场分析师应邀参加"电解产品市场高峰论坛"并发表主旨演讲。锰是制造钢铁的重要原材料，因此他一开场首先介绍了全球不锈钢市场的发展状况，侧重谈论中国不锈钢产业，接下来分享了电解金属锰和电解二氧化锰的市场行情，最后还提到了锰矿市场的近况。演讲中引用了大量的数据，是一篇非常适合练习数字口译的演讲素材。

2. 预习词汇

Compound Annual Growth Rate/CAGR 复合年增长率
Manganese 锰（金属元素）
Manganese Dioxide 二氧化锰
dioxide 二氧化物
stainless steel 不锈钢
metric ton 公吨
restock 重新进货；再储存
bounce 反弹
300 series 300 系不锈钢
400 series 400 系不锈钢
nickel 镍（金属元素）
ore 矿石
export ban 出口禁令
Macquarie 麦格理
EMD/Electrolytic Manganese Dioxide 电解二氧化锰
aluminothermic 加铝热剂的；铝热法的
environmental regulation 环保法规
inventory 库存

Lithium-Nickel-Manganese-Cobalt battery 镍钴锰锂离子电池
cobalt 钴
LMO 锰酸锂
NMC 镍钴锰
R&D/Research and Development 研发
LFP battery 磷酸铁锂电池
lithium-ion battery 锂离子电池
rechargeable battery 可充电电池
alkaline battery 碱性电池
oversupply 过度供给
capacity closure 产能关停
closed manganese alloys furnace 封闭式锰合金炉
skyrocket 快速上升；飞涨
low grade 低品位
high grade 高品位
mining cost 采矿成本
curve 曲线
fall 下跌；贬值

3. 演讲文本

00:00—02:17

Good afternoon, ladies and gentlemen. I'm going to present in English so because I don't speak Chinese very well. So please get some headphones outside the room if you don't speak English and if you don't already have one. This presentation is going to be an overview of the Manganese Metal and the Manganese Dioxide markets with a special emphasis on China. I would like to speak about stainless steel in my introduction. In 2015, global stainless steel production was 42 million metric tons. And this figure was up by 0.7% over 2014, according to Macquarie. As you can see the average growth rate was of 6.3% between 2010 and 2015. And then it's expected to slow down to 4.1% between 2015 and 2020. Last year the only growth markets were India, which has good prospects until 2020, according to Macquarie, and South Korea, which mostly produces 400 series stainless steel for the export market. Stainless steel production in the European Union, in Japan and the USA was very weak last year, but its growth is expected to bounce back this year due to restocking. So the key message here is that global stainless steel production is expected to keep growing from 2015 to 2020, but at a slower pace than before: around 4.1% of Compound Annual Growth Rate. However, 300 series and

400 series (containing less manganese but more nickel) will grow faster than 200 series. This is because of lower nickel prices, and then lower nickel prices are due to the recent Indonesian nickel ore exports ban in Indonesia.

下午好,女士们,先生们。我将用英语演讲,因为我的中文说得不太好。所以如果您不说英语,而且没有领取耳机,请到房间外领取。我将在演讲中概述(电解)金属锰和(电解)二氧化锰的市场,着重讲中国市场。我想开场之前首先谈谈不锈钢市场。2015年全球不锈钢产量为4,200万吨,与2014年相比上涨0.7%,这些数据来自麦格理。大家可以看到,2010—2015年的平均增长率为6.3%。预计2015—2020年会降到4.1%。去年仅有的实现产量增长的市场是印度,根据麦格理的预测,此趋势将持续到2020年,韩国也有所增长,主要生产用于出口的400系不锈钢。去年欧洲、日本和美国的不锈钢产量非常少,但因重建库存,预期这些国家今年的不锈钢产量将会恢复增长。因此,这里的关键信息是全球2015—2020年不锈钢产量预计将会实现增长,但是增长率将低于原来预期的复合年增长率4.1%。然而,300系不锈钢和400系不锈钢(锰含量少,镍含量更多)将会比200系不锈钢产量获得更快的增长。原因是镍价降低,镍价下降是因为近期印度尼西亚的镍矿出口禁令。

02:18—03:34

Now, let's speak a little bit about China's stainless steel industry. Last year, China's stainless steel production was almost 22 million metric tons, up by 0.6% over 2014, according to Macquarie. And as you can see again, the average growth rate between 2010 and 2015 was much higher than the average growth rate from 2015 onwards. The slower Chinese growth production forecasts: China's stainless steel exports are slowing. They were slower by 13% last year because of trade restrictions, especially in the European Union and because of the loss of China's competitive advantage, which is low domestic nickel prices. And the loss of this competitive advantage was due to the Indonesian nickel ore exports ban. China's stainless steel production is forecast to fall slightly this year, and to grow again at a 4.5% average growth rate between 2015 and 2020. So this is a [piece of] good news for the Manganese Metal industry.

现在让我们来稍微谈一谈中国的不锈钢产业。去年中国不锈钢产量接近2,200万吨,同比上涨0.6%,上述的数据来自麦格理。正如大家所看到的,2010—2015年的复合年增长率比2015年以来高多了。中国不锈钢产量降低预示着中国不锈钢出口的疲软。去年中国不锈钢出口量降低了13%,一方面是因为贸易限制,尤其是来自于欧盟的限制,另一方面是因为中国失去了竞价优势,也就是低廉的国内镍矿价。而竞价优势的丧失则是由于印度尼西亚的镍矿出口禁令。中国今年的不锈钢产量预计将会略降,2015—2020年的平均增长率将在4.5%。所以这对锰金属行业来说是个好消息。

03:35—04:12

Now this is the outline of my presentation. I'm going to speak first about Manganese Metal and assure that demand is still rising, but at a slower pace than before. Then the second part of this presentation will be about the EMD market, Electrolytic Manganese Dioxide. And I'm going to show that this market doesn't fully benefit from the growing automotive battery demand. And finally the last part of this presentation will be about the manganese ore market. And I'm going to explain that in spite of recent production cuts, the market will take time to get back to equilibrium.

这是我此次演讲的概要。我将首先谈谈金属锰,可以确定的是,需求依旧会上涨,但增速将放缓。然后演讲的第二部分是关于 EMD 市场,也就是电解二氧化锰市场。我将说明这个市场尚未从对电动车电池增长的需求中充分获利。最后一部分是关于锰矿市场的内容。我将阐明这样一点:尽管近期产量削减,市场仍需时间恢复平衡。

04:13—05:36

So first, manganese metal. Global manganese metal production capacity is around 3.07 million metric tons per year. There are around 130 manganese metal producers in China, with a total production capacity of around three million metric tons per year. Manganese metal production capacity in the rest of the world is very small, around 85,000 metric tons per year. And it's represented by South Africa with a manganese metal company, by Eramet in Gabon. Eramet started producing manganese metal last year, at the beginning of last year, February. And then there is Ukraine. There's a plant called Zaporozhye Steel, owned by Prebates and it produces aluminothermic manganese metal not electrolytic, but it has a manganese content of over 95%. And so in trade statistics, for instance, it's considered as EMM. And on the chart, here you can see the splits, the breakdown of production capacity in 2015 per country. And as you can see, China is by far the world's greatest producer of manganese metal with around 97% of global capacity.

我们来看看第一部分——金属锰。全球电解金属锰年产能大约为 307 万吨。中国拥有差不多 130 家电解金属锰厂,总产能大约为 300 万吨/年。世界其他国家的电解金属锰产能非常低,大约为 8.5 万吨一年。其中有代表性的是南非,该国有一家锰金属公司,然后是加蓬的埃赫曼,这家公司去年初开始生产电解金属锰,还有乌克兰,那里有一家名叫扎波罗热钢铁的工厂,这家工厂为 Prebates 所有,用铝热法生产锰金属而不是电解金属锰,但是锰含量达到了 95% 以上。所以在贸易统计中也可以看作是电解金属锰。从这张图中大家可以看到份额以及2015年各个国家的产能细目。大家可以看到,中国目前是世界上最大的电解金属锰供应商,占全球产能的97%。

05:37—06:31

Now, what about production? Last year, global manganese metal production slowed to 1.1 million metric tons. This was around 10% lower than in 2014. In China, production of manganese metal was around 1.07 million metric tons last year, down by 11% over 2014. Production in the rest of the world increased slightly by around 6% last year to around 39,000 metric tons, because of Eramet starting production in Gabon. So the take-home message here is that China's manganese metal production is slowing, even though global stainless steel production increased slightly last year.

那么产量如何呢?去年全球电解金属锰产量降低到110万吨。这比2014年低了约10%。去年中国电解金属锰产量为107万吨,同比下降11%。世界其他国家产量上涨了约6%,达到3.9万吨,这是因为加蓬的埃赫曼开始生产电解金属锰。所以这里的关键信息是中国的电解金属锰产量不振,虽然去年全球不锈钢产量小幅上升。

06:32—07:13

The reason why China's manganese metal production decreased last year is mostly because of lower manganese metal prices. Also this is due to high inventory, new environmental regulation in China, and all these factors forced many small-scale manganese metal producers using old technology to shut down in 2015. Now if you look at this table here, on the slide you would see that only 20 manganese metal producers in China were still in operation at the beginning of this year, out of a total of 130 producers.

中国去年电解金属锰产量下降主要是因为电解金属锰价格低。同时也是因为高库存和中国新颁布的环保法,所有这些因素致使许多技术落后、规模小的电解金属锰厂在2015年关停。现在大家看这里的表格,在幻灯片上大家可以看到,今年年初,130家电解金属锰厂里,只有20家开工。

07:14—08:53

China now accounts for around 97% of global manganese metal production, but only 52% of global stainless steel production. So of course, stainless steel mills in the rest of the world rely heavily on China's manganese metal supplies. So let's have a look at China's manganese metal exports to supply stainless steel mills in the rest of the world.

These exports have accelerated after the removal of the 20% export tax on manganese metal at the start of 2013. As you can see on the chart, it's very clear, in 2013 these exports increased sharply and last year China's manganese metal exports totaled 323,000 metric tons. This was up by 1.5% over 2014. Demand for China's manganese metal dropped in the EU by around 15%, in North America by around 11% last year, But China's exports increased to Asia by around 8%, to the CIS countries by around 11% and South America by 21%. So the important message here is that China's manganese metal exports are still growing, but at a slower rate than over the last two years, due to the sluggish demand from stainless steel makers in the EU and North America.

中国目前占全球电解金属锰产量的97%，但不锈钢产量仅占52%。因此，很显然，世界其他地区的不锈钢厂严重依赖中国的金属锰供应。我们来看一看中国为世界其他地区的不锈钢厂供应了多少金属锰。自从2013年年初取消了金属锰20%的出口税以后，中国的金属锰出口量大幅攀升。大家可以看到图中非常清晰地展示了金属锰的出口量在2013年大幅增长，去年中国的金属锰总出口量为32.3万吨，比2014年上涨1.5%。欧盟对中国的金属锰需求下降了15%，北美对中国的金属锰需求下降了11%，但是中国对亚洲的金属锰出口量上涨了8%，对独联体国家上涨11%，对南美上涨21%。所以这里的关键点是中国的电解金属锰出口持续增长，但增速会比前两年慢一些，因为欧盟和北美不锈钢厂的需求低迷。

08:54—09:40

Now this slide shows the manganese metal price in China from 2014 to 2016. As you can see, the price of manganese metal in China reduced last year. And this was because of high inventories, low stainless steel prices and low demand from Europe. As I said, the price for manganese metal has been trending down in 2014 and 2015, before increasing sharply in January this year because of an increase in demand ahead of the Chinese New Year in February, and also because of recovering manganese ore prices at the beginning of this year.

现在这张幻灯片展示的是中国金属锰2014—2016年的价格变化。大家可以看到中国的金属锰价格去年是下降的。主要原因是高库存，低不锈钢价格和欧洲的低需求。正如我所说的，在2014和2015这两年间，金属锰的价格一直走低。直到今年一月才大幅增长，因为临近二月中国春节需求有所提高，同时也得益于今年年初锰矿价格的回升。

09:41—10:24

Just a quick demand outlook for manganese metal, manganese ore demand for manganese metal production is expected to keep growing over the next few years, driven by higher stainless steel production. Around 300,000 metric tons of extra manganese units will be needed for EMM production by 2019, according to Macquarie. And it's very clear on this chart that even though the Compound Annual Growth Rate has been to be lower in between 2015 and 2019, it's still positive at around 4% per year.

来稍微看一下电解金属锰的需求前景,由于不锈钢产量的增长,用于生产电解金属锰的锰矿石的需求预计将在接下来的几年里持续增长。根据麦格理的预测,到2019年,大约会有30万吨新增的锰矿石需求,这些新增需求将用于生产电解金属锰。显然,从表格中可以看出即使复合年增长率在2015—2019年间会下降,但增长率仍然有希望保持在每年4%左右。

10:25—11:59

Now the second part of this presentation is about EMD, Manganese Dioxide. First, I would like to show the quick outlook on the auto battery demand. The global auto battery demand will grow from 15GWh in 2015 to around 115GWh in 2020, according to Macquarie. And this growth will mostly be driven by China, where the government, as you probably know, is pushing toward electric vehicle adoption to reduce air pollution and also energy security concerns. At the moment in China, demand for Lithium-Nickel-Manganese-Cobalt batteries mostly comes from electric city buses. But with the improvement of charging facilities everywhere in China, especially in urban areas, demand for private electric passengers cars is on the rise. And demand for auto battery is also expected to increase in the US, where Google and Apple are said to be working on driverless electric vehicles. So the key message here is that demand for batteries in electric vehicles is forecast to grow by 50% per year on average between 2016 and 2020, and this will increase demand for manganese batteries.

演讲的第二部分主要讲讲电解二氧化锰。首先快速看一下电动车动力电池的需求。根据麦格理的预测,全球电动车动力电池需求将会从2015年的15千兆瓦时增长到2020年的115千兆瓦时。而这种增长主要是由中国推动的。中国政府,或许大家都知道,正在推广电动车的使用,以降低空气污染,同时也是出于能源安全的考虑。现在,中国对镍钴锰锂离子电池的需求主要来自城市电动公交车。但随着中国各地充电设施的完善,尤其是城市地区,对私人电动车的需求也在上升。美国对动力电池的需求也有望增长,据说谷歌和苹果都在研发无人电动车。所以这里的关键点是,预计2016—2020年间,电动车电池的需求预计每年将平均增长50%,而这种增长将增加对锰系电池的需求。

12:00—12:51

Now, demand for EMD mostly comes from the battery industry, but mostly for alkaline and zinc carbon batteries, called primary batteries. Rechargeable batteries, including lithium ion batteries for electric cars are the second market for EMD, Electrolytic Manganese Dioxide. And I put this table here so that you can have a quick comparison between all these battery types for electric vehicles. The two battery types in yellow, LMO and NMC, are the two types of batteries containing manganese, and as you can see they have a good capacity, but this is combined with a high cost of production.

现在对电解二氧化锰的需求主要来自电池行业，这其中主要是碱性电池和碳锌电池，这些称作一次性电池或原电池。还有充电电池，包括电动车用锂电池，这是电解二氧化锰的第二大市场。我把这张表格放在这里，大家就能够快速对比所有这些电动车用电池类型。黄色字体的两种电池，锰酸锂（LMO）和镍钴锰酸锂电池（NMC）是两种含锰电池，大家可以看到它们的容量很大，但也有生产成本高昂的特性。

12:52—14:26

NCA batteries are used by Tesla for their electric vehicles because they have a very good energy density, better than manganese content batteries, but they are also very expensive to use in cars, more expensive than NMC batteries (nickel, manganese, cobalt). To reduce the cost of their new cars, Tesla could turn to manganese batteries in the future, because Tesla has a strategy of spending a lot on R&D, research and developments, and then lowering the costs of their vehicles so that more people can afford them. LFP batteries, so LFP is lithium iron phosphate. LFP batteries are only used in China because they have a pretty poor performance. They were used by American automakers before, but these American automakers have gradually abandoned the LFP batteries and now they are purchasing manganese batteries mostly from Japan and South Korea. So the key message here is that among the five different types of lithium-ion batteries for electric vehicles, LMO and LiNMC batteries are the most popular because of good performance, safety and competitive price compared to NCA batteries. And these two types of batteries, LMO and LiNMC contain manganese.

镍钴铝电池用于特斯拉的电动车，因为它们的能量密度非常好，比含锰的电池好，但是它们用在汽车上非常昂贵，比镍钴锰电池还贵。为了降低新车成本，特斯拉将来可能转向使用锰系电池，因为特斯拉的战略是大规模投资于研发，并降低汽车的成本，让更多的人买得起他们的车。LFP 电池，也就是磷酸铁锂电池，只有中国在使用，它们的性能较差。美国汽车制造商以前也用过磷酸铁锂电池，但是他们已经逐渐抛弃磷酸铁锂电池，现在他们主要从日本和韩国购买锰系电池。所以这里的关键信息是，五种不同的锂离子动力电池中，锰酸锂和镍钴锰酸锂电池是最受欢迎的，因为相对镍钴铝电池而言，它们性能好，又安全，并且价格更有竞争力。这两种电池，锰酸锂和镍钴锰酸锂电池都含锰。

14:27—15:38

Now let's go back to EMD. EMD's main application, as I said before, is alkaline batteries, but it is also used in LMO rechargeable batteries, which power traditional phones and laptops mostly, but not smartphones because their energy density is too low. So basically, you will need a huge battery to power your smartphone. Now the table you can see here shows the two types of manganese batteries, LMO and NMC, and their main applications. As you can see, LMO batteries are mostly used in the portable sector, which includes cellphones and laptops, mostly traditional cellphones. The LMO batteries are also used in the automotive sector and LMO batteries use EMD but the EMD in LMO batteries tends to be replaced progressively by Mn_3O_4 and the demands on the sector of course is growing as I've shown in the previous slides.

现在让我们回到电解二氧化锰。我之前说过，电解二氧化锰主要用于碱性电池，但也应用于锰酸锂充电电池，主要是传统手机和笔记本电脑的电池，但由于能量密度太低，不能用于智能手机。所以基本上大家的智能手机需要能量密度高的电池。现在这里有张表格，大家可以看到，表格展示了两种锰系电池，锰酸锂和镍钴锰酸锂电池，以及它们的应用范围。大家可以看到，锰酸锂电池主要用于便携设备行业，包括手机和笔记本电脑，多数是传统手机。锰酸锂电池也会用于汽车行业。锰酸锂电池需要电解二氧化锰，但是其中的电解二氧化锰逐渐被四氧化三锰所取代。我在之前的幻灯片中有展示过，汽车行业对锰酸锂电池的需求当然会上升。

15:39—16:39

LiNMC batteries contain around 30% of manganese, the rest being nickel and cobalt. And they use $MnSO_4$, mostly low grade for portable devices and high-grade for automotive. But the main application of $MnSO_4$ is animal feed and fertilizers. And demand for NMC batteries from the automotive sector is growing sharply. So if you need to remember one thing from that slide is that EMD's main markets (alkaline and LMO batteries for portable devices) are mature markets (demand is not growing). Demand for LMO batteries in automotive is on the rise, but in these LMO batteries, EMD tends to be replaced by Mn_3O_4. So that's the key message here for this slide.

镍钴锰酸锂电池中大约30%是锰，其余是镍和钴。这种电池使用硫酸锰，大多用低品位的硫酸锰来生产便携设备电池，高品位的硫酸锰来生产汽车电池。但硫酸锰主要用于生产动物饲料和肥料。汽车行业对镍钴锰酸锂电池的需求增长迅速。所以如果大家需要从这张幻灯片记住一件事的话，那就是电解二氧化锰的主要市场，也就是碱性电池和用于便携装置的锰酸锂电池是成熟的市场，这个市场的需求不会增长。而汽车行业对锰酸锂电池的需求将会上升，但是这类锰酸锂电池中的电解二氧化锰将逐渐被四氧化三锰替代。这就是这张幻灯片的关键信息。

16:40—17:44

Now, I'd like to focus a little bit on China. China is the world's greatest producer and exporter of EMD. And I've listed here, some companies producing EMD in China as you can see there are six companies in China. These are the main ones. There's one company in Canada, another one in Columbia, India, Japan, Greece, Spain and the USA. If you look at China's manganese dioxide exports by destination, you can see that after four years of reducing exports, China increased its exports last year, by around 19% to 47,000 metric tons. According to industry sources, this increase is mostly contextual, and does not represent an improvement of demand fundamentals because as I've shown in previous slides, the markets of EMD are mostly mature and they are not growing.

现在我想着重谈谈中国的情况。中国是世界上最大的电解二氧化锰生产商和出口商。我在这列出了一些公司，他们在中国生产电解二氧化锰。大家可以看到，中国有六家公司生产电解二氧化锰。这些是比较大的公司。加拿大有一家这样的公司，然后哥伦比亚、印度、日本、希腊、西班牙、美国各有一家。大家看一下中国的电解二氧化锰出口国，你们可以看到，在经历了四年出口量的持续下降后，中国电解二氧化锰的出口量在去年增长了19%，大约4.7万吨。根据行业情报，这次增长极具偶发性，并不意味着需求基本面得到改善，原因正如我在前一张幻灯片所展示的，电解二氧化锰的市场已经几乎成熟，不会再继续增长了。

17:45—19:07

Now this chart shows the price, the average trading price in China of EMD between 2011 and 2015. As you can see, the average price of EMD has been decreasing since 2011. And in 2015, the price decreased by 11% on average. But this price includes all grades of EMD. So it's based on trade stats and trade stats don't make a difference between low grade and high grade of EMD for alkaline or rechargeable batteries. So if we take into account all the prices for EMD traded from China last year, the decrease was around 11% even though it could be bigger for low grade EMD and smaller for high grade EMD. So the take-home message here is that the price decreased and this is due to the main raw material for EMD, which is of course manganese ore. The price of manganese ore decreased by 56% last year. The price decrease of EMD was also due to large supply and stable demand for EMD last year.

现在这张表格展示的是 2011—2015 年电解二氧化锰在中国的平均交易价格。大家可以看到，从 2011 年开始，电解二氧化锰的价格一直在下降。2015 年电解二氧化锰的价格平均下降了 11%。但这个价格包含所有品位的电解二氧化锰。所以这个价格是基于贸易统计数据的，而贸易统计数据并不会区分低品位和高品位的电解二氧化锰，不管它们是碱性电池用还是充电电池用。所以如果我们考虑去年中国所有电解二氧化锰的交易价格，那么价格下降幅度大约在 11%，尽管低品位电解二氧化锰的下降幅度更大，而高品位的下降幅度会小一些。那么这里的关键信息就是电解二氧化锰的价格下降了，原因是受到它们的主要原材料锰矿石的影响。去年锰矿石的价格下跌了 56%。电解二氧化锰价格下降还由于供过于求和去年电解二氧化锰的需求稳定。

19:08—19:59

Now the last part of my presentation will be about manganese ore, the key raw material for both the manganese metal and manganese dioxide markets. The global manganese ore supply last year was around 16.4 million metric tons. I'm talking in manganese units here, not in wet metric tons. This supply was off 14% compared to 2014. And meanwhile, demands decreased by 19% against 2014, to almost 15 million metric tons of manganese units. So even though manganese ore supply reduced last year, it was still larger than demand, so the market remained oversupplied.

我要展示的最后一部分跟锰矿石有关，这是金属锰和电解二氧化锰市场的主要原材料。去年全球锰矿石的供应大约在 1,640 万吨。我这里指的是锰单位，不是湿吨。供应量比 2014 年下降了 14%。同时需求下降了 19%，约为 1,500 万吨锰单位。所以即使锰矿石的供应量去年下降了，但是仍然高于需求量，所以市场仍处于供过于求的状态。

20:00—21:07

And this chart here shows the ascent of the oversupply in the manganese ore market last year. The excess supply we calculate was around 1.5 million metric tons of manganese units last year. So this means stocks of manganese ore increased last year, both at alloy plants (due to overbuying) and at mines (when demand started to decrease). This is especially for Brazil, some African countries, including Gabon, India and Australia. Stocks in these countries increased last year. Supply adjustments have been made at the very end of last year, around November and December, because of price falls at the end of the year. And because of these production cuts announced at the end of 2015 and at the beginning of this year, some of these stocks accumulated in the past between 2013 and 2015 are being consumed this year, and the market is getting

第六单元　行业介绍 Introduction to Industries

more balanced.

这张图展示的是去年锰矿石市场供大于求的上升情况。据我们测算，去年超额供给量大约有 150 万吨锰单位。这意味着去年锰矿石的库存量增加了，因为过量购买，当需求开始萎缩时，合金厂和矿山都增加了库存。这种情况尤其发生在巴西，包括加蓬在内的一些非洲国家，还有印度和澳大利亚。这些国家的锰矿石库存去年都增加了。供应量的调整是到去年年末才进行的，差不多 11 月、12 月的样子，因为价格在年底下跌了。由于 2015 年年底和今年年初宣布的减产，一些 2013—2015 年积累的库存会在今年消耗掉，接着市场将恢复平衡。

21：08—22：02

I would like to focus on a minute on this capacity closure, this production cuts announced in 2015 and 2016 in the manganese ore market. You have the list here per country. We estimate there was around 5.5 million metric tons of production cuts in China. And this is in wet metric tons this time, not manganese units. So there were order production cuts in Australia, South Africa, with Comilog for instance in Gabon and in Georgia. So the total production cuts in the manganese ore market announced in 2015 and 2016 was around 11.1 million metric tons and this was mostly due to low manganese ore prices and high stock levels as I've shown in the previous slide.

我想重点谈谈产能关停问题以及锰矿石市场 2015 年和 2016 年宣布的减产问题。大家看这里列出了每个国家的情况。我们估计中国大约减产了 550 万吨。这里说的是湿吨，不是锰单位。来自澳大利亚、南非、加蓬的公司，如康密劳公司的订单减少了，还有格鲁吉亚订单也减少了。所以锰矿石市场 2015 年和 2016 年共减产约 1,110 万吨，原因我在上一张幻灯片中讲过，主要是因为低廉的锰矿石价格和高库存水平。

22：03—23：14

Now let's compare these production cuts with new projects. There are several new projects going on in the manganese ore industry, especially in Asia. You can see there is one in Australia by South32, which is expected to be completed soon this year. There are a few projects in India, another one in Malaysia, one in South Africa, and one in Togo. But basically all these projects together represent an increase of global capacity of around 2.3 million metric tons, wet metric tons. And even if we assume that all these projects will actually come on line, which is a big "if", the extra capacity will be much lower than the mine closure that we've analysed in the previous slide. It's plus 2.3 million metric tons compared to minus 11.7 million metric tons. So the Manganese ore market is progressively adjusting to the lower demand, and it could return to equilibrium by mid-2017, according to CRU, or even before if more mines cut output.

现在让我们来比较一下这些削减的产量和新建的项目。锰矿行业有几个新的项目，主要集中在亚洲。大家可以看到澳大利亚有一个新项目是South32开发的，预计很快就能在今年内完成。有几个项目在印度，另外有一个在马来西亚，一个在南非，还有一个在多哥。但基本上所有这些项目加在一起相当于全球产能将会增加230万湿吨。就算我们假设所有这些项目都能够实际投入运行，这可是一个很大胆的假设，额外增加的产能也远远低于关闭的产能，这个我们在上一页幻灯片分析过。增加了230万吨，而削减了1,170万吨。所以锰矿市场会日益根据需求情况进行调整，可能在2017年中期恢复平衡。根据英国商品研究所的数据，如果更多矿山削减产能的话，可能在2017年中期之前就能达到平衡。

23:15—24:09

Just a quick focus on South Africa, which is the major producer of manganese ore, as you know. Mid-grade ore production in South Africa has been growing at a 38% average rate between 2009 and 2014. This growth was much bigger than the growth in exports. They increased by 23% on average per year between 2009 and 2014 and it was also bigger than domestic manganese alloys production, which increased by around 18% on average between 2009 and 2014. And this was due to constraints on Transnet's rail capacity, which limited the exports of manganese ore, and also to Eskom's electricity supply and rising prices, limiting domestic manganese alloys production.

现在来快速看一下南非，南非是锰矿石的主要供应商，大家都知道。在2009—2014年间，南非中等品位锰矿的产量增长速度达到38%。这个增速远高于出口量的增长，出口量的平均增长率是23%。同时也高于南非国内锰合金产量的增长，锰合金产量同期平均增长率大约是18%。这受制于南非国家运输公司的铁路运力，铁路运力限制了锰矿石的出口，还有一个原因是南非国家电力公司的电力供应和电费上涨，限制了国内锰合金的生产。

24:10—24:59

Rail capacity in South Africa is now improving following major investments made by Transnet, the rail freight company, and exports have been supported by the fall of the South African Rand last year, but demand for seaborne ore decreased in 2015. South Africa's total manganese ore exports decreased by 8% in 2015 to 11.4 million wet metric tons, forcing several producers to adjust supply. But it's important to know that South Africa's exports of manganese ore into China increased last year by 9.4% to 6.4 million metric tons.

南非国家运输公司是南非国内的铁路运输公司，其在铁路运力改善方面投入了巨额资金,去年南非兰特贬值,拉动了出口,但是2015年海运锰矿的需求量下降了。2015年,南非锰矿总出口量下降了8%,为1,140万湿吨,迫使一些锰矿山调整供应量。但有一点很重要,南非的锰矿出口到中国的部分去年增长了9.4%,达到640万吨。

25:00—25:58

Now I would like to focus on China and compare manganese ore production in China versus imports of manganese ore into China. Due to large manganese alloys production cuts, manganese ore demand weakened in China last year. Manganese ore production and imports followed the same trend. And you can see on the chart, that's the blue curve showing manganese ore production and the red curve showing manganese ore imports into China. Both decreased last year. China imported a total of almost 16 million metric tonnes of manganese ore in 2015, and this figure is down 3% from the previous year. Domestic manganese ore production was around 12 million metric tons, and this was down 23% over 2014.

现在我想重点讲一下中国,比较一下锰矿产量和进口量。去年由于大规模锰合金减产,中国国内锰矿石需求疲软。锰矿石产量和进口量也有相同的趋势。大家看这张图,蓝线代表锰矿石产量,红线代表锰矿石进口量。这两部分去年都下降了。2015年,中国进口了近1,600万吨锰矿石,比前一年下降了3%。国内锰矿石产量大约1,200万吨,比2014年下降了23%。

25:59—26:44

So why did China's manganese ore production drop so much more than its imports last year, 23% versus 3%? This is because of high grade ore requirements of newly built closed manganese alloys furnaces. Domestic output is low grade, so if you want high grade ore, you need to import it. This was also due to depletion of local mines and corresponding higher mining costs. It's more expensive to mine manganese ore in China now because you have to go deeper to get some mineral. And it was also due to the weak incentive to mine domestic low-grade manganese ore in China when the price of imported ore is so low. It decreased by around 57% last year.

为什么中国锰矿产量下跌这么多,远超进口量的下降幅度,产量下跌23%,而进口量下跌3%?这是因为新建的封闭式锰合金炉需要高品位的锰矿,而国内生产的是低品位锰矿,所以如果想要高品位的矿石,就需要进口了。另一个原因则是本地矿山资源枯竭,采矿成本因此增加了。如今在中国开采锰矿的成本更高了,因为矿山不得不挖得更深一些才能获得一点矿石。还有一个原因是动力不足,进口锰矿的价格如此低廉,缺乏开采国内低品位锰矿的动力。去年进口锰矿价格下跌了 57%。

26:44—27:36

And you can see this decrease on the chart here. In 2015, manganese ore prices decreased sharply. They have been increasing over the last few weeks, skyrocketing actually, but increasing very sharply because of recovering demands in China and also because of production cuts in South Africa, in Australia and Georgia, China, all the production cuts I've listed in my previous slides. So in summary, although manganese ore imports in China decreased last year, imported ore is progressively replacing domestic ore at Chinese manganese ore alloys smelters. And that is why China's manganese ore imports reduced by only 3% in 2015, while domestic manganese ore production fell by 23%.

大家可以在这张图里看到锰矿石价格下跌情况。2015 年锰矿石价格暴跌。价格过去两周一直上涨，实际上是飞涨，因为中国需求重新恢复，同时还有我在前几页幻灯片中列举的减产，减产的国家包括南非、澳大利亚、格鲁吉亚、中国。总而言之，尽管去年中国锰矿石进口量下降了，但中国锰合金熔炉日益选用进口锰矿石取代国产锰矿石。这就是为什么中国的锰矿石进口量在 2015 年下降了 3%，而国内锰矿石产量却下降了 23%。

27:37—28:16

Now this chart shows the imports of manganese ore into China by origin between 2002 and 2015. The total import into China was, as I said, around 15.8 million metric tonnes last year, down by almost 3% from 2014. Imports from Australia dropped by 17%, from Malaysia 38%, from Ghana 49% and Ghanaian ore is mostly used for manganese metal production as you know. And from the rest of the world, the imports into China decreased by 47%.

现在这张图展示的是 2002 年到 2015 年中国进口锰矿石的国家列表。我说过去年中国的总进口量大约为 1,580 万吨，比 2014 年下降了 3%。从澳大利亚进口的锰矿石下降了 17%，马来西亚的下降了 38%，加纳的下降了 49%，而且加纳的锰矿石几乎都是用来生产金属锰，这点大家都知道。从世界其他国家进口的锰矿石下降了 47%。

28:17—28:55

So the key message here is that South African manganese ore exporters increased their market share of China's imports, shipping 11% more material in 2015, to 6.4 million metric tonnes. And this growing import from South Africa was supported by the

20% fall of the Rand, the South Africa currency, last year against the dollar. Imports from Gabon grows by 27% to almost two million metric tons, and those of Brazil reached 1.5 million metric tons, up by 90%.

所以这里的关键信息是南非锰矿石出口商扩大了在中国进口市场的份额,他们在 2015 年多运送了 11% 的货物到中国,达到 640 万吨。这是由于去年南非货币兰特兑美元贬值 20%。从加蓬的进口量上涨了 27%,约为 200 万吨,而从巴西进口的锰矿为 150 万吨,上涨 90%。

28:56—29:47

Now this is the end of my presentation. I would like to conclude quickly with a few important things. On stainless steel first: In 2015, global stainless steel production was 42 million metric tons. This was up by 0.7% over 2014. Global stainless steel production is expected to keep growing from 2015 to 2020, but at a slower rate than before, around 4.1% on average between 2015 and 2020. In terms of manganese metal industry: The Chinese manganese metal production decreased last year. That was because of lower manganese metal prices, high inventory of manganese metal and new environmental regulations.

现在我的演讲就要结束了。我想简要地总结一下本次演讲的重点。首先关于不锈钢,2015 年全球不锈钢产量为 4,200 万吨,比 2014 年上涨 0.7%。全球不锈钢产量预计 2015—2020 年间将持续增长,但增速放缓,平均增速约为 4.1%。关于金属锰行业,去年中国的金属锰产量下降了。那是因为低廉的金属锰价格,高库存和中国新颁布的环保法。

29:48—31:10

About the manganese dioxide market: Among the five different types of lithium-ion batteries for electric vehicles, manganese batteries (LMO and LiNMC) are the most popular because of their good performance, safety and competitive price, compared to NCA batteries. Demand for batteries in electric vehicles is forecast to grow by 50% on average per year by 2020, according to Macquarie. And this will increase demand for manganese batteries. EMD's main markets (alkaline and LMO batteries for portable devices) are mature markets (demand is not growing in these two markets). Demand for LMO batteries in automotive is on the rise, but Mn_3O_4 tends to be chosen over EMD in these LMO batteries for the automotive sector. And finally about the manganese ore: The manganese ore market remained oversupplied last year, as demand fell faster than production, but recently announced production cuts could re-balance the market by 2017 or even before if more production cuts are announced. Thank you very much for your attention!

  关于电解二氧化锰市场：在五种不同种类的电动车锂离子电池中，包括锰酸锂电池和镍钴锰酸锂电池在内的锰系电池最受欢迎，因为它们同镍钴铝电池相比，性能优良、安全系数高、价格更有竞争力。根据麦格理的预测，2020 年电动车对电池需求的年均增长率将达到 50%，这将拉动对锰系电池的需求。电解二氧化锰的主要市场包括碱性电池和便携式锰酸锂电池，是一个成熟的市场，需求在这两个市场不会增长。汽车行业对锰酸锂电池的需求将会上升，但汽车行业趋向于用四氧化三锰代替电解二氧化锰生产锰酸锂电池。最后关于锰矿石：锰矿石市场去年依然处于供过于求的状态，因为需求下降的速度比供应下降的速度快，但近期宣布的减产可能让市场在 2017 年重新获得平衡，甚至更早，如果有更多减产计划宣布的话。非常感谢大家的聆听！

第三部分 交传实战

第七单元 时尚潮流
Fashion Trend

I. 实战练习一

1. 演讲背景

2014年11月1日，在线时尚潮流预测公司Fashion Snoops的亚太区总监应邀参加"广交会设计潮流趋势研讨会"，发布2015—2016年秋冬女装时尚趋势。下文摘自第一个主题的内容"平静之心"，他在演讲中详细介绍了该主题产生的背景、色系、造型、材料、印花图案、设计细节、重要单品。演讲的部分内容抽象难懂。

2. 预习词汇

contemporary women's wear 当代女装
wood cabin 小木屋
cocooning 保护层；与世隔绝
fur pelt 毛皮
oatmeal 米灰色；浅棕色；燕麦黄
dusty rose 灰玫瑰色
pale pink 浅粉色
oyster 乳白色
look 造型
asymmetric blanket coat 不规则毛料大衣
elongated layer 长款的层次感
suede 绒面革；仿麂皮
slouchy 没精打采的；懒散的
ribbed knit 罗纹针织
chunky knit 粗棒针织
mohair 马海毛
brushed wool 拉绒
Teddy Bear fur 泰迪熊毛皮
prints & patterns 印花图案

ice shavings 刨冰
water color dye 水彩
surface element 表面元素
cracked surface motif 裂纹图案
oversized 大号的
scooped back neckline 勺形后领口
extra long sleeve 超长袖子
soft pocket 软口袋
draping 垂感
exaggerated rib cuff 夸张的罗纹袖口
layer 层次感
long layering 长长的层次感
key item 重要单品
self belt 同料腰带
cocoon coat 茧形大衣
style guide 款式指南

3. 演讲文本

00:00—01:20

Our first story for Contemporary Women's Wear is something we call Inner Calm and this story for autumn/winter is really all about being wrapped in cozy plush textures, lots of chunky knits, and looking at cold weather dressing and how it really should look. It's something to cozy up to in terms of dress as well as your surroundings. This is actually a theme. If you look behind this theme, this is actually really a big life-style trend that's happening in several… really in all product areas. So we have themes similar to this in men's, in kid's, in accessories. Where the background to the theme is that people, whether it is women's, men's or kid's, there is so much danger in our world today. You know, there is terrorism and there is Ebola that we all worry about. I think in Guangzhou there is dengue fever. We are all looking for safety, for a haven. We are all turning inwards. We are looking to our homes for that sort of safety, soft, cocoon feeling that we all really want in these sort of times of danger. Inner Calm is really playing to that story.

关于当代女装，我们要分享的第一个主题是"平静之心"。这个主题与保暖的绒毛衫、粗棒针织衫有关，看看大家在秋冬季中穿什么，讨论在秋冬季节该如何装扮。无论是穿着打扮，还是家居环境，我们都需要保暖。这实际上是一个主题。如果回顾一下这个主题，您会发现这是一种生活方式的潮流趋势，影响了所有的产品领域。所以我们在男装、童装和配饰等领域也打造了类似的主题。无论主题的背景是什么，无论是女装、男装还是童装。如今，我们的世界存在许多危险，有恐怖主义，有埃博拉病毒，我们都为此担忧，广州还有登革热。我们都在寻找安全，寻找避风港，所以我们都转向内心寻找平静。我们正在寻找家一般安全、柔软、呵护的感觉。这种感觉，是处于这个充满危险的时代的我们所需的。"平静之心"就致力于此。

01:21—02:59

So the story for Inner Calm is that tucked away from civilization, the Inner Calm woman lives outdoors, in a minimalist wood cabin where she has created a cocoon atmosphere in her home as well as in her way of dress. This whole notion of cocooning, you know, goes back to what I am saying of people wanting to find that haven, that sort of comfort or safety net, so features are a lot of… As you can see on this mood board page, it features a lot of sort of knit heavy textures and plays a very important role with chunky yarns everywhere, particularly for those of you who work in sweaters. You would be happy to see that, sort of a knitted armchair and fuzzy textured pillows to match her coziest sweater. Nature factors in not only with natural fibers but also with a lot of high pile fur pelts and prints. A very neutral color palette to keep it clean yet warm, and minimalist lines add a very modern edge to this trend. Again, other things that feed into this Inner Clam trend is this whole notion of the world really understanding more about climate change and becoming more climate conscious. You know, we all worry about greenhouse gases and global warming. This cozy dressing of wearing, fur and thick pile of sweaters and things like that even in our homes helps us sort of to reduce the heating bills and things like that, and really perhaps to save the planet.

因此，"平静之心"的故事隐匿于城市文明之外。代表"平静之心"的女性生活在户外，居住在一个简约的小木屋中。她在屋中营造出一种与世隔绝的氛围，她的穿着也有这种感觉。与世隔绝的概念，可以追溯到我刚刚说的人们想要的那种避风港，那种舒适又安全的保护网，种种特征无法一一细述……正如您在这页情绪板所能看到的一样，它的特点是有很多厚重的针织纹理，再加上粗毛线，这在任何地方都能起到很重要的作用，尤其是对于那些从事毛衣行业的观众来说。您会看到编织扶手椅和毛茸茸的枕头，搭配最舒适的毛衣。自然元素不仅存在于天然纤维之中，也体现于长绒毛皮和印花。中性色系使其干净而温暖，简约线条则增添了现代时尚感。同时，世界对气候变化了解增多，变得更有气候意识，这一认识也影响了"平静之心"的潮流。我们都担心温室气体和全球变暖等问题。这种舒适的穿着，皮草和厚毛衣之类的衣物，能帮助我们减少暖气费用，这也许真的可以拯救地球。

第七单元　时尚潮流 Fashion Trend

02:59—03:57

So again, this is our trend map. We have a trend map for each of our themes, explaining a little bit more details for our clients how the trend has evolved from something, as I said, called haven into cocooning modern comfort and eventually to Inner Calm. So I have a little video that I'd like to play for you. Each one of our themes, this is something new we've introduced this year where we've introduced videos to our site for our clients to see. Basically these videos are made by us, so everything that you see in the video is there for specific reason. The colors support the theme like the video is there to demonstrate it. It is really trying to give our clients through vision and through music a little bit of better appreciation of the trends that we are talking about.

这是我们的趋势图。我们每个主题都有一个趋势图，以便详细地向客户解释这一趋势的演变历程，即如我所说的从所谓的避风港，演变至与世隔绝的现代舒适感，再发展成"平静之心"这个主题。这里我想播放一个小视频。这是我们的所有主题，是今年新发布的，这些视频已经上传到我们的网站，供客户观看。这些视频基本上都由我们制作，所以视频中出现的所有东西都有特定原因。如视频中展示的一样，各种颜色撑起了整个主题。通过影像和音乐，我们希望客户能够对这些潮流趋势有更多的了解。

03:57—05:11

So hopefully that gave you a bit more feel for the theme. So here is your colour palette for Inner Calm. It is really one of the softest colour palettes that we have this season. It has a lot of sort of great new base colours, like oatmeal that you see near the top and mushroom. Then you have sort of your soft pinks that balanced it out, such as your dusty rose, and your pale pink. There's also this sort of a recurrence of your nude buff tone and the continuations of grays from the previous spring/summer is also really important, as you can see in the middle which is an oyster tone. So it is really sort of a very soft neutral color palette that hopefully makes you sort of feel calm, sort of calms you down if you know the color theory, and makes you feel secure. If you look at the color usage, you can see how we are using those beautiful pinks with the grays to create… that emphasis on warmth and on colors. We use the grays obviously for the calming and the pink tones for the warmth.

希望这能让你们对这个主题有更多的了解。这是"平静之心"的色系，是我们本季最柔和的色系之一。色系上新增了许多美丽的底色，如靠近上方的燕麦黄，还有蘑菇色。粉色系能平衡色彩搭配，比如灰玫瑰色和浅粉色。还有再次出现的裸米色调。延续自春夏季的灰色也很重要，如中间的米灰色。希望这个中性色系能让您感到平静。如果您懂得色彩理论，您会平静下来，也会更有安全感。如果您看一下颜色的用法，您就会发现我们是如何用那些漂亮的粉色和灰色来强调温暖和色彩。显然，我们用灰色系呈现平静，用粉色系强调温暖。

05:11—06:12

This is a page that we have on each of our themes which we called the Look for those of you who haven't seen our site before. What we are trying to do with this one page and this one piece is to really illustrate how the whole look should be. This is the girl that best represents this entire theme. Really this is… what you see here the key is the really sort of long heavy outerwear coat that gives the sense of… This is an Asymmetric Blanket Coat of course, but sort of elongated layers that gives you that sense of calmness and security. Your texture interest comes in from suede that you see on the shoes. Again, you know, you can use a circle scarf in there. You can use the fitted gloves, the slouchy beanie. Accessories there are important to accentuate that sense of calmness and warmth.

这一页我们称为"造型"，每个主题都有，给之前没看过我们网站的人参考。我们希望以此来说明应该如何打造整体造型。这个女孩完美呈现出了整个主题。这是件长款大衣，一款不规则毛料大衣，这种长款层次感让人充满平静感和安全感。大衣的材质为绒面革，这种材料常用于制作鞋子。您可以搭配围脖，也可以搭配手套以及慵懒的针织帽。配饰对于增强平静感和温暖感十分重要。

06:12—07:01

Your materials that we're looking at here, keeping in mind that it's such a huge knit conversation. This is such a perfect theme for sweater manufacturing. It is really gonna be such a huge sweater season in general, we're looking at highlights in terms of knitwear, such as No. 2, your Ribbed Knits, your Chunky Knits, and No. 5, your Tissue Knits. Tissue Knits there are for something a little bit thinner, something a little more trans-seasonal. Then, you have this huge hairy component, such as, you see on No. 3, which is Mohair, Brushed wool at No. 7 and very, very plush textures which you see on the bottom of No. 9, which is your Teddy Bear Furs.

这是本主题的服装材料，如同一场针织盛宴。对毛衣制作来说，这是一个完美的主题。一般而言，盛大的毛衣季，我们会关注针织纹理的亮点，如2号的罗纹针织和粗棒针织，以及5号的组织肌理。组织肌理适用于换季所需的轻薄衣物。接下来看一下毛绒质地的材料，如3号的马海毛，7号的拉绒，以及底部9号毛绒绒的泰迪熊皮毛。

第七单元　时尚潮流 Fashion Trend

07:01—07:54

In terms of your prints and patterns that we're looking at here, it really stems from… we mentioned that this is a girl who lives in the woods far away from civilization. So this is where we can bring in that sort of earthy aspect to it, that sort of woody aspect to it. So we have some sort of earth-inspired things, such as Ice Shavings which you see at No. 3, Water Colour Dyes at No. 2, Clouds, sort of very natural prints that would work. Also, there's some sort of nice surface elements, which you see at No. 8, which is a Cracked Surface motif, and Faux knit textures which look like knits but are in fact printed.

接下来谈谈印花图案。前面提到过一个远离城市文明的森林女孩,她是我们在印花图案中添加大地元素和森林元素的灵感来源。所以我们使用了很多大地元素,如3号作品中的刨冰纹,2号中的水彩纹、云纹,这种印花在自然中很常见。同时还有一些美丽的表面元素,如8号中的裂纹图案,以及看起来像针织但实际是印花的人造针织纹理。

07:54—08:31

Now one thing you can't do, unfortunately, during your free trial is to download our artwork. We have tons and tons of artwork that is dyed in house by our design team that allows our clients… they can download these graphic files. They can change it because it's available on AI (Adobe Illustrator). You can use it as your own. This is that beautiful crack surface to mimic a broken rock or broken concrete pile that gives that sort of earthy-grounded aspect to this particular theme.

遗憾的是,在免费试用期间,你们无法下载我们的作品。我们有大量由我们的设计团队进行着色的作品,客户可以下载这些作品图片。客户可以在AI修图软件中修改或者自行使用这些图片。这就是美丽的裂纹,模仿破碎的岩石或混凝土桩,将赋予这个独特的主题大地元素。

08:31—09:05

Design details here, and again, and keeping in mind that it's really about knits, it's all about oversized shapes. So you have No. 3, your Scooped Back Necklines, Extra Long Sleeves at No. 7, Soft Pockets, No. 8. Then obviously when it comes to knits, it's perfect for draping, so you have Draping at No. 6. But what I particularly love is at No. 1. You see the Exaggerated Rib Cuff there. That's a fantastic new look for the season.

这是设计细节,许多关于针织或超大号型服装的细节。比如3号的勺形后领口,7号的超长袖,以及8号的软口袋。显然,谈及针织,垂感非常重要,因此您在6号中可以看到垂感。但我最爱的元素在1号,您可以看到夸张的罗纹袖口,这是本季的绝妙新样式。

09:05—09:30

Looking at some key styling and shaped items for Inner Calm, this first one is all about knit dressing. But it's also all about oversized and sort of long cozy comfy layers. Again you see that sort of long-layering coming into play there as well.

再来看看"平静之心"一些关键的款式和成形的单品,有针织装,也有超大号型款式,款型长,具有让人感到舒服的层次感。不难发现长款层次感也发挥了作用。

09:36—11:02

What we have on our site again not available for our people taking a trial but for our clients that they can download the key items or key silhouette. How this slide works is basically you have the silhouette and then right next to it you have some suggested ways of updating it to make it relevant for the season, and to make it look new, and to make it look yours. So for Inner Calm, again speaking to this sort of huge knitwear component, the matched set on the left is something really really important. This is something that we're seeing done in rib-knit, but we're also seeing updates in elongated styles, elongated tunics, pared back to the pants. Also towards the right, you have the sweater dress, right on the right hand side. This is also really important and a style that will not only have application in this particular trend but will come back again and again throughout my presentation today. What's nice about it here in this trend, is that it's oversized, so that it does provide that, you know, further options when it comes to layering. You have your knit pants. Again something very important this season, and we're seeing a really... with some relaxed fits and also with a self-belt.

客户可以下载网站上的重要单品和主要服装廓形的相关图片,但试用人群暂时无法享用这项服务。这张幻灯片展示了某种服装廓形,旁边有设计建议,帮助您更新设计出符合本季的服装图片,让其面目一新,更具您的风格。对于"平静之心"这种以针织品为主的潮流趋势,左边的套装非常非常重要。这在罗纹中已有体现,但我们的长款款式有所更新,长款无袖上衣长度裁至裤子处。向右看,有毛衣连衣裙,就在您的右手边。毛衣连衣裙非常重要,不仅应用于这个独特的潮流趋势之中,也是贯穿我今天的整个演讲的重点。这个潮流趋势中,毛衣连衣裙也设计成超大号型,因此在层次感上会有更多选择。针织裤也是本季重点之一,版型宽松,配备同料腰带。

第七单元 时尚潮流 Fashion Trend

11:02—12:00

Some more key items here and towards the right on the slide, you have your cocoon coat. This is really all about taking outerwear to the next level; so we're seeing that with sort of this cocoon shape and playing into this sense of seeking comfort or a haven. This cocoon shape is really a great new shape for your outerwear options this particular season. Again the notion of elongation comes back into play, so on the left hand side of your screen you see an elongated sweater. Again that sort of sense of layering and elongating to create very nice cozy layers. Again, all of our sketches on our site are download-able by our clients, but unfortunately, for trialors, you just have to take a look at it.

幻灯片上的右边展示了更多重点单品,如茧形大衣。由此,外衣进入另一层次。茧形给人以追求舒适的感觉,让人感觉像是避风港。在本季当中,茧形是外衣的新选择。长款的概念再次归来,在屏幕左边您可以看到一件长款毛衣。层次感和长款型让这款衣服既好看又保暖。网站所有草图仅供客户下载,试用者只能在线观看。

12:00—12:40

Finally, for Inner Clam, at the end of every theme, we have this page which is called a style guide. Our clients love this page. Basically, we are taking all the essential elements of the theme, the colors, the mood board, the color combinations, the materials, the shapes, we are putting it all on one page. This is again available for our clients to download in high resolution. So you can print it out as big as in an A3 size. They tend to put it in their design studios and reminds them of the entire themes that they are working towards. So that really wraps up Inner Calm.

在每个主题的最后,都会有一页款式指南。我们的客户非常喜欢这一页的内容。基本上,我们把该主题的所有要素,如颜色和情绪板、色彩组合、材料和形状,都放在这个页面上。客户可以下载高分辨率的版本,打印在A3纸上。他们一般会把这页内容张贴在设计工作室内,提醒自己在这个主题上下功夫。"平静之心"主题就介绍到这里。

II. 实战练习二

1. 演讲背景

下文同样摘自"广交会设计潮流趋势研讨会",演讲嘉宾介绍了第二个时尚潮流趋势"都市丽影",他介绍了该主题产生的背景、色系、造型、材料、印花图案、设计细节、重要单品。演讲的部分内容同样抽象难懂。

2. 预习词汇

contemporary women's wear 当代女装
City Slicker 都市丽影
collection 系列
active wear 运动服
androgynous suit 中性套装
architectural element 建筑元素
technical material 技术材料
colour palette 色系
salmon pink 橙红色
sky blue 天蓝色
steel blue 钢蓝色
orchid 兰花紫
city jogger pants 城市慢跑裤
outerwear 外套
tailored jacket 紧身夹克
mesh 网眼
wet look nylon 光亮尼龙
PVC 聚氯乙烯
wool shirt suitings 羊毛衫西装料
tweed 粗花呢
double-faced technique 双面布料
prints and patterns 印花图案
men's wear 男装
windowpane check 窗格状
linear 直线
dropped shoulder 落肩
rounded shoulder 圆肩
tearaways effect 撕开效果
zipped front 前拉链
side panel 侧边嵌条（裤子）
elastic band 松紧带
color splashed trim 饰边
mixed media 混合拼接

sheer panels insert 透明嵌条
cocoon coat 茧形大衣
tailored jacket 紧身夹克
tailored pants 紧身裤
rounded tailored jacket 圆领紧身夹克
cropped pants 半截裤
oversized sleeveless coat 大号无袖大衣
shirt 衬衫
full skirted shirt dress 宽下摆衬衫裙
white shirt 白衬衫
Bermuda shorts 百慕大短裤
parka 风雪大衣
short pants 短裤
shants（sheer + pants）褶皱裤
mixed media top 混合拼接上衣

3. 演讲文本

00:00—01:46

We are moving into your second theme for contemporary women's wear which we've called City Slicker. This really embodies the ultimate urbanite in an active setting. Active wear is really a very important part for fashion right now. There are a lot of, even the luxury brands, like the Dior's, the Chanel's, who are taking a lot of active influences into their main collections. What's new about City Slicker? And this may look a bit familiar to you. It's very much a city metropolis setting. But that setting is reflected in her everyday wardrobe with androgynous suits and tailored aspects that command that she's taken seriously. But she's not just another suit. There are a lot of architectures in play here. You know, her admiration for architects like Zaha Hadid keeps her pulse on the future with a vision that is inspired not only by Gotham, but by edgy shapes and curves that reflect a lot of different architectural elements. Really we've seen androgyny in the women's wear market for the past several seasons. But what we are doing really is that we are adding that sort of active influence to bring much needed newness to the look. The active wear elements are coming through the detail or coming through sort of technical materials that you would traditionally see in active wear. This is the trend map of City Slicker which you could see on the site.

我们现在进入第二个主题，即我们称之为"都市丽影"的当代女装，这也的确体现了运动背景下的终极都市人。运动服是当前时尚非常重要的组成部分，很多奢侈品牌，比如迪奥、香奈儿等，都在为其主要系列女装注入众多运动元素。那么"都市丽影"主题有什么新鲜之处呢？这看起来可能有点熟悉，因为这就是一个大都市背景。但这种背景会反映在日常穿着中，以中性套装和紧身款使其得到认真对待，但这不只是另一套装，这里面包含很多结构设计。您知道，对扎哈·哈迪德一类建筑师的钦佩使她放眼于未来，这不仅受到纽约市的启发，其前卫的形状和曲线也反映出很多不同的建筑元素。我们在过去几个季节的女装市场上确实看到了中性元素，但我们切实在做的就是增加这种运动元素，以便给造型带来亟需的新鲜感。通过细节或通过传统上在运动服中所能看到的各种技术材料，可以体现出运动服元素。这是您可以在网站上看到的"都市丽影"趋势图。

01:46—01:58

So you can see from that video obviously that architectural element really comes into play here. A lot of linear lines, very important to this particular theme.

所以，从视频中可以明确地看到，建筑元素的确会在这里发挥作用，很多线条和直线对于这个特定主题非常重要。

01:58—02:48

Moving on to the colour palette, and hopefully you can see here really that the minimalist influence bringing newness here. So here the new shots of colour would include such as salmon pink, which you see sort of there at 161624. That's a salmon pink as well as a sky blue. Sort of those two colors are really bringing something new to the androgynous theme this particular season. There are also shots of steel blue and orchid which are also new. But still really relevant here is the top of the color palette. When it's in sort of urban theme, androgyny theme, your three most important colors are always gonna to be black, white and grey.

再转到色系，希望您能看到真正的极简主义影响带来的新鲜感。这里的新色彩包括橙红色，可在161624处看到。这是一种橙红色和天蓝色，两种颜色的排序会为这个特殊季节的中性元素带来全新体验。还有一些新的钢蓝色和兰花紫，但这里真正相关的仍是色系顶部的颜色。当它属于城市主题、中性主题时，最重要的总是黑、白、灰三色。

02:48—03:14

So you can see your color usage here where we are using the sort of salmon pinks, mixing with your blacks, your grays. Every one of your color palette should include some combination of your black and your white, or your gray, and bringing in the newness through the uses like steel blue, mixing it with the salmon.

因此您能在这儿看到颜色使用情况,我们会将橙红色与黑色和灰色相混合。每个色系都应包括黑、白或灰的一些组合,并通过使用像钢蓝色这样的颜色与橙红色混在一起,带来一种新鲜感。

03:14—04:18

So here is the look. This is our muse, the City Slicker. In terms of shape, we're looking at something like city jogger pants that can either have a wide or a slim leg. Also the elongated shirts. Some of these are not in the main pictures. Some of the things that we are referring to, like the city jogger pants or the elongated shirts and things like that, sort of on site again updating the muse picture. In terms of an outerwear or also of tailored jackets, the dropped or rounded shoulder becomes sort of a new defining silhouette. In terms of looking at your texture, new quilting techniques add something really important that sort of sports aspect. That quilting always gives you that sort of technical or sports aspect, that sort of brings in that sort of active way of lifestyle into this particular theme.

现在来看"造型"。这是"都市丽影"的灵感源泉。就形状而言,我们正在寻找类似城市慢跑裤的东西,它可以是阔腿的,也可以是窄脚的。还可以是长款衬衫。其中有些未涵盖在主图中。比如城市慢跑裤或长款衬衫类似的东西,都是现场展现的亮点。对于外套或紧身夹克,落肩或圆肩变成了一种新的重要廓形。再看质感,新的绗缝技术增加了一些非常重要的运动元素,这种技术总能带来某种科技感或运动风,也会将一种积极的生活方式引入这一特殊主题。

04:18—05:32

So as I mentioned that the style of the theme that again to achieve that sort of active wear look, materials are really really key to sort of effect that sort of active feeling that we want in this particular theme. So you have things such as No. 3, your Mesh, No. 6, your Wet Look Nylon, which is again really great for outerwear. For something a little bit more edgy and fashion forward, you have your PVC at No. 8. The quilting at No. 2 also adds to that active wear element. But there are also, because this is still very much in androgyny, a theme, so the tailored component is still very important here, so we're looking at things such as No. 5, your Wool Shirt Suitings, your Tweed at No. 10, sort of very traditional men's wear suiting fabrics. For your shirting, nothing better than a white cotton poplin shirt and sort of double-faced techniques is also fantastic for the architectural aspect of this particular trend.

当我提到的主题风格再次涉及这种运动造型时,材料对于这个特定主题中所期待的某种运动风而言,非常关键。您有3号网眼,6号光亮尼龙,这对外套来说也是非常棒的。对于一些更前沿更时尚的东西而言,有 8 号聚氯乙烯;而 2 号的绗缝技术还增加了运动元素。但因为这仍然是同一个中性的主题,有些裁剪元素仍然非常重要,我们正在寻找诸如 5 号的东西,比如羊毛衬衫西装料;10 号粗花呢就不失为一种非常合适的传统男装面料。对于您的衬衫,没有什么比白色棉府绸衬衫和双面布料更契合这种特殊潮流的了。

05:32—06:23

In terms of this particular theme, the prints and patterns here is very straightforward, is not really very much driven by prints and patterns. But the men's wear influence obviously comes from things such as your Windowpane Checks at No. 3. But what is really interesting here, would be that sort of metropolis aspect, that city aspect. You see No. 1, which is a fantastic sort of tough marble surface that our design team found, which really gives you that sort of architectural concrete base. There are some sort of dimensional aspects such as negative space. Obviously lines and linears are also very important in this particular trend.

就这个特定主题而言,此处的印花图案非常直接,并不是真正由印花图案驱动的。但男装显然受到了诸如 3 号窗格式样东西的影响,这里真正有趣的是那种城市感或大都市感。您会看到 1 号,这是我们设计团队发现的一种奇妙坚硬大理石表面,会真正带来那种建筑混凝土基础的感觉。有些方面比较立体,比如负空间。很明显,线条和直线在这个特定潮流中也非常重要。

06:23—07:37

Moving on to your design details for City Slicker, and they really speak to... and this is where we mentioned that sort of athletic components. So you have things like Tearaways at No. 1 on a coat on the top left hand corner. That sort of mimics the basketball pants that you see in a lot of basketball players that they can just really pull the pants away. So that gives you your active element. You have things like Zipped Front at No. 6 which is very important; Side Panels at No. 8, again for that athletic effect; Elastic Bands around the waists at No. 3. Then some more sort of novelty applications would include something like No. 7, Colour Splashed; and Mixed Media at No. 5. Mixed Media for a couple of seasons have been very important again to create that sort of interest, that textural aspect. It continues for autumn/winter 2015/2016. No. 9, you have Sheer Panels inserts which again adds to that sort of athletic aspect of the look.

"都市丽影"的设计细节,也就是我们所提到的那种运动元素。所以您在左上角的外套上可以看到 1 号撕拉型。很多篮球运动员的篮球裤都是撕拉型,真的能把裤子撕开,所以这是一些运动元素。6 号会看到前拉链,这非常重要;而 8 号侧边

第七单元　时尚潮流 Fashion Trend

嵌条则是为了提升运动效果,3号腰部周围的松紧带也是如此。然后运用一些更新颖的东西,包括类似7号饰边和5号混合拼接。混合拼接在几个时装季中对于创造出有趣的纹理感非常重要。2015年及2016年秋冬季也将沿用混合拼接,还有9号透明嵌条更是增加了这种运动感的造型效果。

07:37—08:26

So here you have some key shapes or key styling points. oversized tailoring. Oversized is against sort of underline theme that runs cross several of our trends today. So you have your cocoon coat over your relaxed tailored pants, or your rounded tailored jacket with cropped pants, or oversized sleeveless coat for sort of an edgier option. That cotton poplin comes into play with your shirt dressing. So you have your men's shirt with a wrap skirt, or shirt layered under cocoon coat and cropped trousers and that sort of layering very important, or your full skirted shirt dress.

这儿还会有一些关键的形状或式样,比如大号裁剪。大号和某种粗线条主题不同,这与我们今天所提及的几个趋势一致。茧形大衣可搭配宽松裁剪裤,或圆肩紧身夹克搭半截裤亦或是大号无袖大衣,这样更加前卫时尚。这件棉府绸与衬衫穿搭很合适,男士衬衫搭配裹裙,或衬衫搭配茧形大衣和紧身裤或宽下摆衬衫裙,这种层次感穿搭非常重要。

08:26—09:31

In terms of your key items for City Slicker, really keeping in mind that there is…this is still very much a tailored trend and androgyny trend. So you have your elongated shirt on your left, taking that great white cotton shirt, just making it a little bit longer, elongating it, so that allows for it to be visible with layering. So have your long shirt underneath, a little sweater on top. Fantastic for this particular look. There are also the Bermuda shorts which are great for a tran-seasonal item from spring into fall. We really like the sort of slim fit crease front detail on this. The parka obviously for a fall/winter item, a great sports essential item that you can bring into tailoring with a little bit more of your attention to your tailor details, adding it to the parka, and then your wide-legged pants.

就"都市丽影"主要单品而言,切记这仍然是一个紧身和中性化趋势。所以在左边可以看到长款衬衫,搭上这件漂亮的白色棉质衬衫,再稍微拉长一点,则会显得更修长,看起来也更有层次感。修长衬衫穿搭在下面,上搭一件小毛衣,则非常适合这种特殊造型。还有百慕大短裤适合春秋换季时穿,我们真的很喜欢这种修身裤子的正面折痕。风雪大衣显然是秋冬季的一款产品,这是一款非常棒的运动必备单品,大家可以将更多的关注点放在裁剪细节上,可搭配风雪大衣和阔腿裤穿。

09:31—10:25

Some more key items here in terms of your outerwear. We're speaking to that sort of that very rounded shape, that cocoon shape. That's very important. So again you have your cocoon coat that you've seen in two of the themes now, with the rounded shoulders or your bonded mesh. We love the shants. You know, we've been doing slim fit to death for the last five years, so a bit of wider leg we feel is coming back. The shant is a really really good option for this theme, particularly if you want to make it tran-seasonal. So with wide cuffs or crease front, or maybe in tweed materials to bring that back into a little bit more of androgyny suit aspect to it. You have your shirt dress and your mix media top to complete that slide.

就外套而言，这里还有一些重要单品。我们现在说的是那种圆形，就是茧形外套，这点非常重要。现在您可以再次看到前面两个主题中所提到的圆肩或网格的茧形大衣。我们很喜欢褶皱裤，过去5年里，我们一直做修身款，我们觉得阔腿裤可能会重新回归。如果想让阔腿裤成为换季穿搭的话，褶皱裤就非常合适。因此，可以用宽袖口、折痕面或粗花呢材料做成双面中性西装。幻灯片的最后是衬衫裙和混合拼接上衣。

10:25—10:44

Here you have your style guide for City Slicker, again really emphasizing that mix between tailoring and active sportswear as represented by that key drawing that you see, or key photo that you see in the middle of that style guide.

在这里您可获得"都市丽影"的款式指南，也强调了紧身款和运动服装的混合，您看到的关键绘图或该款式指南中的关键样图都有这个特色。

第八单元　国际仲裁
International Arbitration

I. 实战练习一

1. 演讲背景

皇家大律师 Jeremy 应邀参加由香港仲裁事务所举办的"国际仲裁峰会"并发表主旨演讲。他和另一位皇家大律师 Nicholas 共同就"国际仲裁八大制胜法宝"发言，他负责阐述前面四大法宝：一，了解国际仲裁的基本程序，包括开庭程序、书面审理、证人证言和交叉询问；二，重视合同；三，了解仲裁规则；四，寻找事实。

2. 预习词汇

arbitration 仲裁
ground rule 基本规则
representation 代理；代理人
cross-examination 交叉询问
international arbitration 国际仲裁
domestic arbitration 国内仲裁
international arbitrator 国际仲裁员
common law system 普通法系
civil law system 大陆法系
hearing 开庭；庭审
preliminary hearing on jurisdiction 关于管辖权的预审
oral evidence 证言
factual witness 事实证人
expert witness 专家证人
arbitral tribunal 仲裁庭
arbitration clause 仲裁条款
construction contract 建筑合同
ship building contract 造船合同

interpretation 解释
ICC/International Chamber of Commerce 国际商会
LCIA/London Court of International Arbitration 伦敦国际仲裁院
CIETAC/China International Economic and Trade Arbitration Commission 贸仲委；中国国际经济贸易仲裁委员会
arbitration legislation 仲裁法
seat of arbitration 仲裁地
United Arab Emirates/UAE 阿联酋
information technology 信息技术

3. 演讲文本

00:00—01:27

Well, thank you very much, Gavin. I wish I could give you a guarantee of success for every arbitration in which you are acting for a party. Unfortunately, that is not possible. I cannot guarantee success. However, what I will cover with my colleague, Nicholas, is the eight points which will help to improve your chances on your acting for your clients, the points which will be well-known to many of you, but some of them that may give you some useful ideas. And what we are going to cover is eight points altogether. So firstly, understanding the process. Secondly, to focus on the contract, which is always at the heart of any arbitration dispute. Then, to understand the ground rules; then, to find out what happened during the transaction; getting the right representation; getting the evidence; focusing on cross-examination, and very important, to be realistic.

谢谢 Gavin！我希望我能确保您在每一次的仲裁中为当事人代理时都可以成功。遗憾的是这是不可能的，我无法保证成功。但是，我和我的同事尼古拉斯将分享八点内容，它们会增加您为客户代理的成功率。这八点你们可能很多人都听说过，但是有些确实可以很好地帮助你们。我们要讲的一共有八点。首先，我们要了解程序；其次，重视合同，这往往是仲裁纠纷的核心；紧接着，理解一些基本规则；再然后，就是要知道交易过程中发生了什么，找到合适的代理人，获取证据，注重交叉询问，以及很重要的一点就是要切合实际。

01:27—01:47

And I am going to cover the first four of those points in no more than 12 and half minutes. And Nicholas Vineall is going to cover the other four, in, again, no more than 12 and half minutes. So apologies if I take it a little fast.

我会在接下来不到 12 分半钟的时间里阐述前四点，尼古拉斯将会讲后面四点，演讲时间也会限制在12分半钟内。所以如果我讲的有些快,还请多多包涵。

01:48—04:04

Now, the first thing is to understand the basic process of international arbitration. Because it does involve some very major differences with what I understand to be the features of domestic arbitration here in China. And it is very important to understand those. And the four features that I single out are these. First, the importance in international arbitrations or of law. International arbitrators are very interested in the law that they are dealing with. Sometimes it will be a system of law that they are very familiar with; sometimes it may be one that is completely new to them. So they are going to need help with the law. They are interested in what is relevant in a particular case and how it applies to the particular facts. So what you need to do if you are an arbitration counsel in international arbitration is to find out the relevant law and how best to argue your clients' case on it based on the statements of case and in the later stages of the arbitration. If the system of law that you are concerned with is a common law system, such as the United States, or England or Hong Kong, then it is legislation and case law, which are the most important parts of the law. If it is a civil law system, such as, for example, Germany or France, or many other systems that you will be familiar with, then the legislation is crucial, but also textbooks and articles by legal scholars are important. So whichever it is, it is important to find out what that law is as early as possible in the arbitration and to use that for the clients' advantage.

好,第一件事情就是要了解国际仲裁的基本程序。因为它确实和我所了解到的中国国内仲裁的特点区别较大。了解两者之间的不同点至关重要!我在这里会单独将这4个特征列出来。首先就是国际仲裁或法律的重要性。国际仲裁员对于他们要适用的法律非常感兴趣。有些时候可能是他们非常熟悉的法律体系;有些时候可能是他们之前从未接触过的法律体系。所以他们需要帮助,进一步了解法律的规定。他们感兴趣的是和某个案例有关的法律,以及这些法律是如何适用到具体的事实中。所以如果您是国际仲裁中的仲裁律师,您需要做的就是找到相关的法律,以及基于法律文书和在仲裁后面的阶段考虑该如何更好地为您的客户辩护。如果您适用的是英美法系,比如美国、英国或香港,那么制定法和判例法是法律中最重要的部分。如果是大陆法系,比如德国或是法国,或是其他您所熟知的法律体系,制定法是非常关键的,而且教科书以及法律学者的文章也非常重要。所以无论是哪种法系,非常重要的是要尽可能早的知道仲裁的准据法,为客户抢占优势。

04:05—05:19

The second feature is hearings. And it is now the norm in international arbitration that there will be at least one hearing at which evidence is heard, and quite often more than one hearing, for example, a preliminary hearing on jurisdiction. And the main purpose of the hearing is to hear evidence. It's an even more important feature of an arbitration, if the arbitrations are from a common law background, so they will be expecting a thorough and detailed hearing with oral evidence of factual witnesses and also of expert witnesses if there are any. And that is now the common norm in international arbitration that you have that sort of hearing. Sometimes you have international arbitrations which are on documents only, like I understand quite a number of arbitrations in China. But those are the exceptions rather than the norms.

第二个特点就是开庭。现在国际仲裁的常规做法是至少有一次开庭，期间会提交证据，通常都不止一次开庭，比如说关于管辖权的预审。开庭的主要目的是提交证据。如果仲裁是在英美法系框架下进行的，仲裁有一个更加重要的特征，那就是彻底、详细的庭审，期间也许还有事实证人以及专家证人的作证。类似的庭审已经成为了国际仲裁的常规做法。有时国际仲裁只用书面审理的方式开展，像是我所熟知的中国有一些仲裁就是这样进行的。但是这只是例外情况而非常规做法。

05:20—06:12

The next feature that is important is oral evidence of witnesses and cross-examination. And that is particularly important for lawyers from a common law background, who see oral evidence as very important. Civil lawyers possibly tend to be a little cynical about oral evidence. Because they believe that in a harder part, unless something is written in a document and duly naturalized, it is probably not true. And they may well be right. But common lawyers have a little more faith in oral evidence of witnesses. And so from that perspective, the oral evidence is very important.

另一个重要的特征就是证人证言以及交叉询问。尤为重要的是那些英美法系的律师认为证言非常重要。大陆法系律师可能对于证言持怀疑态度，因为他们觉得在比较难处理的部分，只有那些书面的或是本身就存在的事实才有可能是真的。他们可能是对的。但是英美法系的律师却更相信证人证言。因此从这一点而言，证言非常重要。

06:13—07:43

And for cross-examination, that's something that certainly needs skill, experience and very thorough preparation and can be absolutely decisive in the international arbitration. And then there is a different expectation with expert witnesses. In international arbitration, the norm is now to expect experts to be impartial, and objective, and trying to help the arbitral tribunal with what is genuinely their expert opinion on a particular matter. And if it emerges, that in fact, an expert who has been put forward by a party, is not objective and impartial, and it is simply saying what he or she thinks is going to help the clients' case. That is disastrous. And I've known a number of hearings where that has emerged. And the moment that happens, the arbitrators switch off from paying attention to that expert's evidence. And they reject it. So that doesn't help at all.

交叉询问确实需要技巧、经验，同时需要非常充分的准备，而且这在国际仲裁中起着决定性作用。人们对专家证人有着不同的期待。在国际仲裁中，目前的常规做法就是希望专家可以公正、客观，以及协助仲裁庭对某一事件提出他们的专家意见。如果某位专家是由一方当事人选择的，他不公正也不客观，只说那些他认为有利于客户的话，一旦出现这种情况，危害就非常大。据我所知好几次开庭都出现了这种情况，每到这时候仲裁员就不再对专家的证据感兴趣，也不采信他们所提供的证据。所以这一点帮助也没有。

07:44—10:23

Then focusing on the contract. Well, four features of that that I will suggest to you, the first is to find all possible contract documents. So for example, if it is a case where the contract has been made by emails, which incorporate an arbitration clause, then make sure you have all the emails, not just the ones that the client would like you to see. And whether it is a detailed written contract of the sort that you have in a construction contract or a ship building contract, it is not just the main part of the contract that you need to look at, you need to find out what all documents are, which are appended to the contract or referred to in it, and very often in a construction or ship building arbitration, what matters is not the main clause in the contract, but clause number 5.1, .3, .a, that'll deepen some specification which turns out to be absolutely crucial. So it is important to gather that in. Second point is to consider all possible interpretations of the contract on any disputed issue. So don't just accept the obvious interpretation. Think about whether there are other interpretations which could be argued by the for or against the clients. The third point is to look at the commercial purpose of the contract, because very often that will affect the interpretation that the arbitrators may put on the contract, so they won't just look at the words, but also what the contract was trying to achieve in commercial terms. And then, fourthly, if it is a standard form of contract, for example in the construction field, a contract based on one of the phatic switch of contract, then it is a good idea to search for guidance, to see whether there are any cases, possibly from the ICC, or some other source, which you can use to argue in favor of your position.

然后就是重视合同了，我有四点建议给大家。第一个是找到所有的合同文件。

如果某个案件中的合同是通过电子邮件订立的，其中包含了仲裁条款，那您就要确保您有所有的邮件，而不只是您的客户所想看到的那一份。不管是那种详细书写的建筑合同还是造船合同，您要关注的不仅仅包括了合同的主要内容，您需要找到所有的文件，哪些是合同里附加的或是合同里提到的，通常在建筑或是造船的仲裁中，关键部分并不是合同里的主要条款，而是编号为 5.1，.3，.a 这一类的条款，这些是更具体的规定，反倒是非常关键的内容。所以把它们都收集起来是非常重要的。第二点就是要考虑任何争议事项合同的所有解释。所以不要想当然地接受某一个明显的解释。要想到是否还有其他的解释，这可能对您的客户有利或是不利。第三点就是要看合同的商业目的，因为通常这都会影响仲裁员对合同的解释，所以他们不只是看文字，还要看这份合同究竟是想要取得什么商业利益。第四点就是如果这是一份格式合同，比如说在建筑领域，一份合同可能是基于某个交际性合同转变过来的，那么最好找其他的指导意见，去看看国际商会或是其他渠道有没有一些案例是可以用来支持自己的论点的。

10:24—12:08
The next thing is to understand the ground rules behind the arbitration, and that's vital. So you need to look very hard at the arbitration rules, which will typically be institutional rules of the ICC, or LCIA, or CIETAC, or one of the other arbitration institutions. Those are important. The next central focus is the arbitration legislation, so what you have been interested in, is the legislation about arbitration. In the seat of the arbitration, and that can have a crucial effect whatever the arbitration rules say. For example, if you end up doing an arbitration seated in the United Arab Emirates, there is a short but vital piece of legislation, which you really need to understand before conducting an arbitration there. And it contains some very surprising provisions, such as a requirement that all evidence must be on oath and if the evidence is not on oath, you can go through the whole arbitration, and get a very expensive award, and find it as completely unenforceable. Because some of the evidence was not on oath. Then thirdly, extra requirements under the contract, which sometimes affect the way which the arbitration must be conducted. And fourthly, the law governing the contract, which I've touched on already.

另外一点，您要懂得仲裁的根本规则，这非常重要。所以您要非常仔细地看仲裁规则，这通常都是国际商会、伦敦国际仲裁院、中国国际贸易仲裁委员会或是其他仲裁机构的机构规则。这些都非常关键。另外一个关注的焦点就是仲裁法，所以您感兴趣的就是关于仲裁的法律。在仲裁地，无论仲裁规则有何规定，仲裁法都是非常重要的。比如说，如果您在阿联酋仲裁，有一个简短却非常关键的立法，在仲裁之前需要理解它。它包括一些很出人意料的规定，比如说要求先宣誓才作证，否则的话,您的仲裁结束后,花费了大量的金钱才得到裁决,而该裁决完全无法执行,就因为有些证据因为没有宣誓而未被采信。第三点,合同所附带的额外规定有时也会影响仲裁开展的方式。第四点我刚刚也讲过了,就是合同的准据法。

12:09—14:48

Then the last point I am going to remind you, is the need to find out what happened. And that applies to almost any dispute. It's particularly important in a contract concerning a project where events can go on over many months or years. And trying to look back and find out what actually happened is often rather difficult, but it also matters, even in a smaller dispute. For example, where there is an exchange of emails which is crucial to the contract, and there is a mixture of emails, telephone discussions, meetings. It's very important to find out what happened. And the first point that I would suggest you on that, is don't just accept the client's story. It's very attempting just to accept what the client has to say and go with it, but it's much better to look into it, to find whether that really did happen or not. Because if it didn't happen, and that's going to come out, it should be possible to put the client's case in a much better way, and you need to know that. So you need to investigate what happened during the transaction, typically with lawyers, but in a complex case, technically involving a project, information technology, or construction, or shipbuilding, you may well need experts to look into it as well. Because the lawyers, will probably not have the technical expertise to understand all the issues. So that is a good idea to get the experts involved at the very early stage and really dig into the facts, and find out what happened. And for the lawyers, what is a good idea is to identify the crucial documents, and put together a working file of documents. It may be a very thin file. It may be a very long file. But if you can get all the documents in one place, that will help enormously in running the arbitration. And once you've got the key documents, then you can identify who the important witnesses are, talk to them, take witness statements, and you are well on the way to winning the arbitration. Thank you very much!

最后一点我想提醒你们的就是需要知道到底发生了什么,这几乎适用于所有的争议。涉及持续了几个月甚至几年的项目合同尤其如此。调查其经过,看看到底发生了什么通常很难,但这样做非常重要,小的争议也是这样。比如说邮件的往来对于合同很重要,邮件、电话讨论和会议夹杂在一起。清楚到底发生了什么很重要。首先我建议您不要全盘接受客户讲的话。通常我们都倾向于相信客户,但最好去深挖他所讲的话,看看是不是事实。因为如果没有发生的话,最终真相都会水落石出,应当以另外一种更好的方式处理客户的案子,您需要牢记这一点。所以您必须调查交易过程中到底发生了什么,尤其是和律师。但在复杂的案子中,比如涉及到一个项目、信息技术或是建筑和造船,您可能还需要专家帮您。因为律师可能不具备理解这些问题的专业知识。所以最好在初始阶段让专家参与进来,深入了解事实,知道到底发生了什么。对于律师而言,建议找到关键的文件,合在一起制作工作文档。文档可能会比较薄,或是比较长。但如果您能将所有文件放在一起,在仲裁过程中会帮您很多忙。一旦您找到关键文件,紧接着就要找到关键证人,和他们谈话、记录证词,那么您就有很大胜算了。谢谢大家!

II. 实战练习二

1. 演讲背景

皇家大律师 Nicholas 应邀参加由香港仲裁事务所举办的"国际仲裁峰会"并发表主旨演讲。他和另一位皇家大律师 Jeremy 共同就"国际仲裁八大制胜法宝"发言,他负责阐述后面的四大法宝:一,找到合适的代理人;二,获取合适的证据,在国际仲裁中适用《国际律师协会证据规则》,并且仔细选择您的事实证人;三,注重交互询问;四,切合实际,使用多种方式来减少法律成本,如果仲裁胜诉的几率太低,寻找别的解决方案。

2. 预习词汇

European continental system of law 欧洲大陆法系
barrister 大律师
defense 答辩(书);抗辩理由
witness statement 证人证言
advocacy 辩护
LMAA/London Maritime Arbitrator Association 伦敦海事仲裁员协会
solicitor 事务律师
IBA/International Bar Assocation 国际律师协会
IBA Rules of Evidence《国际律师协会证据规则》
core file 核心文件
cross-examination 交互询问
award 仲裁裁决

3. 演讲文本

00:00—00:33
Well I've got the remaining four points to deal with, but there is one other thing that I wanted to say, and I wanted to say it first. Because it's the most important thing. And

it's thank you for coming, thank you for coming today. We are really honored to have you here. It's a pleasure for us to share with you some of our experience. And we would all be really pleased if we have the opportunity in the future working together. But thank you for coming.

我还有剩下的4点要讲。但我想先说一件最重要的事,那就是谢谢大家今天参加此次峰会! 十分荣幸能与大家相聚一堂,也很高兴与大家分享我们的经验。非常期待未来能有机会与你们合作。谢谢诸位前来参会!

00:38—02:54

And maybe that leads into the first of the points I have to deal with, which is get the right representation. Many of you will have experience already in arbitration, many of you will have experience in domestic Chinese arbitration, and I could not begin to help you or advise you in a case like that. But if you do have an international arbitration case, particularly if it's a case under English law or a system of law similar to English law or under a continental, European continental system of law, then we think maybe we can help. Let me tell you a little bit about what Jeremy and I can do as English barristers. What we are used to doing, it is really three things. We don't do everything, I am sorry, but we do not do everything. But what we can help you with, is some of the things at the very early stage of an arbitration, maybe drafting the notice of arbitration, which can be very important, maybe drafting the early documents setting out the statement of case and the defense. We can help you by advising on the evidence which you will need. We won't go and take witness statements, but we might have suggestions as to which witnesses you will need to speak to. And the thing which perhaps above all we do as barristers is provide advocacy at the ultimate hearing. So we can't do everything; you may need no help at all; you may need help from a full service firm used to arbitrating in the jurisdiction where your client is arbitrating; or you may be able to make do just with the help with barristers.

这或许能够引出我想讲的第一点,就是找到合适的代理人。你们当中的许多人已经有过仲裁和国内仲裁的经验了,对于这样的案件,我无法帮助您,或为您提供咨询意见。但是如果您处理国际仲裁案件,特别是适用英国法,类似于英国法的法律体系,或者欧洲大陆法系的案件,那么我们认为或许可以提供帮助。下面为您介绍杰瑞米和我作为英国大律师能够做些什么。我们常做三件事。我们并不是无所不能的,抱歉,我们不是无所不能。但是在仲裁初期,我们可以帮您起草仲裁通知书,这非常重要,或帮您起草早期的法律文书和答辩书。我们可以帮您,为您所需的证据提供建议。我们不会参加证人作证,但我们会为您提建议,如需要跟哪位证人交谈。我们作为大律师所做的第一件事情可能就是在开庭时提供辩护。所以我们不是无所不能，或许您根本不需要帮助。您可能需要擅长在您客户的仲裁管辖区内处理仲裁案件的全方位服务公司的帮助，或者大律师的帮助对您来说就足够了。

02:54—03:54

I just thought I would give you two examples. In the last 12 months, I have done an arbitration in London, an LMAA arbitration, for a Chinese client. Their solicitors in China were Wang Jing, and it's really nice to see some people from Wang Jing here. Wang Jing had retained a London firm of solicitors, to help with preparing the evidence, and then I was retained. So that's an example right down at the bottom. But I also did an arbitration last year in London for Zhong Long, and they instructed me directly, in that case they were able to do everything, really except the advocacy. So there are lots of different ways you could put things in the mix, but the thing we are keen to remind you of is that as foreign lawyers, you can if you want to, come directly to London barristers.

举两个例子。在过去的12个月中，我曾为一名中国客户在伦敦处理了一起伦敦海事仲裁员协会仲裁案件。他们的中国事务律师来自敬海律师事务所，我很高兴能够在现场看到来自这家律所的嘉宾。敬海律所聘用了一家伦敦律师事务所来帮助准备证据，然后也聘请了我。在PPT下方有一个例子。但我去年也为中龙在伦敦处理了一起仲裁案件，他们对我进行了直接的指导。在那起案件中，他们能做除辩护外几乎所有的事情。所以您可以采用不同的办法来处理案件，但我们想提醒您的是，您若想找外国律师，可以直接找伦敦大律师。

03:54—05:57

So that's get the right representation. Point six in our list, get the evidence. Now isn't that obvious, we are all lawyers; we all know that cases are decided on the evidence. But sometimes, we forget to get the right evidence. Remember, and this is the first point, if you know what the issues are in the case, that can help you get the right evidence. You can spend a lot of time, and that means you can spend a lot of money getting evidence about something that the other side agrees about. There is no point in getting that evidence. What you need is evidence about the things where the two sides, the two parties, disagree. And you really need to focus on that evidence, and the only way to do that, is if you have worked out what are the issues on which the parties disagree. We would suggest, sometimes the arbitral rules are a little vague about some of the requirement of evidence, we think it is often an advantage to agree the *IBA Rules of Evidence* for international arbitration. They are quite a good balance between too many documents, having to disclose everything, which is very expensive and often a waste of money, which some systems have, and on the other hand, you have some systems where parties only have to disclose the documents they want to use, and that's maybe a little restrictive. The *IBA Rules of Evidence* are somewhere in between, certainly my view is, they are a good compromise.

所以这就是找到合适的代理人。我们列表中的第六点是获取证据。这一点是显而易见的,因为我们都是律师。我们都知道案件是根据证据裁决的。但是有时候,我们忘记去获取合适的证据。请记住,这是第一点。如果您知道案件的问题,这能够帮助您获取正确的证据。您会花大量的时间,这也意味着你会花大量的资金来获取对方也赞同的证据,那么获取这样的证据就没什么意义了。你需要的是双方持不同意见的证据。您真的需要关注这些证据,而唯一的方法就是,弄清楚双方的争议焦点。我们建议,有时关于证据要求的仲裁规则会比较模糊,我们认为国际仲裁中适用《国际律师协会证据规则》通常是有利的。对于一些体系来说,披露太多文件和所有证据费用高昂,也很浪费钱;另一方面,在一些体系中,当事人只需要披露他们想用的文件,这可能会有一些限制。我认为,《国际律师协会证据规则》介于两者之间,是一个不错的折中方案。

05:57—07:27

Choose your factual witnesses carefully, you know, there is nothing I like more than finding that my opponents are calling 15 witnesses, and my client is only calling two witnesses. This makes me very happy, because I only have two witnesses who could make a mistake, but my opponent has 15 witnesses, and that each of them could make a mistake, and even if all 15 witnesses are good witnesses telling the truth, they will not all remember things exactly the same, because real people don't remember things exactly the same, and then I will say, he says this, she says that, they can't remember what happened. So don't call too many witnesses. And it's a really common mistake. Choose your witnesses carefully, decide if experts are needed. I am not gonna say anything more on that because the time, and as Jeremy said, have a core file, and let me tell you the one thing that always goes in the core file, the contract. It is always in the core file; you cannot spend too long thinking about exactly what the contract says.

仔细选择您的事实证人。我最喜欢的莫过于发现对方当事人传唤 15 名证人,而我的客户只传唤两名证人。这会让我十分开心,因为我只有两个证人可能会犯错误,而对方当事人有 15 个,他们每一个人都可能会犯错。即使 15 个证人都很诚实,说实话,他们所记得的东西也不见得是完全一样的,因为正常人记得的东西不会完全一样。然后我会说,证人说法不一致,他们并不记得发生了什么。所以不要传唤太多的证人。这是一个非常常见的错误。仔细选择您的证人,决定是否需要专家。由于时间原因,我不会再谈这个方面。正如杰瑞米所说的,您需要有一份核心文件,让我告诉您,在核心文件中一定会有的就是合同。核心文件总是涵盖合同;

花在研究合同上的时间越长越好。

07:27—08:08

Focus on cross-examination. This is a real thing for a barrister to say, focus on cross-examination. But from our point of view, if you have an arbitration, which is in the English style, and not all arbitrations are, but if you have an arbitration in the English style, where calling witnesses is important, then cross-examination is important. Not all arbitrations are like that, but some of them are. And if this is going to be cross-examination you need to, when you prepare, think about what might happen in cross-examination.

注重交互询问。作为一个大律师真正要说的就是注重交互询问。但是我们认为如果您使用英国的方式进行仲裁,并不是所有仲裁都采用英国的方式,但如果您使用英国的方式进行仲裁,那么传唤证人和交互询问都十分重要。并不是所有的仲裁都是这样,但有一些是。如果您需要进行交互询问,您在准备的时候,需要思考交互询问中会发生什么。

08:08—10:09

Final point, be realistic. Being realistic means focusing on what will actually make a difference in the case. Sometimes you have a case, and you got a list of 10 issues. But if you lose on issue number one, you are going to lose on all of them. In a case like that, focus on issue number one. Assess your chances and keep the case under review. Now we know, that if your client is a state-owned enterprise, and it's involved in an arbitration, it may find it very difficult to make an offer, it may prefer to have an award against it, then try to compromise with the other side, we understand that. But even so, when we are acting for those clients, sometimes it seems to us a pity that they will not engage more with the other side. If you have a private company as your client, even more important to think what is likely to happen. Then if you lose or don't do as well as you want to, your client is not surprised, they may be disappointed, but they are not surprised. But also, if you know that you are going to lose part of the case, but you might win another part of the case, you are in a good position to try to settle with the other side, because the other side will not be certain that they will win any of the case.

最后一点就是切合实际。切合实际意味着专注于对案件胜诉起决定性作用的事项。有时在案件中,您有一份列举了10个问题的清单。但是如果您在第一个问题上失败了,您就会接连在剩下的问题中失败。在这样的案件中,您应该专注于第一个问题。评估胜诉的几率,并持续审核案件。现在我们知道,如果您的一名国企客户涉及一起仲裁,它可能会不愿主动提出自己的目标诉求,宁愿等对方提出一个和

第八单元　国际仲裁 International Arbitration

解方案然后再试图和对方妥协，我们对此表示理解。但是即便如此，当我们为这些客户代理时，有时候我们会对他们不与对方进行更多的接触而感到遗憾。如果您有一个私营企业客户，更重要的是要思考会发生什么。然后如果您败诉了，或者做的没有您预想的好，您的客户不会感到意外。他们可能会失望，但不会意外。但是，如果您知道案件的部分将会败诉，但您可能会在案件的另一部分胜诉。您就可以试图与对方和解，因为对方也不确定他们会赢得案件。

10:09—12:01

Let me give you an example. It's a case I am involved within at the moment. I am going to change the facts, so nobody could tell what it was. But just imagine a case, where there is a claim against my client for ten million dollars. I know, as certain as a lawyer can ever be, that for six million dollars, I have no defense at all, but I have a reasonable defense for four million dollars, maybe 50-50. My opponent probably thinks about the same, but maybe is a little bit nervous even about the six million. Surely, commercially, I should be making an offer, of six and a bit, in the hope they would take that, and then I win in effect on the bit of the case I counted on. And remember, in cases where the costs, the legal costs are going to be high, that in a case like the one I've just described, even if you can not reach a settlement, there are ways to protect your position in costs by making a sealed offer, or by making it without prejudice offer to the other side saying, if you like, I will settle at six and a half million, but remember that, if you don't accept that, and you continue with the arbitration, but you only get six million, I will expect you to pay my costs, because I have made you an offer. And often by doing that, you can put pressure on the other side. So don't forget that.

举个例子。这是我正在代理的一起案件。我会改动一下细节，这样就没有人知道具体是哪起案件了。但是想象一下在一起案件中，我的客户面临着1,000万美元的索赔。作为一名律师，我很清楚我是完全没有抗辩理由拒付其中的600万美元。但我有合理的抗辩理由拒付剩余的400万美元，或者一半。对方当事人很可能和我想的一样，但是对于其中600万美元，他或许还是有点把握不准。当然，从商业的角度来看，我应该提出和解，赔偿600万左右，希望他们能接受，这样我就能实际上在我代理的案件中胜出。请记住，在这些案件中，法律成本会很高。在我刚刚描述的一起案件中，即使不能达成和解，也有多种方式来减少成本，例如密封和解要约，或者在不影响对方的前提下提出，如果您能接受，我同意用650万解决。但请记住，如果您不接受，仲裁会继续，但您只能获得600万，我希望您支付给我费用，因为我已经提出和您和解了。通常以这种方式，您可以给对方施压。请不要忘记这一点。

12:01—12:25

Final point, I suppose it's obvious, run a profit, cut a loss. If you are going to lose, find a way out of the arbitration. If you are going to win, that's fine, go to an arbitration, spend lots of money on your lawyers, and everybody will be happy. But if that's not gonna happen, try to find an alternative.

最后一点,我认为显而易见就是逐利减损。如果您会输,采用仲裁之外的其他方式。如果您会赢,那就去仲裁,花大钱请律师,大家都满意。但如果不是这样,就找其他解决办法。

第九单元　动漫娱乐
Animation and Entertainment

I. 实战练习一

1. 演讲背景

中东 ASI（Amusement Services International）国际娱乐公司的代表应邀参加"全球室内游乐场商业运营模式高峰论坛"并发表演讲。他在演讲中提到了由于网购的兴起，购物中心客流量下降，我们需要把零售和娱乐结合在一起才能重振购物中心，在运营娱乐中心的时候，需要采取的具体措施如下：处理好 3 个 F 因素、注重娱乐中心的选址、利用社交媒体营造口碑、合理投资和设置娱乐设施和 IP、采取诸如 VR/AR 等新技术。

2. 预习词汇

Indian subcontinent 印度次大陆
Joypolis 梅田欢乐城
Molly Fantasy 莫莉幻想
YuYuTo 悠游堂
customer profile 顾客类型
attraction 娱乐项目
Augmented Reality 增强现实技术
center food court 中心美食广场
casual dining place 休闲餐饮区
dynamic 热闹的
footfall 客流量
height 高度
common area 公摊面积
WahLap 华立科技
pre-open 试业
Minion 小黄人
playground system 游乐场分区

toddler play area 幼童游玩区
F&B 餐饮区
slushie 思乐雪冰沙
token 代币
debit card system 储值卡系统
trampoline park 蹦床公司
Happy Meal of McDonald's 麦当劳的开心乐园餐
graph 饼图
cost of the license 版权费
air hockey 空气曲棍球
Treasure Quest 寻宝
Big Bass Wheel 大转轮
Atlantis Hotel on the Palm Jumeriah in Dubai 朱美拉棕榈岛亚特兰蒂斯酒店

3. 演讲文本

00:00—00:34

Good afternoon! "你好" is one of the few Chinese words that I know, so please bear with me when I speak in English. Thank you! Well, there were many wonderful presentations before this. You know, thank you all for these, educated me a lot in terms of the various points that they've mentioned. Very quick introduction about my company and what we do. We've got three business verticals.

　　大家下午好。"你好"是我会说的为数不多的一句中文,不好意思今天还是得用英文发表演讲。谢谢大家! 非常感谢各位演讲嘉宾做的精彩演讲,他们的真知灼见让我受益匪浅。首先我会快速地介绍一下我们公司和主营业务。我们有三大主营业务。

00:35—02:41

　　One, designs entertainment facilities. We've designed entertainment facilities in about 35 countries across the Middle East, Indian subcontinent, Africa, Russia, Eastern Europe. We would like to soon venture into China someday. The second vertical is a supply arm. ASI is one of the largest distributors in the Middle East and North African market. We're representing the whole of brands, some of the very, very good Chinese brands too, who have really improved their quality and we're very happy with what we do with them. We cater to about 1,700 amusement operations spread across 45 countries. With this end, I want to talk to you all, about dynamics for creating successful entertainment facilities. I have many people here mentioned about lovely concepts in China. We saw pictures of many of them. We saw impressive ones like Molly Fantasy from Aeon. We saw Joypolis. We saw others before these. I thought the YuYuTo was also a very nice concept. But primary to all of these is the business that we are in. We all think the business that we are in, is a business of entertainment, and that is correct. But at the same time, we are also in the business of real estate. Why are we in the business of real estate? Because as amusement facilities, we add value to real estate operations. By adding value to real estate operations, the value of the real estate goes up. If the real estate is profitable, then more people come to your amusement operations, and therefore you make more money. We are going to go through a few factors right now on how do real estate influences this and how entertainment values change.

第一类主营业务是设计娱乐设施。我们设计的娱乐设施遍布中东、印度次大陆、非洲、俄罗斯和东欧等35个国家。我们也希望将来能进军中国市场。第二类业务是供应。ASI是中东和北非市场最大的分销商。我们代理很多品牌,其中不乏中国的知名品牌。这些品牌不断提高自身质量,我们非常高兴地看到我们取得的成就。我们满足了45个国家的1,700家娱乐场所的需求。借此,我想跟大家谈谈创建娱乐设施成功的秘诀。刚刚有很多发言人谈到了中国一些很新颖的概念。我们也看到了很多图片,比如令人印象深刻的就有永旺的莫莉幻想,还有梅田欢乐城。之前我们还看到其他图片。我觉得悠游堂就是个很不错的概念。但是最主要的还是我们身处的行业。我们都觉得自己身处娱乐业,这一点是千真万确。但同时,我们也身处房地产行业。为什么这么说呢?因为娱乐设施可以为房地产业务增加价值。通过为房地产业务增加价值,房地产的价值又进一步上升。如果房地产利润很高的话,很多人就会来您的娱乐场所,这样您就能赚更多的钱。我们现在来看看房地产如何影响娱乐设施以及娱乐价值观。

02:50—03:48

The marketplace today has changed quite a bit. There was a time when we had shopping areas or shopping districts. In our part of world we call them supermarkets. Since then we've seen the emergence of the shopping mall or what we called as the organized retail sector. And since the emergence of the shopping mall, we've seen the emergence of the smartphone and smart devices. And since then all our customers have gotten very wise and they all go online shopping. This trend of changing consumer pattern has led to shopping malls being redefined. We went through a period where attendance to shopping malls went down. Since the attendance went down, we also saw the revenues of entertainment facilities also go down with it. We then saw the reemergence of the shopping malls.

市场发生了不少变化。曾经我们有购物区,我们称之为超市。之后,我们见证了购物中心或者我们所说的有组织的零售业的兴起。购物中心兴起后,我们见证了智能手机和智能设备的兴起。顾客也变聪明了,他们都开始网上购物。这种消费模式的改变也让我们重新定义购物中心。我们也经历过客流量减少的时期。客流量减少后,娱乐设施的收入也随之减少。随后我们见证了购物中心的复兴。

03:48—05:50

Our customer profile significantly changed. Our customers wanted an experience. Now, this is one of the things that I notice in many amusement operations across China, both small and large. There are few that provide very good experience. There are few that don't. Many of them do the same thing as what other people do. Today, our customers purely want an experience. They go to a place because they want that experience. If they don't gain the experience, they don't want to go there. There are two types of attractions that we deal with. I just come to that in a little while. The fact that our customer wants an experience led to the refinement of the mall concept. Before, the shopping mall was all about shopping. It was all about the stores. They wanted stores. They wanted the entertainment facilities to go there. They treated you like another store. They asked you to pay the same rent as what a ZARA would pay, what a H&M would pay, what a supermarket would pay, but they never looked at the importance you meant to the shopping mall. What is it that they were doing different? Why were you so important to the existence of a shopping mall? The malls slowly realized when online retail, the same ZARA store which is in the mall was selling a product much higher than what they were selling the same product that on their website. So, this led the consumer to go more towards the website and refrain from going to shopping malls. So, what made them go back to shopping malls? This led to them changing. Call shopping malls by a new name. That new name was called RETAIL-TAINMENT. RETAIL-TAINMENT is retail with entertainment.

我们的顾客类型发生了很大的变化。顾客希望获得体验。我注意到中国很多大大小小的游乐场所吸引顾客的一大原因就是他们希望体验一下。有的场所可以提供好的游客体验,有的则不能。有些游乐场所只是模仿别人的做法。如今,顾客就是单纯地追求体验。他们就是冲着那些体验才去消费的,否则就不会去。我们主要有两种类型的游乐项目,待会儿我会谈到。由于顾客追求体验,因此,我们需要重新定义商场的概念。以前,商场是用来购物的,里面都是商铺。商场想要店铺和娱乐设施入驻。商场把游乐场所也当作商铺来对待,要求他们支付和ZARA、H&M及超市一样的租金。但商场从来没有意识到游乐场所的重要性。那游乐场所究竟有什么与众不同之处呢?为什么游乐场所对于商场来说很重要呢?商场逐渐意识到,有了在线销售，ZARA 实体店的商品要比网上的价格高得多，这样一来消费者更愿意网购，而不再去商场消费。那怎样才能让顾客重新回到商场呢？商场需要改变，商场就有了一个新名词——零售娱乐，即把零售和娱乐两者结合起来。

05:51—08:18

So, from where, we... where... as amusement operators and in significant portion of a shopping mall, we then became an important driver of traffic into the shopping mall. We, people came to shopping mall not only to buy clothes, shoes, food whatever, they also came there to get entertained. They came there to shop. They came there to watch a movie. They came there to eat food. They came there with their kids to have fun. It's important that we take notice of this. Because with the RETAIL-TAINMENT revolution that came across all the shopping malls, everything changed. I'm sorry. My slides are not as beautiful as some of the other slides. Pardon me for that. Well, the most notable aspects in this, is the development of the digital media. As many people we are talking here, I saw many other people, all of them were on their Whatsapp, some of you were on your Facebook, all of you were still connected with the outside world at the same time as you are listening to some of the wonderful speakers here. Now this says that information goes from one area to another area way too quickly. You all know about this. I'm not telling you anything new. But the digital media change things to the extent that today you can no longer call yourself a shopping mall or even a retail entertaining place. You have now become what we call as a social hub. What is a social hub? People come to you to meet other people to interact with other people. And that is a part of the experience. People don't go to the shopping malls only to shop; people don't go to the shopping malls only because it's a Joypolis; people don't go to shopping malls only because something else. People may go to Disneyland because it's Disneyland. That's what we call as destination environment. They go to Disneyland because they know it's a one-day experience. They are gonna be there on the holiday and they are gonna ride many attractions.

游乐场运营商在商场占据举足轻重的地位，我们能够增加商场的客流量。顾客来到商场不仅是为了买衣服、鞋子或者用餐等等，他们还来享受娱乐服务。我们要明白，他们到商场来购物、看电影、用餐，还有和孩子共度美好时光。我们要注意这一点，这很重要！因为随着各大商场都掀起零售娱乐的变革，一切都发生了变化。不好意思，我的PPT可能没有之前的演讲嘉宾做的那么好看，希望大家不要介意。其中变化最显著的是数字媒体的发展。我发现今天在场的各位一边用脸书、Whatsapp 这样的社交软件和外界沟通，一边在聆听现场精彩的演讲。现在，信息传播速度非常快。大家都非常清楚，我也不需要再赘述。但是，数字媒体带来的改变十分深远,我们已经不能再把商场视作简单的商场或者零售娱乐场所,现在已经变成了社交中心。那什么是社交中心呢?也就是说人们来到这里,互相交流。这也是所说的体验的一部分。顾客来到商场不仅是为了购物,不仅是因为有梅田欢乐城或其他原因。大家可能就冲着迪士尼的名声才去那儿玩,这就是我们说的旅游目的地与环境。大家选择迪士尼是因为可以在节假日好好放松,玩一些游乐项目,然后度过美好的一天。

08:19—11:51

But as amusement facilities within shopping malls, we are targeting them for a couple of hours. We are targeting them for two hours and our task is to find out both as a manufacturer, as an operator, as a designer, is to find out how are we going to engage them for two hours? How am I going to take enough money out of them in those two hours without making them realize that they have spent too much? But that's it. You know retail spaces becoming social hubs, FECs as many people are using the word. Some of them say it's an American concept. Yes, it is. FECs, as family entertainment centers, are no longer family entertainment centers. They have become social entertainment centers or socially engaging centers. Today, in the coming years, we are also going to see a revolution in this front. In the fact that if all will be about sharing your scores on a game, via Facebook, via your Twitter, via other medias and then interacting with your friends, we've also seen the emergence of Virtual Reality. Many of them talk about Virtual Reality. To me, Virtual Reality is just beginning, has just started. We don't even know how the headsets are going to look like six months from now. You know I was speaking to a CEO for very, very big hotel chain recently. And the CEO told me what is the greatest thing that happen to the hotel sector. He said Virtual Reality. And I asked him why. He said, "In the future, every household, every house will have a VR headset. And how would you book a hotel? You wouldn't go on to a website; you would go to a VR friendly environment. You would be able to see that hotel 360 degrees, you will be able to experience the restaurant. You will be able to experience the rooms, and then you decide that I want to stay in this hotel." That is pretty much the same thing that's going to happen in our segment too. But you know Facebook, being Facebook, they would not have invested two billion dollars into Oculus, if they did not see the whole value of how VR is going to change the world. Partly with VR, we have AR. How many of you know about AR? AR? OK. Few of them know. Pokemon Go? How many of you know about Pokemon Go? Come on guys. Let me see your hands. OK. Quite a few. Quite a few. Yeah. Pokemon Go is AR, Augmented Reality. Right? That's another part that's going to totally envision how things change. I have people from Aeon tell me about, you know creating an app. Now, we're just working with the very large park development in Dubai where when you walk through the park, they force you to download the app for the park. And once you have the app for the park, there are many characters in the theme park that will talk to you if you switch on the app and the camera in the app. Through Augmented Reality, we will make Molly talk to you, we will make any of the characters talk to you. We will make them give you special offers. We'll ask you and direct you to a restaurant. That's another part that's redefining how we are going to shop.

但是作为进驻商城的娱乐设施，我们希望让顾客留得久点儿。我们的目标是让顾客可以停留两小时，并且从制造、运营和设计着手，思考如何让顾客可以在这儿待两小时，以及如何让他们消费而没有意识到自己花的钱越来越多。情况就是这样。零售商店已经开始转变为社交中心，很多人都称此发展为FEC。有人说这是美国提出的概念，确实是。FEC，也就是家庭娱乐中心，它已经不再停留在这个层面了，已经变成了社交娱乐中心。在未来，我们还会看到更多这方面的变革。大家将可以在脸书、推特和其他社交媒体上分享自己的游戏战绩，还可以与朋友互动。我们现在还看到了虚拟现实技术的崛起，很多人都在谈论VR。对我来说，VR只是起步阶段。我们甚至不知道这个头显在六个月的时间内又会发展成什么样。我最近和一位大型连锁酒店的CEO聊过。他对我说："VR将为酒店业带来最激动人心的改变。"我问他为什么。他告诉我说："在未来，家家户户都会有VR头显。大家要怎么订酒店呢？不用登录网站，只要在可以应用VR技术的环境就可以360度观赏酒店，感受一下餐厅和客房，再决定要不要入住这家酒店。"这种变化也将发生在我们身处的领域。正是因为脸书看到VR技术改变未来的价值，它才投资了20亿美元来收购Oculus公司。随着VR的发展，我们还拥有了增强现实，即AR技术。有多少人知道AR技术的？好的，还是有些人知道的。大家知道精灵宝可梦吗？有多少人听说过这个游戏的？知道的人请举一下手。好的，还是挺多人的。精灵宝可梦用的就是AR技术，即增强现实技术。从AR技术中，我们可以进一步预见未来的变革。永旺的工作人员就告诉我说，想要设计一个App。我们也正在和迪拜的公园开发商进行合作，当人们走进公园的时候，就要下载一个专属的App。下载完毕后，如果您开启了App和照相功能的话，就可以看到主题公园里很多角色都会跟您说话。在AR技术的帮助下，我们可以让莫莉或者其他的角色和您说话。我们还可以让他们给您一些优惠。我们会询问您的意见，然后带您去餐厅。因此，AR技术也在重新定义购物的模式。

11:51—13:47

The experience is what people think about and the experience is in two forms. The experience is what they see from their eyes, and the experience is what they see on their file and screen and how they perceive that. It is the combination of these two that's going to change the way entertainment just perceived to large extent. The F + F + F Factor and the influence of the F + F + F Factor is critical to every aspect to leisure. When I say F + F + F Factor, I say the food, the fun and the films or the movies or the cinema that we call it. The location of these three in any shopping mall development is critical to the success of your entertainment facility because each of these feeds on each other. And a good shopping mall developer would strategically position where his cinemas are, where his center food courts are, where his casual dining places are, and where the entertainment facility is, so that he can draw his customer to each of these points significantly. Today, in your choice of shopping malls when you open more, better dynamic FECs, you have to ensure that you've got the location right. In the next slide, we'll go through a bit more of this. The most important factor that is critical to us, creating dynamic leisure facilities, is always recognized that the customer is truly the king. You define all your experience looking backwards. What does my customer want? How is it going to influence? How the success of this operation is going to be? When you do it that way, you're likely to be a lot more successful than other places.

顾客体验就是他们在想什么，有两种体验方式。一是亲眼所见的体验，其次是他们从文件和屏幕上得到的体验。将两者结合起来，能够大大改变娱乐方式。三个F因素及其影响对休闲娱乐的方方面面都十分重要。我说的三个F因素是指美食、娱乐以及电影。这三者在购物商场的位置对娱乐中心的成功至关重要，而且这三者相辅相成。一个经验丰富的购物商场开发商会巧妙地安排电影院、美食广场、休闲餐饮区、以及娱乐设施的位置，这样他才能够吸引顾客到相应的地方。现在，当您开设更多更热闹的家庭娱乐中心时，您需要确保购物商场的选址是正确的。在下一张幻灯片中，我将会进一步谈到这一点。对我们来说，最重要的是要意识到在打造丰富多样的娱乐设施时，顾客就是上帝。您可以回头看如何去定义顾客的体验。我的顾客需要什么？我要怎样才能对顾客产生影响？运营会取得怎样的成功？如果在座各位能从这几方面着手，那么各位很可能会比您的竞争对手更成功。

13:48—14:46

I recently visited an entertainment facility and I saw that over the last five years, they haven't changed much of their entertainment offering, they still have the same thing. They said, "Oh no, we don't see anything new, we are very happy with the rides that we have the same thing." Now, how many, how many operators in this room? How many amusement operators? Any? Many? Few? OK. So, this guy had the same machines, pretty much the same rides, everything for the last five years. Now, a lot of the customers that he was getting when he first got this new ride that was ten years old.

Today, they are fifteen years old. Do you think they will have the same thinking or different thinking? Obviously different. So if we don't change to the needs of our customers, we're not going to succeed.

我最近参观了一个娱乐场所，5 年了，他们还是老样子。他们说："我们没有看见任何新的元素，我们对现有的机动游戏已经很满足了。"现场有多少运营商？娱乐设施运营商？有吗？多吗？还是一些？好的。所以这个运营商没有更新设施，同样的娱乐设施已经用了 5 年。5 年前，玩这个机动游戏的大部分顾客是 10 岁，现在已经 15 岁了。大家认为他们的思维还是一成不变的吗？当然不是。如果我们无法适应我们顾客变化的需要，我们是不可能成功的。

14:48—15:37

Today, some of the, I'm going to address some of the factors that we typically look at, looking at creating that dynamic, which is needed to create a successful FEC. Understanding the mall dynamics, very very important factor. Please understand who are the drivers of the shopping mall. Every shopping mall developer will come up and tell you, "I've got this big brand and that big brand and that big brand", and everybody else. You need to know who is really in that mall because the kind of shops they are are the ones who would drive attention and footfall to the shopping mall. If you don't have great shops which cater to all age groups of audience, all types of people, then you're not going to get the right people into the shopping mall.

今天，我会讲讲需要考虑的常见因素，来帮助家庭娱乐中心取得成功。理解商场的动力源泉十分重要。我们需要知道谁能够促进购物中心的发展。每一个购物中心开发商都会过来和您说："我有这个大品牌，我有那个大品牌。"但您需要知道的是真正在这个商场里面商铺有哪些，因为商铺才是商场吸引注意力、带来客流量的动力。如果各位的购物中心里面没有可以满足各种年龄群和各种顾客类型的商店，那么大家将无法吸引顾客前往。

15:37—18:00

The mall developer participation, they need times. Mall developers always think that they want to lease this space to you. They even tell you very nicely that, "I don't know much about leisure in the attractions. It's your job. Please just give me a rent, then I'm very happy with it." But you should understand, tomorrow there will be another operator who comes in. The shopping mall would allow two other entertainment facilities to set up in that same shopping mall. Maybe the same kind, maybe the different kind, but all of which will affect your investment and what you've invested in that shopping mall. It is very important to understand what is the mall developer's vision for the shopping mall. How is he treating you and is he willing to participate with you by helping you with the power, by helping you with heights, by helping you with the many facilities that you need to create a successful entertainment facility? You have to understand how large is the mall and how big is your FEC space. Every shopping mall developer wants to give you 5,000, 6,000, 7,000 square meters of space, or 200, 300, 400, 500 square meters of space. Many a time that space is not where it needs to be. It's probably in the wrong corner. He'll probably give you a better rent for you to take that space. But that need not be the right decision for you. You have to understand what is that right space, what is GLA. GLA is the gross leasable area of the shopping mall. Gross leasable area is the area of all the shops. Sometimes have large shopping malls, they tell you that, "I'm building a ten-million-square-meter shopping mall". Out of that ten million square meters, maybe 50% are for this common area, Right? It's only they say, if they talk about ten million square meters then or, sorry, ten million square feet, then they may only have like two million square feet of actual leasable area. Your relationship was the leasable area because that's where people go to shop. On that basis, you have to target how much time will the consumers spend in the shopping mall? Is it enough time for them to see the entire shopping mall at one time or are they likely to come back again and again into the shopping mall?

商场开发商的参与需要时间。他们会想把场地租给您，而且还很友好地对您说："我们是休闲娱乐领域的门外汉，所以就靠你们自己了。只要给我交租，我就心满意足了。"但是，您要知道，明天可能就会出现另一位运营商。商场会同时允许设置两项相同或者不同的娱乐设施，不管怎样这都会影响您在商场的投资。重要的是要明白开发商对商场的愿景，他会如何对待您？他是否会帮您解决电力、高度和设施的问题，来确保娱乐设施顺利运转？您要清楚商场和您的家庭娱乐中心有多大。商场开发商会给您几千平方米或者几百平方米的场地空间，但这个场地的位置可能并不好，他就会便宜一点租给您。但这并不是好的选择。您要明白什么是好的选址，什么是GLA，也就是商场的总可出租面积，就是所有商铺的面积。有时候一些大型商场会告诉您，他们在建一个1,000万平方米的商场。而在这1,000万平方米里面，50%是公摊面积，对吧？当他们说1,000万平方英尺时，实际只有200万平方英尺是可出租面积。和您相关的是可出租面积，因为那才是人们逛街的地方。另外，您要考虑顾客会花多少时间在商场里？要让他们有足够时间一次性逛完整个商场，还是要让他们成为回头客呢？

18:00—19:53

Therefore, how should, how should I size up my FEC? How big should it be and what sort of footfalls are the mall expecting to do? There is a relationship normally we give anywhere between 2-3% of the gross leasable area. Sometimes they are really small, more up to 7% of the gross leasable area to the size of an FEC. Similarly, about 2-7% of the footfall that comes into the mall translates as footfall to the FEC. So it's important for you to understand this number right in the very early business planning stage. Selecting the ideal spot for the FEC, vis-a-vis food, vis-a-vis fun, vis-a-vis cinemas, these are very very critical if you have too many competing factors. Sometimes customers come in, they spend very little time and they go away. It's very important that you position it correctly so that when they come in, you're right there and you're able to keep them in your facility for a longer period of time. The simple understanding that is something you know, lot of you may see in Las Vegas. Many of you have been to Las Vegas here? Gambling? Anybody? Las Vegas? No? OK. Few in the back. All right. When you're going to any casino floor in Las Vegas, you never know if it's night or day. All the time it looks the same. The machines are always inviting, they're always calling you in and you don't know how much time you spend. The only time you actually get out is when you've lost everything. So, the idea is they keep making you win some, lose some, win some, lose some, so that they are able to keep you there as long as you can. The longer you stay, the more you will pay.

所以，如何扩大家庭娱乐中心的区域？要有多大？我们希望客流量有多大？通常家庭娱乐中心会占到2%～3%的可出租面积，有时候小的商场就会有7%的可出租面积提供给家庭娱乐中心。商场大约2%～7%的客流量会成为家庭娱乐中心的客流量。所以在一开始做商业规划时就要知道这些数据。如果您有很多竞争对手，不管您的家庭娱乐中心是以美食、娱乐还是电影为主题，选取最佳位置都至关重要。有时候顾客来了，他们只是呆一会儿就走。重要的是您要选址正确，他们来了之后才会停留更长的时间。要知道拉斯维加斯就是很好的例子。你们去过拉斯维加斯吗？去赌博？有人去过吗？拉斯维加斯？没有。好的，坐在后排的有些观众去过。好。当大家去拉斯维加斯的赌博层的时候，您会赌到不知昼夜，感觉时间不变。机器一直在引诱着您，您根本不知道赌了多长时间。输光了您才会出来。所以，他们的做法就是让您赢一点，输一点，赢一点，输一点，这样才能留住您。您逗留时间越长，输得也越多。

19:54—24:13

As I said earlier, one of the critical factors in the somewhere right below the screen, one most critical factors is the rental. Different malls will charge different rentals, and it's very important for you to know the importance of this rental. Rental is a part that you pay irrespective of the money you make. And for any good business model, you have to ensure in a really really good mall which is possibly you can call as a great mall. You can pay up to 15-17% as rental. But in most malls you wanna try and keep that rental as below 15% as possible so that you can actually make your model work for you. We actually came up with this method, chart and that you know I wanna talk the, thanks Mr. Benny for actually asks me to share this thing. Mr. Benny Zhu from WahLap. You know I'm not sure if this is a very clear resolution for you. When you start investing in a family entertainment center concept, or any form of entertainment concept, you start here, at this point. From there on, you're going to design it, you have to build it, you have to project manage it, you have to purchase your equipment, you have to install and commission, you have to pre-open it, you have to hire your staff and train and one day you open. Now, under that point and time, all you're doing is you're spending money. But you start earning money only after you open. Right? So, any mistake, initially, all entertainment facilities do well, which is what we call as a honeymoon period. Right? So, everybody seeing, clapping, increasing. You're growing in popularity. You're really good. Any mistake that you have done in your design, in your selection of equipment, in the way you build it, everything will show up around the six-month range. When your honeymoon is over, and then you will start seeing your declining revenue. Then you start understanding your competition, then you start analyzing your competition. Then you start understanding I bought the wrong equipment from the wrong supplier and many a time that equipment is not working. When do I buy the right equipment? All those thoughts come to you at the later stage. At the same time, you're not there to provide the right customer service, you also have enough staff. And therefore, you're carrying a lot of operating expenses. Now, it's very important to remember that along the time when your revenue dips that's when you really have to look at your business, and then see what are things that I can do, to do this, this could include purchasing new machines, this could include understanding your customers. This could include a lot of other parameters in today's world that we call social. Something wrong happens in your shopping mall; something wrong happens in your entertainment facility. Even before the owner of the FEC knows about it. The social media knows about it. Correct? Because your customers already uploaded it on a YouTube. Customer already put it on Whatsapp and everything else. So today, how many of you in your entertainment facilities actually engage on social media? And you guys do. But, how many more? If you don't, how many of you hire one person in your amusement operation to only take care of social media? Or more than one person. You know, I was opening a new facility recently in India, and one of the first thing I did was to go to the social media and find out everything about my competition. How many bad reviews they had? How many people said they were good? Who were the people who said they were

第九单元　动漫娱乐 Animation and Entertainment

good? Who were the people who said they were bad? And then, the first person I actually engaged, hired for this project was a social media manager. Not many of us are keeping track of what our customers write about us.

正如我之前所说的，在屏幕下方可以看到其中的一个重要因素就是租金。不同的购物商场收取的租金不同，明白租金的重要性对您来说非常关键。租金是无论盈利多少都得开支的一部分。对于可行的商业模式，您得确保是在一个好的商场，也就是您称之为最佳的商场。您可以支付15%～17%的租金。但是大多数的商场都要把租金尽可能控制在15%以下，这样商业模式才会行之有效。谢谢Benny先生让我分享我们之前想出来的一个方法和图表，其实这也正是我想谈的。Benny先生来自华立科技。我不知道大家能不能看清楚这个图。当您开始投资家庭娱乐中心，或其他形式的娱乐时，您从这个点开始。从那时起，您得设计、建造、管理项目、购买设备、安装、调试、试营业，您还得招聘、培训员工，然后正式开业。大家看到屏幕上这个点位的下面，您能做的就是投入资金。但是您只有在正式营业后才开始赚钱，不是吗？当然最初所有这些娱乐设施都运行良好，我们称之为蜜月期，对吗？因此，大家看到，每个人都喜欢这里，收入在不断增加。您的娱乐场所越来越受欢迎，生意越来越好。一些设计、设备选择和建造方式的失误，所有这一切会在6个月的时间显现出来。蜜月期结束后，您会看到收入不断下降。您开始了解到竞争，开始分析竞争对手。然后您开始认识到从不良供应商那里买了有问题的设备，许多情况下根本无法运作。我什么时候买好的设备？您在最后阶段才意识到所有这些想法。同时，您不仅要保证顾客服务质量，还要有足够的员工。因此，您要付很多营业费用。大家要记住，当您的收入暂时下降时，您需要分析自己的业务，看看自己能做什么，比如包括购买新机器，了解顾客，还有我们现在称之为与社交有关的其他参数。一旦您的购物中心或者娱乐设施出现差错，甚至FEC的老板还不了解相关情况，社交媒体就知道了。对吗？因为您的顾客已经将这些事情上传到YouTube、Whatsapp等其他社交媒体上。所以，今天在座各位有多少在经营娱乐设施的运营上加入社交媒体的？你们会关注社交媒体。还有多少人会关注呢？如果不关注，你们有多少人会聘请一个人或者更多人员来管理社交媒体？我最近在印度运营一个新的娱乐场所，我做的第一件事就是去社交媒体关注所有的竞争对手。他们分别有多少差评和好评，哪些人给了好评，哪些人给了差评。我会聘请一个经理来管理社交媒体。我们中很多人从不跟踪了解客户对自己的评价。

24:13—25:01

Previously, it was just the discussion between themselves. Today, it's no longer a discussion just between consumers. It's a discussion that is on virtual space, everybody else is reading about it. If you don't handle what are the good reviews you get and therefore go back to your customer, and if you don't handle what are the bad reviews you get and these two go back to your customer and turn that into a good review, you are not going to be able to retain your customers. Those are some of the new expenses that you should incur in order to succeed in this business, preferably from an operating expense perspective. Sorry about that again.

之前,这只是顾客之间的讨论。今天已经不再是顾客之间的讨论了,而是网络虚拟空间上的讨论,其他人都可以看到。如果无法处理好评、差评,并给顾客反馈,并且将差评变成好评,那么,您就无法留住顾客。从运营费用的角度来看,这些就是您要想在行业中取得成功需要承担的新开支。抱歉这张幻灯片不是特别清晰。

25:01—27:15

Today, I said that, we will talk about different kinds of entertainment facilities. We often get request from a lot of our clients to say that we want the biggest, we want the best and we want to be different from others and everything else. Now many a time all of these cost you a lot of money in terms of investment. I have customers who come in and say, "I want the best roller coaster inside my FEC". We do that for them if he thinks it's right. We have to know what type of a customer base am I dealing with. Am I a Disneyland, Universal Studios that kind of a project? Or am I a neighborhood local demographic based person? Your investment judgment is mostly dictated by that. When I say a Disneyland kind of a project, means I get a million new visitors every time. I don't need to change my attractions regularly. I can afford to spend a hundred million dollars or so on a great roller coaster and everything else and still make money on it. But when I am dealing with a local demographic, I want that customer to come back again, and again and again. How many times do we, how many times are you likely to visit Disneyland in Shanghai? It looks beautiful. Once? May be twice? May be twice in a life time? Right? Or maybe every time they bring a new attraction. You know, Universal Studios, their footfall was going down and they brought *Harry Potter*. Their footfall went up again because they brought a new attraction and that attraction was significant and it brought them almost MYM290 million of revenue just in the first year, because they had the *Harry Potter* attraction, right? So, but we can't do the same. We can't expect the same in the FEC market. In the FEC market, we are all about providing variety; we are all about planning a try; we are all about doing things right to attract our customers again, and again and again. How do we bring them back? That's the only thing that drives us. And therefore, we study the demographic factors and the repeat business value closely.

今天,我会谈到不同类型的娱乐设施。我们的顾客经常要求说要最大、最好、最与众不同的设施。通常这些东西会花很多钱,需要很多投资。我有位顾客走进来说:"在家庭娱乐中心里我想要最好的过山车。"只要他认为好,我们就满足他的要求。我们要弄清楚哪类顾客群是我们要吸引的。我是要建像迪士尼、环球影城那样的项目?还是要建以当地居民为主的家庭娱乐场所?您的投资决定主要是看这个。谈到一个迪士尼项目时,就意味着有一百万新增游客。我不需要定期更改设施。我可以花上亿美元投资建设大型过山车和其他设施,还可以盈利。如果我们的目标客户是当地居民,我希望我的顾客能成为回头客。大家会去多少次上海迪士尼乐园?它看起来非常漂亮。一次?两次?还是一辈子只去两次?或许每次他们引进新的娱乐项目时你们都去。大家都知道环球影城,他们的客流量一直在减少,然后他们推出了哈利·波特主题项目,客流量又增加了,因为他们引进了新项目,这个新项目非常重要,给他们带来了2.9亿美元的收入,这只是第一年的收入。但是我们无法做同样的事,我们不能指望家庭娱乐中心市场也是这样。在家庭娱乐中心市场,我们要做的是提供多元化服务,不断进行新尝试,把事情做好来吸引回头客。我们怎么吸引他们回来?这是推动我们前进的唯一力量。因此,我们研究人口特征,不断地创造商业价值。

27:16—30:03

Again, the other request that I have is I want a IP; I want a Sonic; I want a Minion; I want a universal thing; I want a, you know Angry Bird something and everything. IPs are great. IPs are great because they give you visibility. Your customers know about the product immediately. You tell everybody you are doing an Angry Bird theme park. Your customers are already looking forward to it. This is again great if you are doing a visitor attraction that can attract more than three, four million customers a year easily, new customers a year… every year. Then those sort of IPs are great. If not, for especially for indoor amusement projects, 5,000, 6,000, 3,000 square meter projects. If you are going to be IP based, you have to think how many brands are there in the IP? How many elements can I customize on that IP? What is the cost of customization of those elements from an IP perspective? And how easily can I upgrade it? I know for already the IP project in Dubai. When that IP project opened, when it first opened, the attractions they had was already from Japan and the technology inside that attraction was already five years old. Today, that FEC is open for ten years with the same attraction. So the attraction, in fact, is 15 years old. So our customers have changed the kind of vision. We didn't have LED screens like this before. We had a simple projector showing us what we saw. The resolution has changed; people have changed; everything has changed. But the cost of upgrading that attraction to a new attraction will cost my customer three million dollars. In FEC environment can we invest three million dollars into one attraction? We can't, because we are catering to the same people over and over again. But maybe in a Disneyland kind of the environment if I am in the best shopping mall attracting hundred million visitors a year, maybe I can. So your choice of IP or non-IP based should be based on this logic on what is my investment, how upgradable is the IP, how regularly can I get it, how many machines or rides do I have based on that IP. You know it would be nice to go like the Aeon people, open, you know, four hundred locations across the, you know, across Pan-Asia to a large extent because they have become a brand by themselves. They don't need some of the IP. They have created their own IP and they have successfully managed to expand.

另一个要求是我想要一个IP，我想要索尼克，我想要小黄人，我想要世界知名的东西，我想要愤怒的小鸟等等。IP很好，因为可以吸引眼球。顾客能够立刻了解到您的产品。当您告诉所有人自己正在做愤怒的小鸟主题乐园，您的客户就已经满心期待。如果您做的娱乐项目可以每年新增超过三四百万的游客，那么IP对您来说也是一件好事。否则，对于只有几千平方米的室内游乐项目就不适合购买IP。如果大家要IP化，就要知道IP有多少品牌？需要定制多少元素？定制那些IP元素的成本是多少？升级的难易度怎么样？我了解迪拜的IP项目。第一次开业的时候，他们的娱乐设施是从日本引进的，娱乐设施的技术也有5年历史了。今天，家庭娱乐中心开业十年了，娱乐设施还是不变，所以这批娱乐设施已经用了15年。我们的顾客已经改变了观念。以前没有像这样的LED屏，只要简单的投影仪就可以向我们展示产品。现在分辨率、顾客等等一切也都发生了变化。升级娱乐设施的成本是300万美元。在家庭娱乐中心，我们可以投资300万美元到一个娱乐设施吗？当然不能，因为我们的客户群体没有改变。可能像迪士尼这样的游乐园或顶级购物中心，每年能吸引上亿游客，这样做也许可行。是否IP化应该考虑投资额是多少，IP升级的空间有多大，升级的频率有多高，有多少娱乐设施要IP化。如果能像永旺一样运营就很好了。永旺在泛亚地区开了400家分店，因为他们本身就是大品牌。他们不需要其他IP，因为他们创造了自己的IP，并且成功扩展了这些业务。

30:04—31:22

Creating the entertainment mix is a really, really important strategy. It's always a question in the next graph you will see a bit more about creating the entertainment mix. What do I need to have more of? One of the things I said earlier was the fact that we are all about the real estate space. In many FEC operations that I see here, they have 20 basketballs, 15 basketballs, all lined up each other. Yes, they are very, very popular. Have you ever tried removing ten of them instead of twenty? You make only ten basketballs. What happens to the revenue? Let's say 20 basketballs made 10,000 RMB. Do ten basketballs means 5,000 RMB? Or to do ten basketballs means 8,000 RMB? If you do this analysis, you will then know that the real estate space taken by the other ten basketballs is not worth it. You'd rather have ten basketballs with 8,000 RMB than 20 basketballs with 10,000 RMB because in that space you can bring something different and dynamic.

创造娱乐项目组合是一项非常重要的策略。在下一张图中，大家可以了解到更多这方面的信息。我还需要什么？我之前说过我们需要房地产的场地空间。许多家庭娱乐中心有20台或15台并排的篮球机，非常受欢迎。大家有没有试过去掉10台而不是20台篮球机呢？如果您只留10台篮球机，您的收入会怎样？如果说20台篮球机能挣1万块人民币，10台就意味着能挣5,000或8,000块人民币吗？如果按照这样分析，您就会知道另外10台篮球机不值得去占用地方。宁愿用10台篮球机挣8,000块也不要用20台篮球机挣一万块，因为您可以腾出空间放不一样的娱乐设施。

31:22—34:48

When choosing, what type of entertainment machines I need to have? You need to understand that this ratio and relationship between games, playground systems, toddler play areas and attractions, possibly F&B. When a consumer walks in, you have to think about the player. But you also have to think about who's paying the bill. Many a times, when we are dealing with a 12-year-old and below, the person paying the bills is the parent. If your entertainment concept turns out to be too expensive for the parent, the parent will not bring their child back again the next time. They probably take them for a movie, buy them a popcorn, buy them a slushie that actually work out cheaper than going to an entertainment facility. Because when they come into the entertainment facility, they would always think that "Oh my god, if I go in there and I am going to spend lots of RMB. I would rather not take my son there." So in selecting your entertainment equipment, you have to select those things that make money for you, and those things that can keep your customer inside your facility for a longer time. You need to have a balance of both, because children today are very smart. Everybody talks about education and entertainment, education and entertainment. We do a lot of education and entertainment. Children, these days in school, do the same. Education has become fun even at school, lots of schools, right? Do they necessarily want to come into your entertainment facility sit down all day and paint? Some of them do, most of them don't. They really want to play games; they really want to run around; they really want to be themselves. So there is a ratio. The educational aspect is to bring the parents in; the entertainment aspect is to keep the children in. So this is something that you really need to understand and your operations strategy needs to be derived around that. And many times, we like to target a good return of investment. Now how do you do this? We understand from a market what is it that we will spend. What is it that my demographic and my customers will feel comfortable spending? Is it five dollars per visit? Is it seven dollars per visit? Is it twenty dollars per visit? And then we make it affordable for all. For that twenty dollars, how can I keep it in my entertainment facility for two hours or one and a half hours whatever you target per visit? Accordingly, I then decide what sort of amusement equipment do I need to have inside my facility. And then I catch all my staff and I tell them "Look, guys. we're working on a strategy of ten dollars per consumer per spend. Now here is an incentive. If you're able to do the upsizing of the meal like McDonalds do and everything else, how do I get the extra two dollars out of them without them realizing? Many a times, you, otherwise, is significantly influenced when you get that extra two dollars instead of making your money in three years, you probably make them in two years because of the extra two dollars you got. But at the same time, you've kept your consumer happy at all times.

　　选择合适的娱乐设施时，您需要了解这个比例以及游戏、游乐场、幼童游玩区与其他场所，例如餐饮区之间的关系。当一位顾客入场时，您需要考虑到玩家是谁。但是也需要想到是谁来买单。在大多数时候，我们的客人是12岁或以下的儿童，付款的人通常是家长。如果您的娱乐设施对他们来说太贵了的话，那么下次父母可能就不会带孩子来了。家长可能会带孩子去看电影，给他们买爆米花或思乐雪冰沙，这些都要比去娱乐场所来得便宜。因为他们进入到一个娱乐设施中时，就会想到："老天啊，如果我进去了，那得花好多钱。那我宁愿别带儿子进去了。"所以在选择娱乐设施的时候，各位应该选择那些可以赚钱的设施或者可以让您的顾客停留更久的那种设施。现在的孩子可是非常聪明的，所以您需要在其中找到平衡。每个人都会谈到教育和娱乐这两件事。我们事实上也将两者紧密联系起来。今天，孩子们在学校也是寓教于乐。教育在学校也变得更加有趣了，很多学校都是如此，不是吗？所以孩子们会真的想进入娱乐设施后，一整天都坐在那儿静静地画画吗？有些孩子可能想，有些可能不这么想。他们真正想做的是玩游戏；他们想要跑来跑去，放飞自我。所以这里就出现这样一个比例，教育的部分是吸引家长的，而娱乐的部分是留住孩子的。所以各位要明白这个道理，并据此来制定自己的运作策略。很多时候，我们的目标都是丰厚的回报。那要怎么做到呢？我们要根据市场来进行投资。要如何才能让我的目标人群和顾客们觉得花钱也是舒心的呢？是应该定价每张门票5美元？还是7美元、20美元呢？我们需要让所有人都付得起钱。如果是20美元的话，我要怎么在不管定价多少的基础上，让顾客在我的设施里留一个半或两个小时呢？只有想清楚，我才能决定在设施中应该购置什么样的娱乐设备。我会召集所有的员工，然后告诉他们："各位员工，现在我们的策略是每次让顾客消费10美元。"我们可以为顾客提供奖励。如果大家可以像麦当劳和其它餐厅那样做套餐升级的话，我们要怎么让他们不知不觉多花两美元呢？在很多情况下，那额外的两美元对您影响很大，您不需要三年时间才能回本。如果可以每天多赚两美元的话，您可能两年就回本了。同时，您还得让顾客一直保持好心情。

34:48—36:29

You know, here is an interesting graph, and I've sort of seen this with pretty much FECs, I did compare a lot of numbers with some of the Chinese operators here also in Austin. How does it work? We look at... lots of our operator on debit card system where it's easy for us to get these data. Many of you operate on tokens or debit card system? Today, tokens or cards, how do you operate? You operate tokens? Do you use tokens to operate or do you use a card system? Both? OK. With a card system we get significant data, and today, every, almost for all businesses including the likes of Apple and all of the big corporations, even companies like WahLap should be doing this. In the fact that you analyze what did your customers buy? How long did they stay? How long is it my customers? So data analytics is a very, very important subject. When we did that data analytics of this, we found out typically how does a customer spend his time in an FEC. 47% of the time, he was on amusement rides. 13% of the time, he was in playground systems, toddler-play areas and things like that, 11% of the time, he played video games, 21% of the time, redemption games, 8% of the time with novelty games and carnival games, games where you throw something and win a prize that those sort of games.

这儿有一张有趣的图。我也发现很多家庭娱乐中心都符合这个统计结果。我对比了许多中国与奥斯汀的家庭娱乐中心。这是怎么运作的呢？我们看看……我们有许多运营商都使用储值卡系统，所以我们很容易就拿到这些数据。在座各位有多少用代币或储值卡系统运作的？现在，大家如何用代币或者储值卡运作呢？你们是用代币吗？是用代币去运作还是储值卡？两者兼有？好的。有了储值卡系统，我们就会获取重要的数据。而今天几乎每一家公司，包括苹果或者其他大公司，比如说华立科技，都是要收集数据的。事实上，您需要分析顾客买了什么？他们留在那儿多长时间？那属于我的顾客又留在娱乐设施多久了呢？因此数据分析是一个非常重要的问题。当我们完成像这样的数据分析时，就会找出一位顾客通常是怎样在家庭娱乐中心分配时间的。玩机动游戏的时间占47%。使用游乐场、幼童游玩区以及其他类似设施的时间占13%。玩电子游戏的时间占11%，还有21%的时间会用在有奖游戏上，8%的时间花在新奇的游戏和嘉年华游戏上，这类游戏是那种可以通过投掷来赢得奖品的游戏。

36:29—39:00

When we looked at how the revenue allocates, on the revenue side, we only have 23% from attractions, even though 47% of the time was spent on attractions, only 23% gain on its revenue. Even though 29% of the time was spent on redemption games, we got almost close to 53% of our revenue from redemption games. So typically, when we are designing an entertainment facility, we would put a nice ride in the middle, and surround that with many good-looking games. So that this child is going on the ride, he is looking at all the games and he's being influenced to play them. Now, attractions such as rides, rope courses, trampoline parks anything else that you want to call it as an attraction, they give you dwell time, they help you keep your customers in for a longer time. But games give back a lot more to the customer. Today, all of our customers want rewards. One of the reasons, redemption games, particularly in these days, have grown in popularity. Because children think they win tickets and they can exchange those tickets for prizes, so much like the Happy Meal of McDonald's, the happy meal sells week after week because they give away something. Customers want prizes and therefore would play for it. And that graph clearly indicates so the… by chart they clearly indicate that customers want to spend their money on that. So here is on the attraction site, is where on the playground, is where you have value for the parent, between the redemption, video, and novelty games as where you have your profits hidden. If you run that operation properly, you can be significantly successful. You know, I want to keep this brief, because, you know, my gentleman who is seated next to me is the next speaker. I want to make sure that I finish as quickly so that he takes over next. So, the key takeaways from what I am really trying to convey is that always know your customer, understand your customer, relate to your customer, ensure that your customer knows you care. Get active on social media, try to know them even more, know their spending habits and then plan your FEC.

当我们看收入配比时，23%的收入来自娱乐设施，即使47%的时间是用在娱乐设施上的，然而只占收入的23%。即使顾客在有奖品游戏上只花了29%的时间，我们却从中获得了53%的收入。我们设置娱乐项目时，在中间放一个机动游戏，旁边再放一些好玩的游戏。因此，小朋友在玩游戏时，他会看到其他的游戏，就都想去玩。现在各种机动游戏，比如绳索游戏、蹦床，或者其他您称之为娱乐项目的游戏，它们能让顾客花更多时间在里面，但是游戏又会给顾客很多奖励。现在大家都想要奖励。有奖游戏变得越来越受欢迎的一大原因就是孩子们认为可以得到票券然后兑换礼物，就像麦当劳的开心乐园餐一样，它每周都卖得很好，因为顾客可以拿到奖励。顾客想要奖励就会去买。这个图清楚地显示顾客想在那上面花钱。所以，这些娱乐设施、游乐场对于父母来说是有价值的，有奖游戏、视频游戏、新颖游戏都是有隐含利润的。如果各位能够合理的经营，就会很成功。我不想讲太长时间，因为坐在我身边的是下一位演讲嘉宾，我想快点结束，让他赶紧上台。所以我想传达的主要观点就是了解、理解自己的顾客，与他们建立联系，确保自己的顾客知道他们受重视。在社交媒体上保持活跃，尝试着更多了解顾客的消费习惯，然后相应地规划自己的家庭娱乐中心。

39:02—40:05

Big is always not the best. Sometimes, a big name, you know, be the Transformer or something, be something else is great when you bring it. What's the cost of the license that you are going to pay? What is it going to do for you? How repeatedly do you need to change it? How easy is it for you to get an update on it? Sometimes, simple stuff, in terms of, you know, having a hammer hitting on something can make a lot more money for you. So it's a question of your understanding: What is there? A lot of the times, with redemption operations particularly as you saw on the previous graph, you know, redemption, novelty, carnival is what makes all the money for you. It makes money for you because customers get something back, right? So if you don't give something back, the customers also never come in there and put you money. In order for you to bring your customers back, run a very successful redemption operation where you're able to give you a lot back to the customer. The more you give, the more they'll come back and play.

名声大并不意味着最好。有时候一个响当当的名字，如变形金刚或者其他的大品牌，在您引进的时候是好的。那您要交多少版权费呢？引进之后可以为您带来什么？您要多久改变一次？升级容易吗？有时候，一些小东西，就是用锤子敲敲打打也可以赚钱。所以大家要想明白的一个问题就是：那里有什么？很多时候，在有奖游戏中，特别是在上一个图中，大家也可以看到，有奖品游戏、新颖游戏和嘉年华游戏可以帮大家赚钱。为您赚钱是因为顾客得到了一些奖品，对吗？如果您不给顾客提供奖品，顾客就不会来消费。为了吸引回头客，您就得经营一个成功的有奖游戏，给顾客很多奖品。您给的越多，回头客就更多。

40:06—42:10

Structure your business model to succeed, negotiate the rent right. Tell the shopping mall operator, "Look, you have toilets in your shopping mall, correct?" He would say, "Yes." "Do you charge for toilets?" He would say, "No." "Do you pay for rents for toilets?" "No." "We are as important as toilets to shopping mall." People don't go… A survey done in the United States across seven big malls, said that the cleanliness of the toilet and the facilities that they have in the toilet influences where the shoppers go. And a lot of mothers said, "Where do I have, where is my child best entertained that is where I go." The father said the same, and they all said, "because both me and my wife were working on the weekend, we spend time with our kids and they influence where we go." And where will the child go? The child always wants to go to a facility where he's made to feel like the king, where he or she is made to feel important. So structure your business model around that. Everybody wants something more. Everybody wants a wide range of stuff. So please don't try to put ten air hockeys, because they take up a lot of space. Don't try to put 25 fishing games and use up your real estate space. Your real estate space is important to you. Don't calculate your revenue as revenue per store, calculate your revenue as revenue per square feet. For each square foot of your space that you have is important for you. How are you maximizing this? Do you have the right variety to get that extra hundred RMB from your customers into your machines or into your rides? That is really really important.

打造成功的商业模式并且把租金谈妥。您问购物中心的运营商："商场里面有洗手间，对吗？"他会说："是的。"您接着问："洗手间收费吗？"他说："不收钱。"您又问："洗手间需要收租金吗？"他说："不收。"那么您就可以说："我们就像洗手间一样重要。"美国做了一份研究，调查了7家大商场。研究表明洗手间的卫生情况和里面的设施影响商场的人流量。很多妈妈反映说："孩子哪里玩得最开心，我就去哪里。"很多爸爸也是这么说，他们反映说："平时我们夫妻俩都要上班，只有周末能陪陪孩子。孩子影响我们出行的选择。"那么孩子会去哪里玩呢？他们想去那种能让他们感到像小皇帝一样的地方，能让他们找到存在感。所以您的商业模式得围绕这个展开。所有客户都想享受更多、更多样的服务。所以千万不要放置10种空气曲棍球，因为这样太占空间。不要设置25种钓鱼游戏，占用自己的租地面积。租地面积对您来说很重要。不要光计算每家店铺的收益，要计算每平方英尺的收益。每一平方英尺都很重要，您要思考怎样实现利益最大化？产品是否足够多元化，是否能够让顾客多花100块钱玩您的机器或者机动游戏？这些都非常重要。

42:10—44:59

At the same time, remember with VR. You know, we are already as a business, we're already competing with the whole entertainment market in a big way. There're Internet games, there're VR games, there're console gaming, there are pirated DVDs, there are pirated games. We are competing with all of that. Somebody came and told me, "Oh, VR is going to take over; our business is dead." Is it? But how? You know, I sit down with four of my friends on a Storm Racer G. And we were all racing. I went the first race and my friend wants to have another race with me. And we look at each

第九单元 动漫娱乐 Animation and Entertainment

other and then say, "Wow, that was great, I want to do this again." And we get the next coin in. But VR… headsets and then I'm going to walk around. I'm gonna to be doing my stuff, and how am I connecting? How am I engaging? VR is still not so social; VR will come. There is a time for VR as the technology gets evolved and VR will come in. But until that time, believe it or not, the most simple thing in your entertainment center always makes more money than any other center, than any of the highly technological product. I don't know how many of you have this game. There are many versions of it, called Treasure Quest or Big Bass Wheel. You know, I have a location inside the Atlantis Hotel on the Palm Jumeriah in Dubai. One machine Big Bass Wheel that costs 13,500 dollars. Every year makes half a million dollars for me, just one amusement machine. And all the customer does it. He hits the handle; it spins and it stops at the ticket value. That's it. And I have seen this all my 23 years in the amusement business: The simpler, the better. The more simple it is, the more easy it is in the customer's eyes. At the same time, I'm also saying this for a lot of the manufacturers. It could be cultural. But at the same time, I do wish to say this. Sometimes manufacturers do too much to a game. They put so many features into a game. They give kids ten buttons to press. The size is cheating me. The child doesn't understand all of that. They're just showing there to have a good time. The more simpler you can manufacture your products do in terms of game play, when the customer looks at it, he should understand how to play the game, and how can I score big in this game. The more you can look at it from that perspective, the more winners will you create, and therefore, your operations will be very very successful. I hope you'll find what I say informative. I thank you very much for giving me the opportunity. Thanks!

与此同时，还有VR。我们娱乐中心已经和整个娱乐市场展开了竞争。我们还得和网络游戏、VR游戏、单机游戏、盗版DVD、盗版游戏竞争。有人走来跟我说："唉，VR要取代我们了，我们要没落了。"是吗？怎么个没落法？那时候我和4个朋友一起玩雷动G赛车。我拿了第一名，我的朋友想要再玩一局。我们看着对方说："哇塞，太好玩了。我还想玩。"我们又投了一枚游戏币，但是戴着VR头显走来走去，我也要做自己的事情，但是我怎么和其他人互动呢？怎么交流呢？VR的互动性不是那么强，但是VR时代将会来临。随着技术不断发展，VR时代也将迎来自己的时代。在那之前，不管各位信不信，娱乐中心最简单的东西赚取的利润会超过其他中心和高科技产品。我不知道你们有多少人玩过这个游戏，它有很多个版本，叫寻宝或者大转轮。我在迪拜的朱美拉棕榈岛亚特兰蒂斯酒店内有一个娱乐中心。有个机器大转轮耗费了13,500美元，每年能给我带来50万美元收入。这还只是一个游戏设施而已。每一个顾客都会玩。操纵手柄，机器会旋转，然后停在票值上。就是这样。过去23年我在这一行明白了一个道理：越简单，越好。越简单，顾客就越容易上手。我也对很多制造商说过，可能每个地方情况不一样。但是同时，我真想说有些制造商把游戏做得太复杂，给游戏设置太多功能，让孩子按十个按钮，尺寸太大了。孩子根本不知道怎么玩，他们来到这里只是想玩得开心而已。游戏设计得越简单，孩子看到一款游戏时，就知道怎么玩，怎么拿高分。如果大家多从这个角度思考的话，就会有更多的游戏赢家，各位的运营也会更顺利。我希望在座各位能有所收获，感谢大家让我有机会发表演讲。谢谢大家！

II. 实战练习二

1. 演讲背景

紫水鸟影视的制片主任应邀参加"东莞动漫展高峰会"并发表主旨演讲，她在演讲中介绍了公司的基本情况以及作品，包括《珍妮与龙》《太空娃娃》《雷鸟神机队出发》《天赋异人》，同时还介绍了自己作为制片人参与制作的多个作品，分享了官方合拍的好处和经验。

2. 预习词汇

Pukeko Pictures 紫水鸟影视公司
Head of Production 制片主任；制作总监
co-production 国际合作拍片
entertainment production company 娱乐节目制作公司
contractual equity 合同股权
New Zealand screen industry grant system 新西兰影视业补贴制度
Weta Workshop 维塔工作室
Miramar Peninsula in Wellington, New Zealand 新西兰惠灵顿密拉马半岛
Portsmouth TV 朴茨茅斯电视公司
Park Road Post 公园路后期制作公司
Lord of Rings《魔戒》；《指环王》
The Hobbit《霍比特人》
Weta Digital 维塔数码
Stone Street Studios 石街工作室
Avatar《阿凡达》
co-founder 联合创始人
co-owner 共同所有人
Academy Award 奥斯卡奖
British Academy of Film and Television Award 英国电影和电视艺术学院奖

第九单元 动漫娱乐 Animation and Entertainment

Knight Companion of the New Zealand Order of Merit 新西兰一等功骑士勋章
Thunderbirds《雷鸟神机队》
Thunderbirds Are Go《雷鸟神机队出发》
Jane and the Dragon《珍妮与龙》
Fifty the Tractor《拖拉机50号》
The WotWots《太空娃娃》
Cleverman《天赋异人》
Executive Producer 执行制片人
Chief Creative Officer 首席创意官
illustrator 插画家
motion capture 动作捕捉
steam-powered spaceship 蒸汽宇宙飞船
preschooler 学龄前儿童
live-action background 真人实景
CGI animation 电脑生成动画技术
live-action model sets 真人实景模型
creative and technical excellence 原创和技术优势
licensing programme 授权计划
CG（Computer Graphics）计算机视觉设计
CGCG 中国西基动画创意学院
Primetime Drama Series 黄金时段播出的电视剧
factual 纪实片
documentary 纪录片
comedy 喜剧片
animation 动画片
drama 话剧；电视剧
Production Accountant 制片会计
Drama Co-production Executive 电视剧联合制作总监
satirical puppet show 讽刺木偶剧
Spitting Image《一模一样》
Peter and the Wolf《彼得与狼》
European Chamber Orchestra 欧洲管弦乐团
short film 短片
feature film 长片
The Full Monty《一脱到底》
Slumdog Millionaire《贫民窟的百万富翁》

This Is Not a Love Song《这不是一首情歌》
Mrs Ratcliffe's Revolution《老娘闹革命》
Kevin & Perry Go Large《蒲精放暑假》
The Escapist《逃亡》
Hustle《飞天大盗》
Trainspotting《猜火车》
Four Weddings and a Funeral《四个婚礼和一个葬礼》
Secrets & Lies《秘密与谎言》
Sword of Honour《荣誉之剑》
Fever Pitch《极度狂热》
Hilary & Jackie《她比烟花寂寞》
The Theory of Everything《万物理论》
Show of Hands《举手表决》
Heavenly Creatures《罪孽天使》
Two and A Half Men《好汉两个半》
Apron Strings《家事美人》
Separation City《男人的真相》
Hercules and Xena《战士公主西娜》
Bad Taste《宇宙怪客》
The Frighteners《恐怖幽灵》
King Kong《金刚》
Not Only But Always《不仅总是》
top class crew and cast 顶级的剧组
post production 后期制作
main cast 主要演员
set build 场景建设
minor cast 配角
co-production agreement 合拍协议
Weight of Elephants《大象的重量》
Slow West《西部慢调》
official co-production status 官方合拍资格
Screen Production Grant 影视制作补贴
cash grant 现金补贴
Aboriginal mythology 原住民神话
VFX 视觉效果
sound design 音效

creature work 道具造型
crew to produce hair and prosthetics 制作头发和负责修补工作的人员
funding body 资助机构
international premiere 国际首映式
creative 创意人员
look of the show 作品的外观
production schedule 制作进度

3. 演讲文本

00:00—00:33

Greetings. my name is Angela Littlejohn and 2 years ago I was privileged to join the award-winning team at Pukeko Pictures created in partnership by Sir Richard Taylor, Tania Rodger and Martin Baynton. I am a producer and head of production of Pukeko Pictures and I will be sharing with you my life as a producer as well as my experience in international co-production.

大家好！我叫 Angela Littlejohn。两年前我很荣幸加入了由 Richard Taylor 先生、Tania Rodger 女士和 Martin Baynton 先生共同创立的紫水鸟影视旗下的获奖团队。我是一个制片人，也是紫水鸟影视的制片主任。我想和大家分享我作为制片人的生活以及我的国际合拍经验。

00:37—01:46

Let me talk a little about Pukeko Pictures and its creators Sir Richard Taylor, Tania Rodger and Martin Baynton. Pukeko Pictures is an independent entertainment production company focused on the development and production of world-class, multi-platform entertainment for a global audience. Pukeko Pictures takes a contractual equity position on the properties we produce through direct investment and through the renowned New Zealand screen industry grant system. Pukeko Pictures, with a connection to the world-famous Weta Workshop, is a world-leading entertainment company, harnessing the best in global talent and world-class production processes.

让我简单介绍一下紫水鸟影视公司以及公司创始人 Richard Taylor 先生、Tania Rodger 女士和 Martin Baynton 先生。紫水鸟影视是一家独立娱乐制作公司，主要发展和制作面向全球观众的世界级、多平台的娱乐作品。通过直接投资和为人熟知的新西兰影视业补贴制度，紫水鸟影视以合同股权的方式管理我们制作的作品。紫水鸟影视和世界著名的维塔工作室紧密联系，是全球领先的娱乐公司，掌握着最优质的世界人才和一流摄制流程。

01:47—03:00

Based on the Miramar Peninsula in Wellington, New Zealand, Pukeko Pictures is part of this network of creative companies and home of some of the world's finest filmmaking talent and technology. The companies include Weta Workshop, which is owned by Sir Richard Taylor and Peter Jackson; Portsmouth TV which is another company owned by Sir Richard Taylor and Peter Jackson which supplies world class equipment and lighting; Park Road Post, which is Peter Jackson's world-class postproduction facility that he has made his famous films *Lord of Rings* and *The Hobbit*; Weta Digital, which is the world famous digital affix company and Stone Street Studios, which has housed the world famous *Lord of the Rings*, *Avatar*, and various other big productions.

位于新西兰惠灵顿密拉马半岛的紫水鸟影视是这个创意公司群的一部分，拥有世界顶尖的制片人才和技术。公司群包括 Richard Taylor 先生和 Peter Jackson 先生的维塔工作室；还有他们名下另外一家提供世界一流设备与灯光的公司，朴茨茅斯电视公司；公园路后期制作公司，Peter Jackson 先生将这家公司精湛的后期技术用于他的著名电影《指环王》和《霍比特人》；维塔数码，世界著名的数码技术公司；还有石街工作室，这家公司制作了全球著名的《指环王》《阿凡达》及其他大片。

03:06—04:26

Richard Taylor is the co-founder and co-owner of Pukeko Pictures and Weta workshop. Richard began Pukeko Pictures with his wife Tania Rodger and Partner Martin Baynton due to their combined love of children's television and the desire to deliver highly compelling programming through the medium of locally-made high quality television to children globally. Richard has won numerous awards for his endeavours and film and television including five Academy Awards and four British Academy of Film and Television Awards. In 2010, he was awarded a Knight Companion of the New Zealand Order of Merit for his services to film. Richard started Weta Workshop over 28 years ago with Tania as it was their dream to establish a special effects facility to enhance and support the New Zealand film and television industry. Richard has been working in China for the past 17 years and brings a strong working relationship with the Chinese creative industry to his endeavours at Pukeko Pictures.

Richard Taylor 先生是紫水鸟影视公司和维塔工作室的创始人和共同拥有人之一。他和妻子 Tania Rodger 女士，还有合伙人 Martin Baynton 先生创立紫水鸟影视公司是因为他们都热爱儿童影视，并且希望通过国产高质量的电视媒介为全球小朋友带来精彩的节目。Richard 以其对影视界的贡献获得了很多的奖项，包括5项奥

第九单元 动漫娱乐 Animation and Entertainment

斯卡奖，4项英国电影和电视艺术学院奖。2010年，他凭借对电影的贡献荣获新西兰一等功骑士勋章。Richard和Tania在28年前创立维塔工作室，创立一个特效设施来促进和支持新西兰影视业是他们夫妻俩的梦想。Richard已经在中国工作了17年，极大地促进了紫水鸟影视公司和中国创意产业之间的紧密工作联系。

04:27—05:35

A life-long *Thunderbirds* fan, Richard is the Executive Producer of the new series *Thunderbirds Are Go* which is sold over 40 countries internationally. Martin Baynton is the co-owner of Pukeko Pictures and Chief Creative Officer where he leads the creative and development teams to build the Pukeko Pictures' properties from conception through to production and beyond. He has an international reputation as a writer and illustrator of more than 30 children's books including *Jane and the Dragon*, and *Fifty the Tractor* series. Since it was first published in 1986, the *Jane and the Dragon* book series has never been out of print. He created the *Jane and The Dragon* TV series based on his books and co-created *The WotWots* with Richard Taylor. He is the executive producer on our latest drama series called *Cleverman*.

作为《雷鸟神机队》的忠实粉丝，Richard执行监制了新系列的《雷鸟神机队出发》，并在全球40多个国家上映。Martin Baynton是紫水鸟影视公司的其中一位共同拥有人和首席创意官。他带领创意发展团队创作属于紫水鸟影视的资产，包括概念、作品的制作等等。他是世界著名的作家和插画家，著有30多部儿童读物，包括《珍妮与龙》和《拖拉机50号》系列。自1986年出版以来，《珍妮与龙》系列丛书从未绝版。以他的书为原型，他创造了《珍妮与龙》电视剧，还和Richard Taylor共同创造了《太空娃娃》。他也是最近播出的《天赋异人》系列剧的执行制片人。

05:45—08:01

Now, let me just talk a bit about some of our shows. *Jane and the Dragon* is the award-winning CG, motion capture animated series and is co-produced by Weta Workshop and Nelvana Limited in Canada. *Jane and the Dragon* follows the adventure and comedic exploits of Jane, an adolescent girl training to be a knight and her friend, Dragon, a talking, flying, 300-year-old, fire-breathing dragon. The series is based on the books of the same name by Martin Baynton. *TheWotWots*. Two friendly aliens traveling in a steam-powered spaceship explore Earth in this series for preschoolers. Made for kids, the show's computer-animated characters are seamlessly integrated into live-action backgrounds. It has aired in over 100 territories. We are currently working with China on a spinoff of *The WotWots* called the *Space Kiddets*. *Thunderbirds Are Go* is a co-production between Pukeko Pictures and ITV Studios produced using a unique mix of CGI animation and live-action model sets. Showcasing Pukcko Pictures and Weta Workshop's ground-breaking creative and technical excellence, it delivers a whole new level of action-adventure animation for today's audience whilst also affectionately paying tribute to the legacy of model locations from the classic 1960s series. *Thunderbirds Are Go* has been broadcast in over 40 countries worldwide and has an extensive licensing program, and it is a truly global production with writing being done in the USA, design and asset CG built in New Zealand, character animation with CGCG in China and post production in the UK. *Cleverman* is our current show we are producing. It's Pukeko's first prime time drama series. I would take you through the show later in my talk.

现在让我稍微介绍一下我们的作品。《珍妮与龙》是一部使用了电脑动画和动作捕捉的获奖动画片,由维塔工作室和加拿大 Nelvana 公司共同制作。《珍妮与龙》讲述珍妮和龙的冒险和有趣壮举。珍妮是一个训练有素的年轻骑士,而她的朋友是一条已经 300 岁并且会讲话、会飞、会喷火的龙。这个系列改编自 Martin Baynton 的同名丛书。《太空娃娃》是关于两个有爱的外星人乘坐蒸汽动力的飞船探索地球的故事。这个系列是面向学龄前儿童的。在这个专为儿童打造的系列里,电脑生成的角色完美嵌入实景环境。这个系列已经传入 100 多个国家和地区。我们正在和中国打造《太空娃娃》的续集,中文名字也叫《太空娃娃》。《雷鸟神机队出发》由紫水鸟影视公司和英国 ITV 工作室共同制作完成,独特地混合了电脑生成动画技术和真人实景模型。它展现了紫水鸟影视公司和维塔工作室极具开拓性的原创和技术优势,为今天的观众诠释了全新水平的动作冒险动画片,同时表达了对 20 世纪 60 年代经典同名电视系列剧经典拍摄遗迹的真挚敬意。《雷鸟神机队出发》已经在全球 40 多个国家播出,并且有大量节目授权计划。它是货真价实的世界性作品,美国负责书面剧本,新西兰负责设计计算机视觉设计用的相关软硬件设备,中国西基动画创意学院负责角色动画,而英国负责后期制作。《天赋异人》是我们目前正在创作的剧。它是紫水鸟影视公司首个黄金时段播出的电视剧。待会儿我带大家一起欣赏一下这部剧。

08:05—10:27

A little bit about myself. I have been working in the TV and film industry for over 25 years, working in all aspects of production and covering all genres. I have worked in factual, documentary, comedy, animation and drama. Prior to joining Pukeko Pictures in 2014, I worked as an independent producer in the film and television industry. From 1986 to 2000, I worked in the UK film and television industry as a production accountant, production manager, producer and finally for six years as drama co-production executive at Channel 4 and Film 4. I worked for a number of years on the famous British satirical puppet show *Spitting Image* whose creator Roger Law's work was one of Richard Taylor's main inspirations behind his award-winning workshop at Weta Workshop. During this period, we made *Peter and the Wolf*, a retelling of the Prokofiev Fantasy narrated by Sting with music from the European Chamber Orchestra. I also worked on a number of TV shows with British comedians Steve Coogan, Jonathan Ross, Frank Skinner, Rob Newman and David Baddiel. At Channel 4 and Film 4, I mentored a lot of writers, producer and directors from short films through to feature films. Some of these filmmakers have gone on to write, produce and direct awarding winning films for example, such as Simon Beaufoy (*The Full Monty*, *Slumdog Millionaire*), Billie Eltringham (*This Us Not a Love Song*, *Mrs Ratcliffe's Revolution*) and Jolyon Simmonds (*Kevin & Perry Go Large*, *The Escapist* and *Hustle*). Other films made during my tenure were *Trainspotting*-director Danny Boyle, *Four Weddings and a Funeral*—starring Hugh Grant, *Secrets & Lies* - director Mike Leigh, *Sword of Honour* - starring Daniel Craig, *Fever Pitch* - Starring Colin Firth, Writer Nick Hornby and *Hilary & Jackie* starring Emily Watson and Rachel Griffiths.

简单介绍一下我自己。我已经在电视电影行业工作了25年多，做过制片的所有工作，涉及所有的影视题材。我做过纪实片、纪录片、喜剧片、动画片和电视剧。在2014年加入紫水鸟影视公司之前，我是影视界的独立制片人。1986年至2000年间，我在英国影视业做过制片会计、制片经理和制片人，最后在第四频道和第四电影频道做了长达6年的电视剧联合制作总监。我还为英国讽刺木偶剧《一模一样》工作过几年。这部剧的创作人Roger Law的作品是Richard Taylor先生的主要灵感之一，助力了他在维塔工作室的成就。在这段时间，我们创作了《彼得与狼》，这是普罗科菲耶夫狂想曲的旁白复述，由欧洲管弦乐团配乐。我还参与过很多电视剧，合作伙伴包括英国喜剧演员Steve Coogan, Jonathan Ross, Frank Skinner, Rob Newman和David Baddiel。在第四频道和第四电影频道时，我指导过很多作家、制片人、导演，包括短片和长片。其中一些电影制作人已经投身编剧、制片，还执导许多获奖电影，例如Simon Beaufoy的《一脱到底》和《贫民窟的百万富翁》，Billie Eltringham的《这不是一首情歌》和《老娘闹革命》，还有Jolyon Simmonds的《蒲精放暑假》《逃亡》和《飞天大盗》。我任期期间还参与制作过其他电影，包括Danny Boyle导演的《猜火车》，Hugh Grant主演的《四个婚礼和一个葬礼》，Mike Leigh导演的《秘密与谎言》，Daniel Craig主演的《荣誉之剑》，Colin Firth主演的、Nick Hornby所著的《极度狂热》，以及Emily Watson和Rachel Griffiths主演的《她比烟花寂寞》。

10:31—13:23

I returned to New Zealand in late 2000 as I wanted my children to experience the childhood I had growing up in New Zealand. I had also been following the huge success of Richard Taylor and Peter Jackson. We're having with the blockbuster trilogy *Lord of the Rings*. Having settled in Wellington, New Zealand I started to work with writers and directors on the ideas and scripts for both short films and feature films. I worked closely with them on helping shaping their scripts for the screen. Filmmaking is a collaborative process so I would encourage writer and directors to work with script editors to help make the best script possible. One of my proudest moments was seeing my writer, director Anthony McCarten of my very first feature I produced win the British Academy Film and Television Award last year for *The Theory of Everything*. He was also nominated for an Oscar in the 2015 Academy Awards. Another of my writers who I worked with in Britain during my tenure at Channel 4 won an Oscar at the Academy Awards for his adaptation of *Slumdog Millionaire*. I made *Show of Hands* with Anthony McCarten, starring Melanie Lynskey who starred in *Heavenly Creatures*, and the hit USA show *Two and A Half Men*, *Apron Strings* starring Laila Rouass and *Separation City* starring Joel Edgerton. As well as working closely with New Zealand filmmakers, I was keen to keep my relationships with the networks, with the UK television and film industry. On one of my trips back to the UK, I spoke with one of my UK drama producer friends about the amazing cast and crew I had experienced working in New Zealand. The cast and crew in New Zealand had gained their international experience working on TV shows like *Hercules and Xena* and Peter Jackson's films *Bad Taste*, *The Frighteners*, *Heavenly Creatures* as well as the Oscar winning *Lord of the Rings*, *King Kong* and *The Hobbit*. They have become one of the top-ranking crews internationally. We started talking about a TV show they were making for my old company Channel 4 in the UK called *Not Only but Always*. It was the story of famous British comedians Peter Cook and Dudley Moore. I described the locations that could be found in New Zealand to my producer friend who said New Zealand sounded a perfect place to come and film. Within a month the producer, director and his team were in New Zealand reckoning locations.

我于2000年底回到新西兰，因为我希望我的孩子们感受一下我在新西兰长大的童年。我也一直追随理查德·泰勒和彼得·杰克逊的成功脚步。我们创作出了成功的《指环王》三部曲。在新西兰惠灵顿定居后，我开始与编剧和导演合作，为短片和故事片构思和写剧本。我与他们密切合作，帮助他们打造电影剧本。电影制作是一个协作过程，所以我会鼓励编剧和导演与剧本编剧一起工作，齐心协力制作最好的剧本。我感到最骄傲的时刻就是看到我第一部作品的编剧兼导演安东尼·迈卡腾去年凭借《万物理论》获得了英国电影电视艺术学院奖。他还获得了2015年奥斯卡奖提名奖。我在第四频道任职期间合作的另一位英国作家因其改编了《贫民窟的百万富翁》而获得了奥斯卡奖。我与安东尼·迈卡腾合作了《举手表决》，由梅

第九单元　动漫娱乐 Animation and Entertainment

兰尼·林斯基主演的《罪孽天使》，热门美国节目《好汉两个半》，莱拉·罗斯主演的《家事美人》以及乔尔·埃哲顿主演的《男人的真相》。在与新西兰电影人密切合作的同时，我还积极维持与英国影视行业的同行人脉关系。在我返回英国的一次旅途中，我与我的一位英国影视制片人朋友谈到了我在新西兰遇到的出色的剧组。新西兰剧组在参与制作的电视节目如《战士公主西娜》和彼得·杰克逊的电影《宇宙怪客》《恐怖幽灵》《罪孽天使》以及获得奥斯卡金像奖的《指环王》《金刚》和《霍比特人》中获得了国际经验。他们已成为一支国际一流的剧组团队。我们开始谈论他们为我的老东家第四频道制作的一个电视节目，叫做《不仅总是》。这是关于英国著名喜剧演员彼得·库克和达德利·摩尔的故事节目。我把在新西兰可以找到的拍摄地点介绍给我的制作人朋友，他说新西兰听起来是一个拍电影的好地方。制片人、导演和他的团队用了一个月的时间在新西兰选址。

13:24—17:22

　　We managed to double New Zealand for many overseas locations such as London, Devon in the UK, Mallorca in Spain, the Caribbean, Los Angeles and New York in the USA. We were also able to find top class crew and cast. *Not Only But Always* was nominated for a BAFTA for best TV feature and won a BAFTA for Rhys Ifans for his portrayal of Peter Cook. This co-production between UK and New Zealand was totally reliant on two producers from each country, the UK and New Zealand, coming up with an agreement on what countries responsibilities would be. In the case of this TV show, the UK was responsible for the script, director, main cast and all the post production, New Zealand was responsible for all the shooting including all the locations, set builds and all the creative heads of department and minor cast. It is important to make sure when doing a co-production that both countries are absolutely clear about what the co-production duties of each country will be and outline this in a co-production agreement which I will talk about later. I then went on to work on a number of official and unofficial co-productions including *Separation City* which was a New Zealand/Australia co-production starring Joel Edgerton, *Weight of Elephants*, a New Zealand/Denish co-production, *Slow West*, a New Zealand/UK co-production starring Michael Fassbender and just recently the TV series *Cleverman* which was a New Zealand/Australian co-production. I just talk a little bit about official co-productions. Official co-productions are film and television projects made between New Zealand and other countries which we have a formal treaty agreement with. New Zealand has 17 official co-production treaties with other countries. This includes China. In China we have a film and a television co-production agreement, an official agreement. Official co-productions are an increasingly attractive option for many producers. There are numerous potential benefits including the sharing of creative and technical resources.

There are other benefits:
- access to local incentives and subsidies
- access to the domestic market of the other co-producer
- the ability to pool financial resources and share the financial risk
- the ability to deliver projects of a larger scale

In New Zealand, if you qualify for official co-production status you may also qualify for the New Zealand screen production grant. This grant is a 40% cash grant that forms part of the New Zealand Producers equity and is an important source of finance for a TV and films budget. It is calculated on the New Zealand spend as per criteria set. Productions must be an official co-production or qualify under the Significant New Zealand content test. There is also a cash grant available to larger international productions whose budget is in excess of New Zealand MYM15 million. This grant is equal to 20% of qualifying New Zealand spend.

我们设法使新西兰成为英国的伦敦、德文郡，西班牙的马略卡岛，加勒比海，美国的洛杉矶和纽约等许多海外地区的第二取景地。我们也能找到顶级的演员和剧组工作人员。《不仅总是》获得了英国电影电视艺术学院最佳电视长片奖提名，并且因为莱斯·伊凡斯生动地演绎了彼得·库克而获得了英国电影电视艺术学院奖。这部英国和新西兰的合拍片完全有赖于这两个国家（英国和新西兰）的两名制作人就双方的责任达成协议。在这个电视节目中，英国负责剧本、导演、主演选角和所有后期制作。新西兰负责所有拍摄，包括所有拍摄地点、场景建设以及部门的创意主管和配角选角。大家要记得重要的一点，那就是拍摄合拍片时，双方必须明确各自的义务，并要在合拍协议中清楚列明相关义务，这一点我后面会谈到。接下来我将接着讲一些官方和非官方合拍片，有新西兰/澳大利亚联合制作的、由乔尔·埃哲顿主演的《男人的真相》，新西兰/丹麦联合制作的《大象的重量》，新西兰/英国联合制作的、由迈克尔·法斯宾德主演的《西部慢调》，以及最近由新西兰/澳大利亚联合制作的电视剧《天赋异人》。我再稍微讲一讲官方合拍片。官方合拍片是新西兰与其他国家一起制作的电影和电视项目，我们与这些国家都签署了正式的条约协议。新西兰与其他国家有17个官方合拍片协议，其中包括中国。在中国，我们有一部电影和一部电视剧合拍协议，这是一份官方协议。官方合拍片对许多制片人来说越来越有吸引力。这有许多潜在的好处，其中就包括创意和技术资源的共享。

还有其他好处：
- 获得当地的奖励和补贴
- 更容易打入联合制片人的国内市场
- 能够融合财务资源并分担财务风险

第九单元 动漫娱乐 Animation and Entertainment

- 能够开展更大型的项目

在新西兰,如果您符合官方合拍资格,您就可能还有获得申请新西兰电影作品资助金的资格。这笔补贴是 40% 的现金补贴,它构成了新西兰制片人的部分股权,同时它还是影视作品预算的重要资金来源。它是根据在新西兰拍摄标准的开销进行计算的。影视作品必须要通过一项重要的新西兰内容测试。对于预算超过 1,500 万新西兰币的国际合拍项目,也是可以申请现金资助的,资助的金额相当于在新西兰拍摄花销的 20%。

17:30—20:27

One of the first productions, one of the first co-productions I was involved with when I joined Pukeko Pictures two years ago was a project called *Cleverman*. We were approached by Goalpost Pictures producers of the award-winning feature film *The Sapphires* directed by Wayne Blair. The six-part television drama series they brought to us had been developed by a young aboriginal filmmaker Ryan Griffinand and they were looking for a co-production partner to help finance and produce the series. Ironically despite Australia being our closest neighbour we were introduced to each other by a USA partner, thousands of miles away. *Cleverman* is a smart, sexy and startlingly original drama that sees a group of non-humans battling for survival in a world where humans feel increasingly inferior to them and want to silence, exploit and kill them. Central to the story is the story of two estranged indigenous brothers who are forced together to fight for their own survival. Other worldly creatures also emerge into this fragile and dangerous place in this action-packed new series. *Cleverman* was a perfect fit for us at Pukeko. The subject material based on aboriginal mythology meant there was a natural fit with our sister company. Weta Workshop producing the design and manufacture of our supernatural creatures and Peter Jackson's Park Road Postproviding visual effects, sound and music. All filming took place in Sydney, Australia. Weta Workshop provided all the creature work and crew to produce hair and prosthetics. All post production including visual effects, a lot with 3D visual effects performed in Wellington, New Zealand. The production was financed by ABC in Australia, Red Arrow International in Germany, Sundance TV in the USA, Goalpost in Australia and Pukeko Pictures with support from both the New Zealand and Australian Screen Grants and funding bodies. It has been sold to many countries and has had rave reviews. As well as airing on the ABC in Australia, Sundance TV in the US, TVNZ in New Zealand and the BBC in the UK next month. *Cleverman* made its international premiere at the Berlinale Special program at the Haus der Berliner, Festspiele and was selected to screen at the 2016 Series Mania TV festival in Paris. *Cleverman* has been nominated for the AWGIE awards, the Australian Guild awards, and for Best Original Miniseries. Here is a little taste of *Cleverman*.

《天赋异人》是我两年前加入紫水鸟影视公司时参与的第一批联合制作的作品之一。我们接触了 Goalpost Pictures 公司，它旗下曾制作了由 Wayne Blair 执导的获奖长片《蓝宝石》。这部由六季组成的电视剧是由一位年轻的原住民电影人 Ryan Griffin 制作的，他们当时正在寻找合拍合作伙伴来帮助融资和制作该系列剧。具有讽刺意味的是，尽管澳大利亚是我们最亲密的邻居，但我们却是通过远在数千英里外的美国合作伙伴相互介绍的。《天赋异人》是一部充满智慧、值得玩味和令人叹为观止的原创电视剧，它描述了一群非人类生物为了生存而抗争的故事，在那个世界里人类越来越逊色于这些非人类生物并且想要奴役并杀害他们。故事主要讲述了两个感情疏远、土生土长的兄弟，他们被迫一起为了生存而战。其他人间的生物也出现在这个脆弱但危险的地球上，使得这部电视剧充满了打斗的场面。《天赋异人》对紫水鸟影视公司来说十分契合。基于原住民神话的题材意味着与我们的兄弟公司维塔工作室有着天然的契合，他们负责超自然生物的设计和制造，彼得·杰克逊的公园路后期制作中心提供视觉效果、音效和音乐。所有的拍摄都在澳大利亚的悉尼进行。维塔工作室提供道具造型，并有工作人员专门负责制作和修补道具头发。包括视觉效果在内的所有后期制作，其中还有大量 3D 视觉效果全部在新西兰的惠灵顿进行。该作品的投资方包括澳大利亚的 ABC 电视台、德国的红箭国际、美国圣丹斯电视台、澳大利亚的 Goalpost Pictures、紫水鸟影视公司，还得到新西兰和澳大利亚影视作品补贴和资助机构的大力支持。它已经销往许多国家并且广受好评。除了在澳大利亚的 ABC 电视台播出，美国的圣丹斯电视台、新西兰的国家电视台和英国的 BBC 电视台下个月也会播出。《天赋异人》在柏林艺术节馆进行的柏林影展特别节目中进行了国际首映式，并被选在巴黎 2016 Mania 电视节播放。《天赋异人》已经获得澳大利亚作家协会奖提名，角逐最佳原创迷你剧奖。接下来是《天赋异人》的一些片花。

20:29—22:49
Video.
播放视频。

22:52—26:14
So what makes a good co-production and what are the things we have learnt from *Cleverman*? Choose your partners well. Make sure you are on the same page creatively and you are making the same show. To achieve this, you must spend time in each other's country planning the whole production. This is very very important. You must make sure the creatives including the producers, writers and directors meet with and have a say in the teams they will be working with. You have to like them a lot as you will be

第九单元　动漫娱乐 Animation and Entertainment

seeing them more than your family and friends when you are making your show. Make sure you have the same creative goals. These need to be worked on together. Film and television is a very collaborative process so make sure there is an agreement on all things creative every step of the way. This includes the script, design and look of the show, all the key heads of department, sound and music. This requires a lot of planning and you will know very early on if you are a good fit and a good team to be working together. Have a good production agreement in place. This agreement sets out all the expectations on both sides. What co-producing partner is doing what. It will include the list of duties assigned to each country, the financial split and the time frame. You will need to make sure you have a good production and financial team to support all the creative vision. The producer's job is to facilitate this vision as well as keep the production on schedule and on budget. Make sure you have the right creative team in place and everyone is playing in position. A good analogy is the famous New Zealand All Black rugby team who all play in position and are disciplined and always achieve amazing results. Make sure each partner is aware of the other country's cultural and production processes. Don't take for granted their processes will be the same as yours and how it is done in your country. Make sure there is careful planning on the overall production schedule. You need to be sure that the other country's schedule is achievable as this will impact on your schedule and more importantly your budget. The schedule needs to be written into the co-production agreement and any changes to this need to be agreed in advance as to how it is dealt with in the budget and whose responsibility is for the overages. Most importantly it is communication. Set regular meetings with your co-production partners and make sure you are updating each other daily. My experience in production is that you will be working alongside your co-production partners right throughout the production. As I said before, you will end up knowing them as well as your friends and family by the end of the process.

　　那么怎样制作一个优秀的合拍片？从《天赋异人》身上我们学到了什么呢？选好合作伙伴。确保你们在创作上想法相同，并且朝着同一个目标前进。要做到这一点，您必须在合作双方的国家花点时间做好整个制作的规划。这一点非常重要。您必须确保所有创意人员包括制作人、编剧和导演，能够与他们合作的团队见面并有发言权。您得多喜欢他们一点，因为当您在制作时，您见到他们比见家人和朋友还多。确保大家都有相同的创意目标。这需要大家通力合作。电影和电视是一个协作的过程，所以确保在创意的道路上都能达成共识。其中包括剧本、作品的设计和外观、所有部门主管人员、音效和音乐。这需要做大量的规划，之后您很快就知道自己到底适不适合，是不是一个好队友。制定完善的合拍片协议。协议要列出双方所有的要求、合拍合作伙伴的责任和义务。这包括分配给每个合拍国家的任务清单、分摊的费用和时间安排。确保有优秀的制作和财务团队来支撑所有的创意想法。制作方的职责是协助实现创意想法，并且把控拍摄进度和预算。确保有合适的创意团队，并且所有人都各司其职。一个很好的例子就是著名的新西兰国家橄榄球队，每位队员都各司其职并且高度自律，所以总是取得惊人的成绩。确保所有合作伙伴都了解其他合作国家的文化和制作流程。不要想当然地认为对方的流程与自己的国家是一样的。确保对整个制作进度进行详细的规划。要确保其他国家的拍摄进度是可行的，因为这将会影响到您的进度，更重要的是会影响到您的预算。进度安排需要写入合拍片协议中，如果有任何变更都要提前商定，这关乎如何在预算上进行调整以及工作延时由谁承担责任。最重要的是沟通。定期与合拍方伙伴举行会议，确保每天都会更新彼此的进度。我的制作经验是您与您的合拍片方伙伴全程都要并肩作战。正如我之前所说的那样，在这个过程结束后，你们会像朋友和家人一样了解彼此。

26:17—28:40

So what is next for us at Pukeko Pictures? We are currently in production on Series 2 and 3 of *Thunderbirds Are Go*. We have started pre-production of Series 2 of *Cleverman* which starts filming next month again in Sydney. We are also pleased to announce our first official co-production with China. It is a co-production with local Guangzhou company Huawen Century. It is a 52 episodes animated kids series called *Space Kiddets*. We have been working with Huawen Century for the past couple of years developing the series. It is a terrific creation partnership with all the scripting and 3D design being created at Pukeko Pictures and Weta Workshop in New Zealand. Character build, modelling and storyboarding at Mechanic in New Zealand, who currently do a lot of the Marvel comic work for the US. Animation will be done with Blossom in Beijing with the post sound and music finishing at Park Road Post (Peter Jackson's post production facility). We are very excited to be working with China on this co-production and hope this is the beginning of a very long and happy relationship. We at Pukeko are so pleased that I have been invited to speak at this prestigious event and I hope this is my first trip of many as along with my colleagues, Sir Richard Taylor, Martin Baynton and Clive Spink. And we will get the opportunity to meet you all later to talk about our experiences and your experience with working with other countries. Please feel free to come and talk to me after this talk. I am very happy to share my knowledge. I am happy now to answer questions, any questions you have for me. 谢谢！

那么紫水鸟影视公司的下一部作品是什么呢？目前我们正在制作《雷鸟神机队出发》的第二和第三季，也开始了《天赋异人》第二季的前期制作，该系列将于下个月在悉尼再次开始拍摄。我们很高兴地宣布我们首次与中国进行官方合拍。这部官方合拍片是与广州的华文世纪公司合拍的,制作一部叫做《太空宝贝》的52集动画片。过去几年我们一直在与华文世纪合作制作这个系列。这真是一次特别好的创意合作,新西兰的紫水鸟影视公司和维塔工作室创作了所有的剧本和3D设计,而新西兰的Mechanic则负责模型制作和故事板制作,他们目前为美国制作了很多漫威漫画作品。动画、后期音效和音乐由北京花开影视有限公司在公园路后期制作中心(彼得·杰克逊的后期制作设备)完成。我们非常高兴能够与中国合拍这部作品,并希望这是我们建立长期、愉快合作关系的开始。我的公司非常高兴我能受邀在这次活动中发言,我希望以后还有很多机会与我的同事Richard Taylor先生,Martin Baynton先生和Clive Spink一起出席。稍后,我们几位将有机会与在座各位见面,分享我们的经验以及大家与其他国家合作的经验。这次谈话结束后可以随时与我交流。我很乐于分享我所了解的一切。现在欢迎大家向我提问,大家有任何问题都可以问我。Thank you!

第十单元　绿色建筑
Green Building

I. 实战练习一

1. 演讲背景

比利时 LTB 建筑事务所的建筑师应邀出席"比利时中国绿色建筑经验分享会"并发表主旨演讲。他在演讲中着重介绍了公司的团队、四大核心业务、年营业额，以及公司已经完成和正在开展的建筑项目。其中谈到了如何因地制宜地选择建筑材料、采用节能技术、循环利用材料，从而实现建筑的节能减排。

2. 预习词汇

Brussels 布鲁塞尔
aesthetic 审美的
Flanders 佛兰德斯
Wallonia 瓦隆
social care center 社会保健中心
turnover 营业额
chamber 协会
University of Louvain 鲁汶大学
Architects' Council of Europe 欧洲建筑师理事会
sustainability 可持续性
low energy 低能耗
BREE-AM 英国绿色建筑评估体系
sustainable energy 可持续能源
translucid 半透明的
blinding 令人眩晕的
sports hall 体育馆
fiber glass 玻璃纤维
fiber cement 纤维水泥
insulated 绝缘的

heat pump 热泵
biofuel 生物燃料
night cooling 夜间辐射制冷
concrete 混泥土
cladding 覆盖层
coral 珊瑚
auditorium 礼堂
atrium 中庭
ventilation system 通风系统
acoustic 声学的
Heist-op-den-Berg 海斯特奥普登贝尔赫
University of Ghent 根特大学
Vilvoorde 菲尔福尔德
compact 紧凑的
E level 能源水平
Halle 哈雷
Langemark 朗厄马克

3. 演讲文本

00:00—01:21

Yes. Thank you, Mattias. First of all, welcome here. I'm very glad that I'm able to be with you, and first of all, I'd like to thank Her Excellency of Minister Cécile Jodogne, who took me with her on her expert visit to China. So thank you very much that I could join in this group going to China. I also would like to thank Mattias and his team, for the excellent organization of these events that we could join in this week, as well as Robert, this organizing trip from Belgian signed out. Thank you very much for your organization. So I'm going to present my company, and I'm also going to present a little bit about sustainability in our country. This was not prepared, so I just knew one day ago, yesterday, that I was able to give some words about my activities in Belgium on buildings and sustainability more particular. So I'm going to try to do that in a short time that this has been prepared.

好的，谢谢您，马蒂亚斯。首先，欢迎各位的莅临。我非常高兴能够与大家相聚一堂。首先，我想感谢乔茜乐部长阁下携我来到中国进行专家访问。谢谢您，让我能够加入这个团队，来到中国。我也想感谢马蒂亚斯及其团队，谢谢你们出色地组织了本周我们参与的活动。同时，我也想感谢罗伯特签字批准了本次组织的访问。非常感谢诸位的组织。所以接下来，我将介绍我的公司，以及我们国家的可持续发展。这不是事先准备好的，我是在昨天才知道可以介绍我在比利时建筑领域，特别是可持续发展方面的工作。所以我尝试在短时间内将这些准备好。

01:26—03:19

So first of all, the team, we're an architect office situated in Brussels. We are about 35 people, most of them architects or engineers, or the combination of both because we have the education of architects, and we have the education of engineers in Belgium, but we also have the combined education of engineer architect, which combines a bit technical aspect of our profession, together with more aesthetic aspect of profession. As a team, we're working on a lot of projects, mostly in four fields. We're active from 1993. I founded the company. And now we have 35 people in the company. We have four activities. First of all, we're working on quite a lot of schools in Belgium, in Flanders, and Brussels and Wallonia. In fact, we have had lots of building built in the 60s, in the 50s and the 60s. It's quite a while ago. So most of our patrimonial school buildings is old and so we're renewing part of it, and also building quite a lots of new schools. Schools is the first activity we're working on, but also social care centers, sport and leisure facilities as well as residential project and housing. These are the four core businesses from our company. We're working with a team of 35 people, which means that we need to make a turnover of about 100,000 Euro per person, so this makes 3 to 3.7 million Euro per year that we need to have as a turnover to be able to give enough work to all these people.

首先介绍一下我们的团队。我们是一家位于布鲁塞尔的建筑师事务所，大约有35名员工，其中大多数是建筑师、工程师，或者两者皆备。因为比利时不仅有建筑师、工程师的教育，还有工程建筑师的联合教育。这种教育将我们职业的技术方面，与更多的审美方面相融合。作为一个团队，我们正开展着众多项目，主要涉及四个领域。1993年，我创立了公司。现在我们公司已有35名员工。我们的工作有四方面。首先，我们正在比利时的佛兰德斯、布鲁塞尔以及瓦隆进行着许多学校项目。实际上，我们大部分建筑都是于20世纪50年代或60年代建成的，年代颇为悠久，所以我们大部分的学校建筑都是旧的。我们正对部分进行翻新，同时也在建设着大量的新学校。学校是我们工作的第一个方面，除此之外，我们还有社会保健中心、运动休闲设施，以及住宅工程和住房。这是我们公司的四大核心业务。我们的团队有35名员工，这意味着每名员工需要达到约10万欧元营业额。我们则每一年需要有300万到370万欧元的营业额，这样我们才能为员工们提供足够的工作。

03:19—05:26

I have something about myself, because it was somehow asked by Mattias to explain a bit whom I am myself. So I, as he told already, I got some presidencies in the field of architecture in Belgium, as there're the chamber of all the architects in Belgium, as well the local chamber and national chamber. Also that's perhaps important for those who're working on the scientific fields, or working together with universities, or education centers. The faculty of science, engineering sciences of university of Louvain is where I studied in the past. I'm still linked to the university. And we would be pleased to work together and collaborate with universities here in China, of course, also International Chamber of Architect Society, I mentioned already, and also the Council of Architects of Europe. You need to know that we have a group in Europe, which is called the Architects' Council of Europe, and the Architects' Council of Europe has a couple of work groups on specific issues. And we have a work group on sustainability, and low energy buildings. So it must be interesting, I think, to get in touch with this European organization. It's going beyond of the national level. It's international. So it's covering the whole of Europe, and you might be interested in having contact with these people. So I can bring you the references and bring you in contact with them. In Belgium, and more specific in Brussels, we have an organization which is called the G30. We as an office, a member of G30, which groups the bigger offices in our country, and also we're working around this specific issue of sustainability and low energy. So we could be of somehow also of course and I have the honor actually to be designated as dean of the Royal Institute of the Elites of Labour, for the professional architect.

我打算介绍一下我自己,因为马蒂亚斯刚刚让我做一个自我介绍。正如他所说,我在比利时建筑行业担任着一些主席的职位。在比利时,有所有建筑师都参加的协会,当地协会,以及全国协会。所以,对于那些从事于科学领域,在大学或者教育中心工作的人来说,这或许是重要的。我曾就读于鲁汶大学工程科学系。现在我和我的大学仍有联系。当然,我们很乐意与中国的大学、国际建筑师协会以及欧洲建筑师协会合作。您需要知道,我们在欧洲有一个叫欧洲建筑师理事会的组织,它有针对确切问题的工作组。另外,我们有一个可持续发展以及低能耗建筑的工作组。我认为与欧洲组织一同工作肯定非常有趣。这超出了国家层面,是国际性的,它覆盖了整个欧洲。您可能有兴趣与这些人接触,所以我可以为您引荐,并帮助您与他们取得联系。在比利时,更确切地说是在布鲁塞尔,我们有一个叫做G30的组织。我们作为一个办事处以及G30的成员,将我们国家的大型事务所聚集在一起,我们也在围绕可持续发展和低能耗这个确切的问题而努力。另外,我也十分荣幸作为职业建筑师被授予劳动精英皇家学院院长的职位。

05:26—06:40
So now about the office, what we're doing, so I'm going to present you a couple of

projects we're working on or we were working on in the past. So we recently developed the British school of Brussels, which is quite a sustainable building. In fact, this building got a BREE-AM rate of excellence with 75%, so it's a quite high rating. You could compare it, if you compare it to your system, with a five star building, this is a building. This is based upon global sustainability, not only low energy. So we're looking to lots of elements. That's a composite of sustainable buildings. And first of all, if you talk about sustainability and energy use, first of all, the best is not to use any energy at all. But of course it's hardly possible. So you need some and if you need some energy that it's best that you use sustainable energy. And if you don't have enough sustainable energy, you use energy but you're going to treat it in a proper way, and to use some techniques, some special techniques to work with this long sustainable energy for the best.

所以现在请允许我介绍一下我们的事务所,以及我们目前在做什么。我将为您介绍一些我们正在开展或者已经完成的项目。我们最近建设了布鲁塞尔英国学校的一幢可持续建筑。实际上,这栋建筑的英国绿色建筑评估体系等级达到了75%,这是非常高的等级。如果您将其与您的体系进行比较,这就是一栋五星级类型的建筑。该建筑不仅仅低能耗,而且是建立在全球可持续性基础之上。我们关注的要素很多。这里有一些可持续性建筑的图片。首先,若您谈论可持续和能源使用,最好就是不要使用任何能源。但当然,这几乎是不可能的。所以,如果您需要一定量的能源,最好使用可持续能源。如果没有足够的可持续能源,您可以使用其他能源,但要妥善处理,并且采用特殊技术来使用这些长期可持续能源。

06:40—08:04

So what we did, first of all, for this building, is a building of about 11,000 m^2. It's a school, it's a primary and secondary school for the British community in Belgium, and first of all, was the choice of materials. So we used materials which are specific, for example, for the wall cladding, we used a material that is not very often used in Belgium. It's coral, and coral is for the parts in white you see, and these parts are translucid parts, so you'll get some lights throughout these parts of the building without being blinding, because these… the building, it serves this part of the building, it's a sports hall. And so in sports hall, you don't need too many lights. You need lights, but not too many, and especially not glassing, because you will be blinded throughout the glass and that cannot be the case. So we used another material, which is a thin material, consisting of fiber glass. And the other part is fiber cement, so we have a very thin skin of the building. We have a very well insulated parts. It's about 25 cm of insulation that we use into the walls. And we use 25 cm insulation into the roof part. So the building is extremely well insulated, and that makes it use already less energy.

我们首先需要完成的是一栋面积约为11,000平方米的楼宇。这是比利时英国社区的一所小学和中学。首先,是材料的选择。我们使用的材料是特定的。例如墙面覆盖层,我们使用了一种在比利时较少使用的材料。那就是珊瑚,珊瑚就是您看到的这些半透明白色部分。因此,建筑的这些部分可以透光,而不至于令人眩晕。它为建筑的这个部分所使用。这是一个体育馆。体育馆内部需要光线,但不需要太多,尤其是不需要玻璃。因为玻璃会令您眩晕,所以玻璃这种材料用在这里不合适。我们使用了另外一种由玻璃纤维构成的轻薄材料,那就是纤维水泥。所以建筑的表面是非常薄的。我们使用了很好的绝缘部件,我们在墙壁中和屋顶部分使用了25厘米厚的绝缘层。所以这个建筑绝缘性高,这使得它消耗更少的能源。

08:04—09:44

About the energy provision for the building, we use different techniques. We have a system of heat pump that we use, and also what we call biofuel. So we use the energy that we can get out of the soil, due to differences in temperature you have in the soil. So we use that energy to bring heat into the building. On the other hand, there is no cooling, no artificial cooling, there is night cooling, but not artificial cooling, because in fact, air conditioning is completely opposite to any sustainable measurements you take for a building. So we try to prohibit for the maximum, using air conditioning. For example, using materials, it didn't only use concrete, I see here in China, you use enormously a number of concrete for most of the buildings. Well, we use lots of steel, very fine thin steel structures, which are more sustainable, we think, than using concrete. Concrete has a lot of capacities, but for such kind of building, it's better to use frames in steel, combined with concrete, of course, because you need concrete for the soils, and also combined with wooden structures. We use wooden structures for the swimming pool, and also the swimming pool itself is sustainable, because we use the water of the swimming pool, which is about 28 degrees normally, and they only use it during the day. We use it by night in the cold period to heat up the building. So we reuse somehow the heat that is put into the water to bring it up to 28 degrees.

在建筑能源供应方面,我们采用了不同的技术。使用了一个热泵系统以及我们所说的生物燃料。土壤的温度差异使我们能够从中获得可以利用的能源。所以我们利用该能源将热量引入建筑。另一方面,建筑内没有人工制冷,而是采用夜间辐射制冷的技术。因为实际上,空调与建筑的可持续性评估是完全相违背的。所以我们尽量禁止使用空调。例如在材料使用方面,我看到在中国的大部分建筑中,不仅使用混凝土,而且是大量地使用混凝土。我们则大量地使用钢铁和非常精炼轻薄的钢铁结构,我们认为这比使用混凝土更可持续。混凝土十分有用,但对于这样的建筑，将钢铁构架与混凝土结合会更合适一些。当然，因为泥土需要混凝土，我们也将其与木质结构相结合。我们在泳池中使用了木质结构，同样，游泳池本身也是具有可持续性的。因为我们使用的游泳池中温度通常为28度的水，并且仅在白天使用。在寒冷的夜晚，我们会用其来为建筑供暖。所以在某种程度上，我们重复使用了水的热量，来将建筑升温到28度。

09:44—10:30

Here you can see that we also use normal glass. But this is normal glass inside the building between different functions of the building. So the swimming pool has also partly all claddings as well as normal windows. Did you have a view into the sports hall part? And you see these parts in coral, which are bringing light, naturally light inside. So you have to use less energy, less electricity to make artificial light. This is about the British school. I think we got this BREE-AM rating. It's the first BREE-AM rate of school in Belgium, so we're very proud of this project. We hope that in the future more buildings will be able to get this BREE-AM rating.

在这里您可以看到，我们也使用了普通的玻璃。但是建筑内的普通玻璃是用于不同的功能区。游泳池有部分采用了覆盖层以及普通的窗户。您能看到体育馆的部分吗？您可以看到这些部分由珊瑚构成，来将自然光引入内部。所以您使用了更少的能源和电力来制造人造光。这是关于英国学校的项目。我记得我们已经获得了英国绿色建筑评估体系的评级。这是比利时第一所拥有英国绿色建筑评估体系评级的学校，所以我们引以为傲。我们希望在未来有更多的建筑能够获得英国绿色建筑评估体系评级。

10:30—11:23

But I am immediately to tell you something about ratification of buildings. We have to pay attention with this, because it's not always needed to have a BREE-AM, or a very very high standard to sustainable system, or labelling, especially in a lot of labelling, because you need to see what's the best for a building. And you need to make kind of an analysis when you see how many efforts, and how many money do you put inside, and what do you get out. There are some analysis and there are some balance to obtain, and not going always for a very very high rating which is not appropriate for the use of the building for some buildings is a bit overkilled as you could say. So this building is a very sustainable building and our client is very happy with this result.

但是，接下来我会为您介绍有关建筑批准事宜。我们必须注意这一点，因为我们并不是一定要拥有英国绿色建筑评估体系，或者一个高标准的可持续体系，或者标签，特别是标签，您要清楚什么才是最适合这幢建筑的。而且要进行分析，看看

第十单元　绿色建筑 Green Building

您投入了多少精力和资金，又能从中能得到什么。我们需要进行分析、取得平衡，而不是一味追求不适用的高标准建筑评级，因为您可以看到，这对于一些建筑来说，有点强人所难了。所以这栋建筑是非常可持续的，我们的客户对这个结果十分满意。

11:23—12:21

We use for the maximum opportunities that also were able to be found on the area itself. We had to break down the building, so we had some waste. Breaking down the building is never a good idea, but we couldn't do else way. OK. Because the building was far too old. But with the materials we broke down, we reused them to make the paths and the underground of the building, the structure of the underground of the building, we used it for that purpose. So we use for the maximum, everything we can get out of the original situation we got when we started. Another thing is that we use, of course, the water. There is a kind of, well, quite an area of roof, we use the water we get for reusing in its school. They have a lot of toilets, so of course we take that water, which is for free so far.

我们尽量将这个区域的机遇最大化。我们不得不拆除建筑物，难免会造成一些浪费。拆除建筑从来都不是一个好办法，但却是我们唯一能做的。因为建筑物太破旧了。但我们再利用拆除的材料来修路、打地基。我们最大化利用从原来建筑中获得的材料。另外就是用水。建筑物的屋顶有一定的面积，可以将收集来的水在学校中再利用。学校有很多厕所可以使用这些水，目前来说水是免费的。

12:21—13:34

Another project I'd like to present you is also a school building. And this is a passive school. It's a passive school. It's all the buildings are in the neighborhood of Brussels, surrounding of Brussels. This school is a passive school, is a secondary school and consisting of a lot of classrooms, 18 classrooms all together, auditorium, atrium, lots of different functions. And what we did is we made it passive, so that it means that it's completely automatically regulated. We are not able to open the window, so we have a ventilation system which is also completely automatic. But we... in the architecture of the building, we organize it that way that we have some overhang on the floors to what's the underlying level. So that's the heat of the sunlight. Sunlight is somehow covered and brought to a reasonable level, so that would be kept... no system of overheating inside of the classrooms. So we use this kind of technology.

我将为您介绍的另外一个项目也是一所学校建筑。这是一所被动式学校。所有的建筑物都邻近布鲁塞尔。这所被动式中学由多个教室组成，共有18间课室，还

209

有礼堂、中庭，有各种功能分区。我们采用了被动式的建筑概念，所以这意味着该建筑完全是自动调节的。不能打开窗户，因此，它有一个完全自动化的通风系统。在建筑架构方面，地面上有悬挑部分垂挂在基础层中。所以这是阳光的热量。阳光以某种方式被遮挡，并调节到一个合适的水平，教室没有安装过热探测系统，因此，我们采用了这种技术。

13:34—14:42

What we also use in the passive school is a carbon measurement to get the air quality as good as possible. So we measure the carbon that you have in the room. Because the students in the room, they are breathing, and due to that there are of course carbon production. And when the carbon production gets to a certain level, automatically we have the ventilation system which is going to start. So we have air quality, because this is a big problem in our schools. Actually in Belgium. There is the quality of the air, all the buildings, OK. The ceilings are mostly high. But even though the air, after a while, after one, two, three lessons, is very bad. And so you have to renew the air, because if the air in the classroom is not to a certain standard, the pupils are going to become tired much more quickly, and they pay no attention any longer. And the class results will drop down. So there're some analysis made about this. So air quality is extremely important.

在被动式学校中，我们也采用了碳测量，尽可能改善空气质量。我们会测量房间中的碳含量。因为课室中的学生都在呼吸，因此会产生碳。当碳产量达到一定程度时，通风系统就会自动开启，因此，空气质量得以保证。这在我们学校是一个很重要的问题。比利时所有建筑物的空气质量能都得以保证。这里的天花板大多很高，但是在一节，或两三节课后，空气就会变得浑浊起来。这时就需要换气，因为如果课室内的空气达不到一定标准，学生很容易疲惫，无法专心听讲，班级成绩会下降。有过许多这样的分析。因此，空气质量非常重要。

14:42—15:48

Also acoustic measurements are extremely important in school buildings because of the noise that you have always in classrooms can be very very embarrassing to pay attention to what's going on in the class. Another element to reduce the energy costs we do in school buildings is the measurement of the light level. So we're going to measure the light which is coming inside from the windows, and based on that, we're going to put on the artificial lighting but that means that the artificial lighting is put on in several stages. So first of all, the area which is most far away from the windows will be lighted, and then afterwards, more in the middle, and in the ends, also approximate to the windows. So this kind of technical systems help a lot to bring down the energy consumption that you have in the school buildings.

此外,声学测量在学校建筑物中也十分重要。因为课室中长期的噪音会让人难以专心听课。我们使用的另一个降低学校建筑能耗的方法就是光水平测量。我们会测量从窗户照射进来的光线,再基于这个测量来使用人工照明,但这意味着人工照明的利用分为不同阶段。所以,首先,离窗户最远的区域会被照亮,然后到中间,最后到窗户附近。因此,这种技术系统有助于降低学校建筑能耗。

15:48—17:45

I'm going to pass through because it wasn't foreseen that I was going to give some explanation on sustainability, I was just going to talk about my work. So a lot of couple of projects that we're working on, as I told you, a lot of schools for the moments, the Flemish, the Brussels, and also the Wallonish governments are investing, highly investing in school infrastructure, because of the facts that our schools are quite old, as I told you. So there's a lot to be done. And this is a new campus we do in Heist-op-den-Berg, which is covering 16,000 m^2. It's a completely new secondary school, also primary school. And also there we use the same techniques to bring down the energy consumption. So this gives an idea of the campus itself. But also there we work with heat pumps, we work with solar panels, and the same measurements we do as in the other projects. We also have a project for the University of Ghent, where we are developing a new college building with the same techniques as I told you before. Also in Vilvoorde, that's just straight behind Brussels. It's a primary school, but I give you an idea, this is a school, it doesn't like compact, but it is very compact. And so we obtain for this school, we obtain an E level of 45, which is very very low. Normally we have to obtain E level of 60 in this period, but we go much further to E45, and the passive school you saw, goes up to E30 level, which means that we just use 50 kW/m^2 per year for the school energy use.

我将跳过这一部分,因为我没想到会讲解可持续性,我原本只打算谈谈我的工作。所以,正如我所说的,我们在做很多的学校项目,佛兰德斯、布鲁塞尔,以及瓦隆政府都正在大力投资学校的基础设施,因为事实上,正如我所说的,我们的学校很破旧。所以,我们所要做的事情还很多。这是我们在海斯特奥普登贝尔赫新做的一个校园项目,其面积为16,000平方米。这是一所全新的中学,也有小学。在那里,我们也使用了相同的技术来降低能源消耗。所以这就赋予了校园一个理念。但我们也使用了热泵、太阳能电池板,以及与其他项目相同的测量方法。我们还有一个根特大学的项目。我们正在那建一栋新学院建筑,使用了我先前说到的技术。同样在菲尔福尔德,就是在布鲁塞尔的正后方,这是一所小学。介绍一下,这所学校不喜欢紧凑,但自身却十分紧凑。我们让这所学校达到了E45的水平,这是相当低的。正常情况下，在这期间，我们必须达到 E60 的水平，但是我们进一步达到了 E45 的水平。刚刚您所看到的被动式学校达到了 E30 的水平，这意味着学校每年仅使用 50 千瓦/平方米的能源。

17:45—18:12

I'm closing down. As I told you, we also do some care centers. This is care center in Halle. We're developing, you see we have lot of glass in the building that although we can go to a passive building with a lot of glass. There are possibilities. And the same we do in Langemark, also a social care center, and with the same principles we use for the development of the building. Thank you very much!

我总结一下。正如我所说的，我们也做一些社会保健中心项目。这是在哈雷的一间保健中心，该项目正在建设中，尽管我们可以建一栋采用很多玻璃的被动式建筑，但您可以看到建筑物中用了许多玻璃。一切皆有可能。我们在朗厄马克也一样，有一个社会保健中心，我们在建筑物中应用了同样的原则。谢谢大家！

II. 实战练习二

1. 演讲背景

奥雅纳董事应邀出席"敢创设·界亚太设计论坛"并发表主旨演讲。他在演讲中分享了世界各地奇特的建筑设计，例如：巴西库里蒂巴禾洛套房旋转大厦、意大利米兰的"垂直森林"、新加坡的翠城新景、香港的移动铝屋、苏州工业园区 3D 打印而成的建筑、阿布扎比投资委员会总部。此外他还分享了现在特别流行和热门的"可植入设备"，最后提出了智能设计的三大原则：前瞻性、能应对目前的挑战、以人为本。

2. 预习词汇

smart design 智能设计
Suite Vollard 禾洛套房旋转大厦
spinning building 旋转建筑
Porta Nuova Isola 垂直森林
vertical garden 垂直花园
Interlace 翠城新景
Alpod 移动铝屋
facade 幕墙；立面
sun photosynthesis 光合作用

第十单元 绿色建筑 Green Building

iris scanning 虹膜扫描

3. 演讲文本

00:00—00:50

Hi, good afternoon. First of all, I would like to thank the organizer for giving me the opportunity to talk to you, you know, about some of the, you know, the things that we have done worldwide. As this forum is focused on architecture and design, and smart design, the ultimate aim is to enhance the quality of life of the people, like smart living, and to make people, you know, having an easier life. So my talk, because of the time, will focus on architecture and design, and how it is gonna influence our life. Towards the end, time permitting, I would talk a little bit about how we extend it to designing and planning, like a city, or bigger, you know, urban development.

大家下午好。首先,我想感谢主办方,让我有机会和大家交流,大家应该知道我们在全球做了什么。本次论坛的焦点是建筑、设计以及智能设计,最终目的是提升人们的生活质量,比如智能生活,使人们生活更便利。由于时间关系,我将重点讲讲建筑和设计及其对我们生活的影响。最后,如果时间允许的话,我想谈谈我们该如何扩展到设计和规划领域,比如城市,或者更大的范围,也就是城市发展。

00:50—02:20

This is a building in Curitiba, Brazil, which is called Suite Vollard. That has been completed in the year 2001. (I am sorry.) This is 15-storey high building and each floor can actually turn independently clockwise or anti-clockwise. And when it was constructed, they called it the futuristic building of the world, because this is the first spinning building of the world and the facade of the building, they make use of different color of glazing, so that when different floors turn at different angles you have a very spectacular view and color of the building. Architect Bruno de Franco, he said all the equipment that he used is off-the-shelf equipment or parts. And he had purposely designed it so that it would require very least you know very little maintenance. And he said that if you believe in everything that he said, you know, in the Internet, to turn around the whole floor it will take about one hour, and the power that is consumed is only equal to using your average hair dryer for the same one hour, so it is very energy, you know, saving.

这是巴西库里蒂巴的一座建筑,叫禾洛套房旋转大厦,于2001年竣工。这是一座15层高的建筑,每层都可以单独顺时针或逆时针旋转。建成时,人们称之为世界的未来派建筑,因为这是世界首个旋转建筑,而且它的幕墙是用不同颜色的玻璃做成的,因此,不同楼层旋转到不同角度时,您会看到不同的景观和颜色。建筑师 Bruno de Franco 说他所用的设备都是现成的或是零部件。他也有意这样设计,这样就不怎么需要维护了。他还说到如果您相信互联网中的一切,整层楼转一圈需要一个小时,所消耗的电仅仅和您用一个小时吹风机一样多,所以这非常节约能源。

02:20—04:08

Now with this, it creates a lot of imagination around the world like spinning building, rotating building as… If you surf the Internet you will find you know place, you know tower or building like a dynamic tower in Dubai whatever floor, it is not circular so when they, every floor turns at a different angle, the building will have a different shape. But those were never constructed. We look at future building, and we think that future building not only could they have you know turning at different direction, but this serves different function as well, within you know the building. Some floors may become you know a factory that is used to produce what we call urban agriculture that produces food for the city. Some floors could be used as the transport floor. And most importantly, future building they would use modular design, and each module could be constructed by robots. Now of course you know we don't know when of this type of building will be fully erected of building like this. But we can see that when you go into a building like this, sometimes you become you know a commuter when you take the bus, take a metro or drive your car to work. From a commuter you switch to another floor then you become a worker you know in the urban farm, or you work in the office. And then after work, you go down to the shopping mall, you know and you become a consumer, or you go to a theatre and then you become, you know, you entertain yourself. So this multi-flexible building actually become what we call an activities interchange instead of just you know a building.

它激发了全世界人们的想象力,像旋转建筑……如果您上网,您会发现像迪拜动态塔这样的建筑。每一层都不是圆的,每一层旋转到不同的角度时,整幢建筑的形状就会发生改变。但是那些建筑从没有被建成。来看看未来的建筑,我们以为未来的建筑不仅仅可以像我们想的那样转向不同方向,而且还有不同的功能。有些楼层可能成了工厂,变成城市农业,为城市生产粮食;有些楼层变成交通层。最重要的是,未来建筑可能会用模块化设计,每个模块都是用机器人建造的。当然,我们并不知道这种建筑究竟什么时候能完全建成这样,但我们可以看到您走进这种建筑乘公交车、地铁或是驾车去上班时,您变成了通勤者。到另外一层楼,您就从通勤者变成了城市农场的工人,或是办公室的员工。下班后,您下楼就到了购物商场,变成了消费者,如果去影院的话,就是在消遣娱乐。所以这种多变的建筑已经不是您认知中的建筑了,实际上变成了活动枢纽。

第十单元 绿色建筑 Green Building

04:08—05:21

This is a building called Porta Nuova Isola in Milan, Italy, that has been completed in 2012. It made use of a lot of what they call innovative construction material like very high strength concrete and high strength steel and of course they use stamper so that they would absorb all the vibration of the building so that it will not affect you know people living in the building. But as you can see from this picture, they have planted 90 different species of trees, bushes, and flowering plants to make it look like what they call a vertical garden in the city. Now French architect Vincent Callebaut, he had designed five buildings in Shenzhen, of course, those have not been built yet. That is very green. And the green plant which is very similar to what you've seen on this Porta Nuova. Actually she said that the plant will actually purify the air and also it will provide food, you know for the inhabitants.

这是意大利米兰的一座建筑，叫"垂直森林"，于2012年建成。用的是非常新颖的建筑材料，比如说高强度混凝土以及高强钢，当然他们也会使用压膜，有防震功能，也不会影响居住在里面的人。但您可以从这幅图看到，他们种植了90多种树、灌木，以及开花的植物，形成了我们所知的城市垂直花园。现在法国的建筑师Vincent Callebaut已经在深圳设计了五座建筑，当然还没有建成。非常环保。绿色植物和您在这个建筑上看到的非常相似。实际上她说这个植物可以真正地净化空气，也可以给居民提供食物。

05:21—06:04

This is the Interlace in Singapore that was completed in 2013 by architect Oma, and this is what people would call a Lego building. But I think this is a too big a Lego actually to be constructed like a Lego because it contains 31 blocks of apartment, each block is six-story high, and you know with the same name, but what architect Oma has said this is the future building that integrates the space within the social and the space using residential, you know recreational.

这是新加坡的翠城新景，于2013年由建筑师Oma设计竣工，人们称之为乐高建筑。但我觉得这个建筑太大了，不能称为乐高，因为它有31幢公寓楼，每一幢都有6层高，而且他们的叫法都一样。但是建筑师Oma认为这就是未来建筑的样子，融合了社交、住宅以及娱乐的空间。

06:04—06:56

This is what the architect James Law called an Alpod, actually it is in exhibit in Hong Kong now in East Kowloon. This is like… the size of it is just slightly bigger than a container box, and the whole thing is made of aluminum. And he said that this is the smart building of the future in the smart city where you can stack, a lot of these boxes together to create you know multi-story building, and of course the core itself have to be constructed in situ. And each you know, each component, some could be you know a living room, some could be an office, and some could be the washroom, kitchen etc. And he said you know because this is constructed from aluminum, this is quite light, and you can transport it anywhere on a container truck.

这就是建筑师罗发礼所说的"移动铝屋",现在正在香港九龙东展览。尺寸比集装箱小一些,且全部都是由铝制成的。而且他说这就是未来智能城市的智能建筑,把这些箱子堆在一起,就成了你们所知的多层建筑。当然它的核心部分还是要在施工现场建设。就各个组成部分,有些可能是客厅,有些是办公室,有些是洗手间或厨房。他还说因为整幢建筑是由铝制成的,重量非常轻,您可以用货柜车把它带到任何地方。

06:56—08:09

This is a building, a five-storey building that the whole building was 3D printed in the Suzhou Industrial Park in 2014. Now after they have printed the whole building actually they have to add installation and steel reinforcement in the building in order just to comply with the local building regulation. Actually they don't have to add that, they said. And the whole building was printed by the contractor WINSUN who has a special-made 3D printer that is 14-meter long, 10 meter by 6 meter. So you can see that with such a special printer, the shape of the building cannot be too irregular. But with 3D printing actually we can make use of 3D printing to print a lot of very complicated and you know technology permitted very high spring joint that can enable the architectural design to be more imaginative in the future. We have seen facade like this. This responds to the sunlight that change the color so that people will feel more comfortable inside the building.

这是一幢5层楼的建筑,整幢建筑是在2014年苏州工业园区用3D打印技术做成的。他们打印了整幢建筑之后,需要在建筑中加一些钢筋强化,从而更符合当地的建筑规定。实际上,他们说没有必要加上这些东西。整幢建筑是由承包商盈创建筑科技公司打印的,他们有特制的3D打印机,14米长,宽和高分别为10米和6米。所以您看有这样一个特制的打印机,建筑的形状不能太不规则。但是我们可以利用3D打印技术打印很多复杂的东西,而且您要知道,技术可以制造较高的弹簧连接,这使得建筑设计在未来会更富想象力。我们已经看到类似的幕墙,它们的颜色会随着太阳光线的变化而变化,人们在屋里会更加舒适。

第十单元 绿色建筑 Green Building

08:09—09:29

This is the Abu Dhabi Investment Council headquarters in Abu Dhabi. The building was completed I believe in 2012, and made use of a system what we call active facade. Each facade you know is like you know a lotus flower, which can open and close by itself according to the intensity of the sunlight. And after three, four years of operation, they said actually it saved 40% of the air-conditioning cost in the whole building. This is another building that is a five-story building in Hamburg that was completed in 2014. This is more or less like a test building. The facade composed of two layers, the normal layer and an outer layer were panel as you can see on the right hand side. This panel insulates the heat from the sun and also the noise from the surrounding road. Inside each of the panel it's a thin thing of liquid which could be used when it reacts to the sun photosynthesis, that would create, using the algae, could create biomass, and the biomass could be used to generate energy for the building.

这是阿布扎比投资委员会在阿布扎比的总部。这座建筑于2012年竣工,使用的是主动式立面系统。每一个立面就像是莲花的一瓣,可以根据阳光的强度自己开合。经过三四年的运作,他们说整栋建筑的空调费用减少了40%。这是汉堡的一座5层建筑,于2014年建成。这更像是一个试验性的建筑。它的幕墙有两层,常规层以及外层就是您看到的右手边这个平板。这个平板能隔离来自太阳的热量以及周边道路的噪音。每个平板里面有薄薄一层液体,在进行光合作用时可以利用水藻产生生物质,为建筑产生能源。

09:29—10:42

Wearable is very common you know nowadays, people you know put on an Apple Watch and other things you know to check their health, and all that. But in the electronic show in Las Vegas, which is one of the foremost you know electronic show in the world, in December of 2015 people find that wearable is out already. Why is wearable out? Because internable are in. Ericsson have done a survey in December of 2015, and it said a lot of people actually nowadays is quite willing to plant certain things within the body so that it would enhance the performance like vision. For example, I don't wear glasses now, because I have all my you know lens, converted to artificial lens already, so I don't have to wear glasses, I have been wearing glasses for 30 years. So you know in terms of vision, almost 65-70% of people is willing to do the implant, memory, hearing, you know, you can see, you know, on the graph.

现今大家都知道可穿戴设备非常常见,比如人们戴苹果手表来监测自身健康状况。拉斯维加斯的电子展是当今世界最重要的一个电子展,在2015年12月份的展览上,人们发现可穿戴设备已经过时了。为什么呢?因为现在流行的是内部植入。

爱立信公司在 2015 年 12 月的时候做了一项调查,据说现在很多人都愿意在体内植入某种东西,从而可以提升各个方面的性能,比如视力。比如我现在不戴眼镜了,因为我现在已经有人造晶状体,所以不用再戴眼镜。我可是差不多戴了 30 年的眼镜。所以就视力而言,几乎 65%~70% 的人都愿意植入,改善记忆或是听力,您可以在 PPT 的图表上看到详细信息。

10:42—12:03

Now internables have a very big impact on the use of space and architecture in future. Imagine if I implant, you know, a key, you know, on my hand, so in the future I don't need to carry my key, I just go to the door, this smart door would open because it knows I am coming home, I just turn the knob and the door will open. But if it is not me the door will be locked. This is happening already around the world. But most importantly, this leads to what we call ticketless technology. Now imaging with 3D scanning, iris scanning, biometric, and all internables, in future if you go to an airport and or you go to a railway station you don't need to have the ticket. Because by scanning you, they know that whether you have bought the tickets or not, and if you go through the airport immigration and custom, there is no need you know for you to stop and show your passport because they know already when you walk in, who you are and scanning you they know what you are carrying. Now image all the space that could be released for other use like retail, commercial use, and the usage, and the application is limitless.

如今内部植入对于未来空间和建筑的影响非常大。想象一下如果我在手中植入钥匙,那我以后就不需要再带钥匙了,我只需要走到门口,智能门就会打开,因为它知道我回来了。我只需要拉一下把手,门就会自动开。但如果不是我的话,门还是会锁着。这在世界各地都已经存在了。但最重要的是这会使我们进入无票时代。现在想象一下 3D 扫描、虹膜扫描、生物识别,所有的这些都是可以内部植入的,那么将来如果您去机场或者火车站,您就不需要拿票了。因为通过扫描您,他们就知道您有没有买票,如果您去机场的入境海关,您也不需要停下来给工作人员看您的护照,因为您走进来的时候,他们就知道您是谁,扫描之后也就知道您携带的是什么行李。现在想象一下所有这些地方都可以腾出来用于其他用途,比如零售、商业用途。内部植入有无尽的用途。

12:03—13:38

On the street level, we can integrate a lot of them more or less. A lot of lower tech, what we call lower tech nowadays actually was quite high tech a few years back, like ways finding, interactive map, and smart bus stop where you can sit there know when the bus is gonna come, you can connect to the wifi, you can charge your phone etc., can integrate you know that on the street level. This is what we call an integrated urban environment. BMW is launching what they call a DriveNow program around the big city in the world like in London, and in you know various cities in America where you don't have to own a car, you just go there you know with a certain card, or you know maybe in the future and implantable, you just open the door, drive the car, and you drive away, and then you leave it you know at the intersection or certain corner. Now what this mean, the sharing economy means maybe in the future a lot of building they do not have to build so many car parks. Right now a big shopping mall they probably have to build 1,500, to 3,000, 4,000 car parks to cater for the customers coming in. If you don't own a car anymore using the sharing economy, just drive the car to parking lot, leave it there, and then other people going home could take the car away. So image all those space that could be released, image how it would change the architecture of a building if you don't have to design you know a car park.

在街上，我们可以进行一些整合，我们现在所说的低端科技在几年之前确实算是高科技了，像找路、互动地图、智能公交车站。有了智能公交站，您坐在那儿就能知道公交车什么时候到，能连接无线网络，还能给手机充电。这就是我们在街上可以进行的整合，我们称之为"综合城市布局"。宝马在伦敦这样的大城市展开了一个名为"DriveNow"的项目，在美国的许多城市，您不需自己有汽车，只需要拿着特定卡片，未来可能这个卡片都可以内部植入，您打开门，开车，上路，之后您在十字路口或是某个角落停下离开。共享经济意味着可能未来很多建筑都不需要建很多停车位。现在一个大型的商场可能要建1,500个到3,000个或4,000个停车位，从而满足顾客的需求。通过共享经济，您就不需要自己有车，只要把车开到停车场，停在那儿，其他人回家时可能就会把车开走。想象一下这些空间都被腾空，想象一下如果不需要设计停车场的话，建筑结构将有多么大的变化。

13:38—15:30

Taking this context of... a wider context like a city or urban development, we have the smart designs, smart architecture, we also have been practicing low carbon development for a long time. Then we have what we call this resilient city. How do we put all these together? So in the last eight and nine years we have developed what we call a smart green resilient thinking that we said we should elevate the science of city making to create secure, open and pleasant living communities for the people. And all of these put together would be like a prism, that converge all the diverging or conflicting sometimes could be conflicting objective of smart, green, and resilient together to come to a holistic you know and satisfactory solution. Now we don't want smart, green, resilient to be very prescriptive just like LEED, LEED certification. LEED certification actually stands for Leadership in Environmental and Energy Design. But as it goes on for many years a lot of the LEED certificates have been downgraded. To a lot of the practitioners it's just a "tick in the box" exercise, instead of taking the leadership in the design. The original idea of LEED is that you think about how your building reacts with your environment or the city that you are in to come up to a holistic and sustainable solution. But by practicing just ticking the box in order to get you know a gold certification, or platinum certification, you lose that leadership in design process. So we don't want smart, green, resilient to be a prescriptive thing.

以一个城市或城市发展为大背景，我们有智能设计、智能建筑，我们长期以来一直实践低碳发展。只有这样我们才能建成弹性城市。我们怎样才能把这些结合起来呢？在最近的八九年里，我们发展的是所谓的智能绿色弹性思维，这可以提升城市规则，为人们创造安全、开放、舒适的居住环境。所有这一切加在一起就成了一个棱镜，集中所有的分散和冲突，有时可以把智能、绿色、弹性这些相冲突的目标结合在一起，变成令人满意的整体性的解决方式。现在我们并不需要智能、绿色、弹性变得和能源与环境设计认证LEED一样规范。LEED的全称是能源与环境设计先锋奖。但这么多年来，该认证级别降低了不少。很多从业者都认为那只是一种"在方框里打钩"的练习（机械地按照认证要求来做），并不能引领设计。该认证起初的想法是考虑建筑该怎样和周边的环境或是城市互动，进而得出全面持续的解决方案。但如果只是为了获得所谓的金级或铂金级认证，那您在设计过程中就难保持领先地位。所以我们并不希望智能、绿色、弹性变成规范。

15:30—16:46
However, we believe that there should be three fundamental principles that should be practised in smart design. First, it should be future-proof, just like in this picture it is an aqua tower in Japan. It has been there for 700 years and it is still serving its function of bringing water to the city just like the Roman aqua tower. The Roman aqua tower is not bringing the water to the city anymore but they become a very big tourist attraction. So they serve, still serve a certain purpose. Then of course it has to be relevant to contemporary challenges because their expectation from the community. Lastly but not least, it got to be people-orientated, smart design should go for future end user not, sorry, the future end user, the actual end user. The end user and it's not your client, your client may be the government, may be the big developer, but actually you should focus on the end user. In order for it, you know, to be sustainable. And because of time, I will stop here. Thank you!

但是，我们认为智能设计应当有三大基本原则。首先，智能设计要有前瞻性，就像这幅图片里的日本水塔，距今已有700年历史，仍然像罗马的水塔一样将水运

第十单元 绿色建筑 Green Building

到城市里。罗马水塔现在已经不运水进城了,而是成了一个非常大的旅游景点。所以它仍然发挥一定作用。其次,智能设计要应对目前的挑战,因为这是社会的期望。最后,智能设计要以人为本,智能设计需要面对的是未来的终端用户,实际终端用户。终端用户不是指您的客户,您的客户可能是政府,可能是大开发商,但您应当关注终端用户,这样您的设计才具有可持续性。由于时间关系,我就讲到这里。谢谢大家!

第十一单元　知识产权
Intellectual Property Rights

I. 实战练习一

1. 演讲背景

英国出版商协会代表应邀参加"广东版权保护大会"并发表主旨演讲。他在演讲中首先介绍了英国出版商协会的工作，包括纸质书和电子书在内的英国出版市场概况，数字化带来的机遇，以及版权的重要性，例如赋予作者财产权、著作人身权、确保作者的权利与消费者的活动保持平衡。

2. 预习词汇

Consul General 总领事
digital age 数字时代
Publishers Association 出版商协会
Elsevier 爱思唯尔
Wiley 威利
Cengage 圣智
Oxford and Cambridge University Presses 牛津和剑桥大学出版社
Pearson 培生
Macmillan 麦克米伦
Random House 兰登书屋
Hachette 阿歇特
Harper Collins 哈珀柯林斯
intellectual property 知识产权
copyright infringement 版权侵权
database retrieval 数据库检索
Copyright Law《版权法》
digital access 数字访问
National Copyright Administration Committee 国家版权管理委员会
digital revenue 数字化收入

第十一单元　知识产权 Intellectual Property Rights

academic journal 学术期刊
physical book 纸质书
e-reader 电子阅读器
property right 财产权利
exclusive right 专有权利

3. 演讲文本

00:00—00:41

Mr. Cheng, thank you very much indeed for that introduction. I would like to start by thanking you and Mr. Hugo Zhang for organizing today's conference. I am afraid, like the previous speaker, Consul General Morgan, I am going to speak in English. Forgive me. I hope the interpreter will... I know the interpreter will convey my words to you. But if I am going too fast, I will look over to you and you wave at me and I will slow down. But I am sure you will keep up.

程先生，非常感谢您的介绍。我首先要感谢您和张玉国先生组织今天的会议。我恐怕要像前一位发言人摩根总领事一样用英语发言，请大家谅解。我知道翻译会把我的话传达给在座各位。但是如果我的讲话速度太快，我会看看你们的反应，你们向我挥挥手示意，我就会放慢速度。但我相信你们会跟上我的发言速度。

00:42—01:01

Thank you very much indeed for inviting me along to speak today on this incredibly important topic about protecting copyright in the digital age. And I would like to give you some perspectives from the British and the European side in which I work.

非常感谢邀请我今天就关于保护数字时代版权这一重要话题进行发言。我想和你们分享我在英国和欧洲工作的一些看法。

01:02—01:36

I will start by mainly talking about what the Publishers Association does. We are a trade body of 150 publishing companies, many of whom, I think, are representatives in this room. And indeed we have offices in China. So as well as Mr. Zhang's Elsevier, we have companies such as Wiley, Cengage, Oxford and Cambridge University Presses, Pearson, Macmillan, Random House, Hachette, HarperCollins and so on.

我首先介绍一下出版商协会的工作。我们是一个由150家出版公司组成的贸易组织，我想其中有许多代表都出席了今天的活动。事实上，我们在中国设有办事处。除了张先生代表的爱思唯尔，我们还有威利、圣智、牛津和剑桥大学出版社、培生、麦克米伦、兰登书屋、阿歇特和哈珀柯林斯等公司。

223

01:38—02:12

We are not a government body. We are entirely run by and run for our membership. Our main role is in making representations to governments and to both British Governments and Parliament, and also the European governments and parliaments on many areas of policy, including some which have been touched on already this morning: intellectual property, role of governments in businesses, in terms of taxes and employment law.

我们不是政府机构,我们完全由会员制经营并运行。我们的主要职责是向政府,英国政府和议会,以及欧洲各国政府和议会就许多领域的政策进行交涉,其中包括一些今天上午已经提到的政策:知识产权以及从税收和雇佣法的角度来看政府在商界的职责。

02:13—02:30

We also spend a lot of our time coordinating the efforts of our members in combating copyright infringement. We do that both in the UK and indeed on an international level, hence our engagement with this conference this morning.

我们还花了很多时间联合会员打击版权侵权。我们在英国乃至国际上都这样做,所以我们前来参加今天早上的会议。

02:32—03:14

And it was very interesting to hear Mr. Cheng's comments on the role of libraries in facilitating access to students, the correct position of fair use, and how best to achieve database retrieval. Because those are the very issues which we are engaged in great debates both in the United Kingdom and the European Union at this very moment. These are clearly the challenges of the digital age that are being confronted, whether it is here in Guangzhou, whether it is in London, whether as you hear from Lui Simpson later, it is in Washington DC.

听到程先生讲图书馆在方便学生访问、合理使用以及如何最好地实现数据库检索方面所发挥的作用非常有意思。因为这些都是目前在英国和欧盟引起热议的重要话题。无论是在广州、伦敦,还是在稍后沈璐怡会提到的华盛顿特区,这些显然都是数字时代正面临的挑战。

03:16—04:01

It may interest you to know that in the United Kingdom at the moment, we are in the final stages of finalizing some updates to *Copyright Law*. As you have heard that it has been around since 1709. But it doesn't mean that it shouldn't change; in fact, that's

第十一单元　知识产权 Intellectual Property Rights

probably the reason that it should change. And so we have the amendments to the *Copyright Law* going through right now, which will allow libraries greater ability to make digital copies for the purposes of archiving and preservation. There are also new laws coming in, which will make it easier for libraries to provide digital access to their users.

您可能会想知道目前在英国,我们正处于修订《版权法》的最后阶段。您可能知道《版权法》是1709年颁布的,但这并不意味着不应该修改;事实上,可能正因为如此,才要修订《版权法》。因此,我们现在正在进行修订,赋予图书馆更大的权限,为存档和保存进行数字拷贝。我们还会出台新的法律,使用户更容易进行图书馆数字访问。

04:03—04:35

We have also, recently, in the United Kingdom, concluded a new arrangement with our national deposit libraries, so the British libraries and also the university libraries and others around the country, whether it is a legal requirement on publishers to deposit works, we have just concluded arrangements to facilitate the digital deposits of works. So again, libraries are getting access immediately to the works of British publishers.

我们最近还与我们的国家图书馆存储库订立了新的协议,所以英国的图书馆、大学图书馆和全国其他的图书馆,无论它们对于出版商存放的作品是否有法律规定,我们都已经立协议,方便作品进行数码存放。同样,图书馆也可以立即访问英国出版商的作品。

04:39—05:20

And in this week we're coming over to China for this conference, we are taking the opportunity, Emma House and Lui Simpson and I, together with Hugo Zhang from Elsevier to visit with the National Copyright Administration Committee and also with Alibaba and Taobao yesterday in Hangzhou, where, we, again, have found we have so much in common in terms of trying to find ways through to make sure that published works are accessible whilst at the same time making sure that copyright infringement doesn't go on.

本周我们来到中国参加此次会议,我和艾玛·豪斯、沈璐怡以及来自爱思唯尔的张玉国先生也借此机会一起参观了国家版权管理委员会,昨天我们也参观了位于杭州的阿里巴巴集团和淘宝总部。在那里,我们再次发现我们之间存在着许多共同点,我们都是一边在想方设法确保用户可以访问出版作品,一边又得确保版权侵权不会继续发生。

05:23—05:54

So what I would like to talk more about this morning is not the negatives about copyright and infringement, but the positive story, and how copyright is actually working for publishers in the digital age. Before I do that, I thought it might be helpful to give you some context about the size and scope of the British market, and the importance, in particular, of digital products and services.

因此,今天早上我想从正面的角度多谈谈版权问题以及版权在数字时代如何为出版商服务,而不是探讨版权和侵权的负面情况。在那之前,我认为向您介绍一下英国市场的规模和范围以及数字产品和服务的重要性可能会有所帮助。

05:55—06:22

In 2012, there were 3.3 billion pounds' worth of book sales in the United Kingdom. Now I know, in an economy as big as China's, maybe that figure doesn't look so big. But the British economy is about one trillion pounds. So you can see we have, we are at least, soaring somewhere on the national radar.

2012年,英国图书销售额达到33亿英镑。我也知道在一个像中国那么大的经济体中,也许这看起来并不是个大数目。但英国经济体量约为1万亿英镑。所以您可以看到,至少我们正在助力英国国民经济的迅猛发展。

06:23—06:55

But the important figures that I want to draw your attention to are the fact that consumer e-books continue to become more popular, up by 134% last year. But digital revenues rising, again, this has happened in previous years as well, to 400 million pounds, and now are some 12% overall of the publishers' revenues. And that figure is tracked to continue to rise.

但我想请您注意的重要数据是电子书依旧畅销,去年增长了134%。而且数字化收入和前几年一样也在上涨,达到4亿英镑,现在占到了出版商总收入的12%左右。而且这一数字还在继续上升。

06:56—07:28

Now the big question in British publishing is where does that figure stop? Are we looking to a future, where perhaps 60%, 70% of revenues of digital? Or perhaps it will level out at about 50%. And there will still be a strong market for physical books. At the moment, we simply don't know. We will just continue to invest in the digital products. As long as readers want those, that is what we will seek to provide.

现在英国出版业面临的一大问题就是这个数字的上限是什么?我们是否期待着

第十一单元 知识产权 Intellectual Property Rights

未来可能有60%、70%的数字化收入?还是说它会达到50%左右的平衡状态?纸质书籍仍然会有强劲的市场。目前,我们根本不知道答案。我们将继续投资数字产品。只要是读者想要的,我们就要提供。

07:29—08:22

The other important figure there is for academic journals, which is, of course, an entire separate business, again, from our book business. That is 1.5 billion pounds to the UK. And practically it is all about digital revenues and that business has been on-line for a very long time. And there are some 109 universities in the United Kingdom. Again, that might sound like a small number, I know, to this audience. But 6% of all the research with British publishers published is derived from the UK. So as the Consul General was saying earlier about the British creativity perhaps being greater than one might expect for our population, also our scientific and academic output is also disproportionately large.

另一个重要数据是学术期刊,当然,这也是我们图书业务的一项完全独立的业务。这对英国来说价值15亿英镑。实际上,这全是数字化收入,而且这项业务实现在线化已经相当长时间了。英国有109所大学,当然我知道这对听众来说可能是很小的数字。但英国出版商发布的所有研究中有6%来自英国。正如总领事早些时候所说的,英国的创造力可能远超过人们的预期,我们的科学和学术成果硕果累累,与人口总数不成正比。

08:25—08:57

British publishers in the United Kingdom, together with their colleagues in the United States and other international companies, are working very closely with the British Government to facilitate open access. British publishers agree with the British Government that academic research, especially when it has been funded by the state, by the taxpayer, should be available for reading as soon as possible, preferably immediately.

英国的出版商与他们美国及其他国际公司的同事正在与英国政府密切合作,以实现开放查阅。英国出版商和英国政府观点一致,即学术研究,尤其是国家或者纳税人资助的学术研究应尽快开放给读者,最好是一发布就开放。

08:58—09:48

And that is why the British publishers support open access and a system that has been developed not just in the UK, but we put it into place in the UK, whereby papers can be immediately available for reading, provided that the publisher has been paid by the author, by the researcher of that paper earlier in the process. And this is a new policy in the United Kingdom, which began on the 1st of April this year. We are also seeing development of the policy at the European Union level. And we are very hopeful that by working with our governments and working with British libraries and universities in this way, we will ensure that the published works are available to everyone who wants them as soon as possible.

这就是为什么英国出版商支持开放查阅和一个并非由英国独立研发的系统,我们把系统应用到英国,只要作者或者论文的研究人员已经提前给出版商付费,论文就可立即供阅读。这是英国从今年4月1日开始实行的一项新政策。我们也看到了欧盟在这方面的政策发展。我们非常希望通过与我们的政府、英国的图书馆和大学合作,我们能确保有需要的人可以尽快获取已发表的作品。

09:49—10:14

But I wouldn't know from those figures that you can see, despite the increased importance of digital, that physical books still dominate for now. So digital technology is clearly changing the landscape of publishing. And it's doing so in ways which are beneficial to all stakeholders.

尽管数字化越来越重要,目前纸质书仍占主导地位,不看这些数据我都不会知道这一点。所以显而易见,数字化技术正在改变着出版业的格局,而且对所有利益攸关方都大有裨益。

10:16—10:47

First of all, authors. Authors are being able to exploit digital opportunities in finding new ways to write. If an author is no longer bound by the physical confines of a book, then their imagination, if they are fiction writers, can develop in ways unconstrained by physical formats. We are already seeing in the development of e-books, authors are writing in different ways, because they are no longer constrained.

首先,作者本身。作者现在能够利用数字化机遇寻找新的写作方法。如果一个作者不再受到纸质书的实体限制,如果他们是小说作家,那么他们的想象力可以不受书本格式的约束而自由发挥。我们已经看到了电子书的发展,因为现在作者不再受到限制,他们正进行不同方式的写作。

10:48—11:17

We are also seeing authors no longer constrained by having to work with publishers. And self-publishing, where an author writes a work and puts it straight onto the Internet. Perhaps by-passing the publisher is becoming more and more common. Of course, we would always say, as publishers, that well, they could do this. They would probably find it better than they did with publishers. But nevertheless, this is a growing trend.

我们也看到作者不再局限于与出版商的合作。他们可以个人出版，即作者自己创作并将作品直接放到互联网上。也许绕过出版商出版作品正变得越来越普遍。当然，作为出版商，我们总是会说，作者可以这样做。也许他们还会发现这种方式比和出版商合作更好。但无论如何，这都是一大趋势。

11:19—12:01

Digital is providing new opportunities for readers, not just as Mr. Cheng said earlier, in university libraries, but also in the wider economy as well. As I have just shown, British readers are enjoying the opportunities to read e-books. 25% of British consumers have an e-reader. 30% of British consumers have a tablet, on which they can also read e-books. So you can see as those devices penetrates the economy, more and more digital reading is taking place. And of course, for publishers, this all means new revenue streams as well. And I'll now talk about those in a moment.

数字化为读者提供了新机遇，不仅仅像程先生所说的在大学图书馆，而且在更宽泛的经济领域中也如此。正如我刚才所展示的，英国读者正在享受阅读电子书。25%的英国消费者拥有电子阅读器。30%的英国消费者拥有平板电脑，他们也可以在上面阅读电子书。您可以看到，随着这些设备渗透到经济中，数字化阅读就也越来越普遍。当然，对于出版商来说，这一切都意味着新的收入来源。稍后我将谈到这一点。

12:02—12:24

And the final benefit, I think, at the moment, from digital opportunities is to all of our society and all of culture. And this is the most exciting thing about the digital opportunities, it's not just publishers and readers, but all of our society can benefit. And it allows us to get access to each other's culture internationally.

我认为最后一个好处是，目前全社会和所有文化都迎来了数字化机遇。数字化机遇最令人兴奋的是不仅仅是出版商和读者，就连全社会都可以受益。它使我们能够了解不同国家的文化。

12:27—12:56

But it is often asserted that in the face of this rapid technical development that copyright is somehow hopelessly outdated. Some people say copyright is a relic that it's not fit for purpose, that we need a whole new system of laws to cope with the 21st century. I happen to disagree with that view.

然而也有人说，面对这样快速的技术发展，版权会过时。有些人说版权是一个遗物，并没有合适的用途，我们需要一个全新的法律体系来适应21世纪。我恐怕不能同意这种观点。

12:57—13:27

While some adaptation will always be required, and as I mentioned just now that adaptation is going on at the moment in the UK and everywhere. Fundamentally, copyright is still the best way to ensure that we can reward creativity and incentivize investment. Because the central tenets of copyright are as important and relevant in the modern age as ever they were.

我们当然需要做一些调整，正如我刚才提到的英国和世界各国目前都正在进行调整。从根本上说，版权仍然是确保我们可以奖励创造力和激励投资的最佳方式。因为在当下，版权的核心宗旨还是和以往一样重要，并具有现实意义。

13:28—14:26

I think this is because copyright does four important things. It secures the property rights of the author. It allows the creator of the work to say, that is mine and then decide how that work is used, how it is traded, how it is reproduced. And it does that by giving the author some exclusive rights. It allows the author to determine how the work is copied. It allows the author to determine how the work is distributed, how it is sold or hired or rented. And it also allows the author to determine how the work is made available to the public. And those three rights of reproduction, distribution and communication sit at the very heart of our intellectual property system.

我认为这是因为版权做了四件重要的事情。它保障了作者的财产权利。它让作品的创作者可以说作品是属于他们的，由他们决定这个作品如何使用、如何交易以及如何复制。这是通过赋予作者一些专有权利来实现的。它允许作者来决定作品如何被复制，允许作者决定作品的发行、销售或租用方式。它还使作者能够决定作品如何向公众开放。复制、发行和传播等三项权利是知识产权制度的核心。

14:28—14:59

Now often, the author will sign those rights to a publisher and that's where we come in. But all the time the publisher is acting fundamentally in the interests of the author. And very often when publishers perhaps get a bad reputation for trying to protect their work, they are actually protecting the work of the author. Because it is part of the agreement that the publisher has with the author that they will do this.

现在作者经常会签字把这些权利转让给出版商，而这也是我们发挥作用的地方。出版商一直以来都从根本上代表着作者的利益。很多时候出版商在试图保护他们的作品时可能会因此而声名狼藉，可他们实际上是在保护作者的作品。因为这是出版商和作者协议里的规定，他们就要做到这一点。

15:01—15:34
Another important facet of copyright, which is all the more important in the digital age, is moral rights. This speaks to the ability of the author to claim acknowledgment for his work or her work to be able to say, I did that. And the moral rights also allow the author to object to derogatory, unfair treatment of their work. And this is very important where we see in the digital age works being taken for uses that they weren't originally intended for.

在数字时代，版权的另一个重要方面是著作人身权。也就是作者可以理直气壮地说作品是他写的。著作人身权还允许作者抗议对其作品的贬损和不公正待遇。在现在的数字时代，我们看到许多作品在使用时都背离了作者原意，从这方面看，著作人身权就显得十分重要。

15:36—16:12
And finally, copyright allows those rights of the author to be balanced with consumer activities. And notice I deliberately don't say consumer rights in this respect. Copyright doesn't give consumers or users rights. Copyright gives the author rights, which has balanced against what consumers might then want to do. Sometimes, a consumer or a user will want to copy a work, and it's up to them the author did decide whether or not they can.

最后，版权确保作者的权利与消费者的活动保持平衡。请大家注意，我在这里故意不提消费者权利。版权并没有赋予消费者或用户权利。版权是赋予作者权利，这正好与消费者可能想要做的保持平衡。有时候，消费者或用户想要复制某件作品，这要由作者决定他们能否这样做。

16:16—16:44
So this combination of digital technology and copyright leads to new services and products. It allows the linking of scientific research as we heard earlier. It allows publishers and authors to determine how their works are put onto the Internet and how they can be linked with other works on the Internet. Copyright provides publishers and authors with the ability to determine that.

所以数字技术和版权的结合产生了新的服务和产品。正如我们早些时候听到的，版权与科研产生联系，让出版商和作者决定如何将作品放到网上，如何将自己的作品与互联网上的其他作品联系起来。版权为出版商和作者提供了决定权。

II. 实战练习二

1. 演讲背景

下文也同样摘自英国出版商协会代表的演讲。他在第二部分的演讲中分享了数字化技术的益处以及如何利用水印技术、密码术和密钥交换、编程技术打击侵权,如何与搜索引擎公司、电影公司、工作室、音乐公司、维萨卡、万事达信用卡和贝宝的等服务商合作阻止侵权行为。最后他还强调最有利的工具是教育公众保护版权的重要性。

2. 预习词汇

watermarking technology 水印技术
cryptography technique 密码术
exchanging of key 密钥交换
data mining 数据挖掘
distribution right 发行权
Visa 维萨卡
MasterCard 万事达信用卡
PayPal 贝宝
moral right 著作人身权;精神权利
text mining 文本挖掘
metadata 元数据
content ID 内容身份识别代码
Copyright Infringement Portal 版权侵权门户
photocopy 影印

3. 演讲文本

00:01—00:53

There is a very exciting new development, again, thanks to digital technology in data and text mining, the ability to use computer technology to go into repositories of academic research and draw from them conclusions which aren't immediately apparent, that can be discovered by computers reading across vast quantity of data. This is a very new, exciting area of development, which publishers are working with researchers to help facilitate. It does blow up questions about copyright, about how that work is

第十一单元　知识产权 Intellectual Property Rights

copied. And that's why, again, right at this moment, publishers are in close discussions with European and British governments about how we can ensure that this activity goes on but without infringing on the rights of the author.

还有一个非常令人兴奋的新发展，这要归功于数据的数字化技术和文本挖掘，它们能够利用计算机技术进入学术研究库，并从中得出并非立即显而易见的结论，这些结论可以通过计算机读取大量数据来获取。这是一个十分新颖、令人兴奋的发展领域，出版商正联合研究人员为此出一份力。这确实让人们质疑关于版权以及如何复制作品的问题。因此现在，出版商与欧洲和英国政府正在密切讨论如何确保继续开展这项活动，但又不会侵犯作者的权利。

00:56—01:23

Digital technology allows, enhances e-books so that readers perhaps aren't just reading a novel or a poem, but are reading that at the same time as hearing actors read it, or seeing films lined behind the book. These are all developments which have come about because we can bring together the copyrights of filmmakers and actors and broadcasters and putting them in one product.

数字技术提升了电子书的地位，通过电子书，读者不仅可以阅读小说或诗歌，同时也可以听到演员朗读文本，或看书后附上的相关影片。这些都是已经出现的发展，因为我们可以将电影制片人、演员和广播公司的版权集合在一起，将之融入到一个产品中。

01:25—02:15

And finally, copyright is allowing publishers to determine how their works are sold and made available in new and exciting ways. For instance, a number of British publishers have tried to link the service in the UK whereby they are selling e-books to a university faculty. And then that faculty is then providing those books completely free to the students on the course for a period of seven years. So the students arriving at the university with their laptops or their PC is able to get access to all those works digitally for nothing for the length of the time they are on that course. And that's possible because of this combination of copyright and technology.

最后，版权允许出版商决定作品以何种新颖且令人兴奋的方式对外销售和开放。例如，一些英国出版商通过向大学教师出售电子书来连接这种服务。然后那些教师随后又将这些书籍完全免费地提供给选修这门课的学生，时效长达 7 年。因此，带着笔记本电脑或个人电脑来到大学的学生可以在选修课程期间无数次免费访问所有这些作品。版权和技术的这种结合使得这一切变为可能。

02:16—02:42

But I want to talk now finally about how we can use that technology to ensure that copyright is not infringed. Because at the same time that digital technology and copyright are combining to provide publishers with new revenue streams, we are using that very same technology to tackle on-line copyright infringement and protecting revenue.

但最后我想谈谈我们如何利用技术来确保版权不受侵犯。数字技术和版权相结合,为出版商提供了新的收入来源,与此同时,我们也在使用同样的技术来解决网络侵权问题,从而保护收入。

02:43—03:49

And here are just some of the ways that British publishers are looking to do this. First of all, if we think about that, first, the most important right of copyright, the reproduction right. How we are using technology to help prevent that being infringed? A number of publishers are talking to provide us with watermarking technology. Now this will allow every single time an individual digital copy is made, a watermark or an invisible electronic protection can be put into that work so that you know precisely where it is. Now this will allow publishers to monitor infringement, if a copy of the work that they have made turns up on the Internet in some distant web-site, they will know precisely where that has come from. They might be able to identify where in the supply chain the infringing copy is taking place. That technology is fast being developed. I think we will see it more prevalent in the market in a few years' time.

以下只是英国出版商为此所采取的一些方法。首先,我们想一下,版权中最重要的权利就是复制权。我们如何利用技术来防止侵权?许多出版商说可以为我们提供水印技术。这将使得每一次复制电子版时,水印或无形的电子保护功能可以嵌入作品中,以便您确切知道它所在的位置。这将允许出版商监控侵权行为,如果他们原作的复制品显示在某个远程网站上,他们就会精确地知道来源。他们也许就能确定供应链中侵权行为发生的位置。这项技术正在快速发展。我认为几年的时间,你们就会看到它在市场上变得越来越普及。

03:52—04:24

When publishers wish to make copies of their work to allow data mining as I've talked about earlier, it is very important that the person making the copy is allowed to do so, but also the people who aren't allowed to make the copy don't. And publishers are already using the cryptography techniques, the exchanging of keys so that only the person who has the right to copy that work is able to do so. This technology is allowing a very safe exchange of information between scientific academic publishers and data

第十一单元 知识产权 Intellectual Property Rights

miners.

出版商希望复制自己的作品,进行我之前提到的数据挖掘,复制作品的人要得到允许,未经允许不能这么做。出版商已经在利用密码术和密钥交换,这样只有有权复制该作品的人才能进行复制。有了这项技术,科学学术出版商和数据挖掘者之间就可以非常安全地交换信息。

04:27—04:52

Now I said, one of most important rights in copyrights is the ability to determine how a work is communicated to the public, especially in the modern age of the Internet. Now as you all know, the Internet, wonderful thing that it is, also allows for large scale of copyright infringement to take place. But we can use technology to protect ourselves or to try to protect ourselves against that.

版权最重要的一大权利就是能够决定作品如何传播给公众,特别是在现代互联网时代。众所周知,互联网精彩纷呈,但也会引起大规模的版权侵权行为。但我们可以利用技术保护自己,保护自己免受这种伤害。

04:53—05:26

And in the UK and elsewhere, we are using the very same algorithm of the world's leading search engines, such as Google, with whom we have a partnership, so we can use their search engine technology to search the world wide web and find infringing copies of publishers' and authors' works. And we are using that very same technology to protect our works. Because one of the main problems with infringement is just finding where the infringing work is in the first place. We are getting better and better in doing that.

在英国或其他地方,我们使用的算法与谷歌等世界一流搜索引擎一样,我们与谷歌也建立了合作关系,因此我们可以使用他们的搜索引擎技术搜索万维网,查找到侵权出版商和作者的作品。我们正在利用同样的技术来保护我们的作品。因为侵权行为的一大问题就是首先要找到侵权作品的来源。我们在这方面做得越来越好。

05:28—06:01

One of those other rights in copyrights is the distribution right, the ability to determine how a work is sold. And again, the Internet is providing exciting new opportunities for this. But it's also allowing people who infringe copyrights to infringe that distribution right. There are websites in the world, happens to be the case that Russia is one of the places where these are more prevalent, where websites are set up and they are selling the work as if it was theirs, a clear infringement of copyright.

235

版权中的另一项权利是发行权，即确定作品如何销售。互联网也正在为作品的销售提供激动人心的新机遇。但侵犯版权的人也会借此侵犯该作品的发行权。世界上有一些网站，例如俄罗斯就有很多这样的网站，这些网站把别人的作品当作是自己的作品进行出售，这明显侵犯了版权。

06:02—06:36

What we are doing in the United Kingdom, together with films, studios and music companies, is talking to the people who facilitate on-line e-commerce. People like Visa and MasterCard and PayPal and saying to them, "when you see works on an infringing site, don't allow people to use your services to buy those works." Again, using that technology, using the same methods that infringers are using, to try and stop that copyright infringements taking place.

我们在英国联手电影公司、工作室和音乐公司与那些促进在线电子商务的人进行沟通。对像维萨卡、万事达信用卡和贝宝等服务商说："在侵权网站上看到侵权作品时，请勿让他人使用您的服务购买这些作品。"正如之前所说，我们要用和侵权者相同的技术、相同的方法来阻止侵权行为。

06:38—07:03

The importance of moral rights in copyright I have touched on earlier, and again, we can use technology to help protect those, when a digital file is sent, be it literary work or film, or a piece of music, the metadata accompanying in that work, that sits over the top of it, has information about who created it and who should get rights payments.

早先我已经谈到了版权中著作人身权的重要性，再说一次，我们可以使用技术来帮助保护这些权利，例如发送数字文件，无论是发送文学作品、电影还是音乐作品，附在该作品顶部的元数据都会显示出创建人以及谁应该获得权利费。

07:05—07:22

It is often people who infringe copyrights are those sometimes who ignore those metadata, or especially in the case of images, they strip it out altogether, so that when an image appears on the Internet, there is nowhere of knowing who created that image and who took the photograph, and therefore who should be paid.

侵犯版权的人通常是那些忽略元数据的人，尤其是在有图像的情况下，他们会将图像全部剥离出来，所以哪怕是一张图像出现在互联网上，大家都不清楚图像到底是谁创建的，照片是谁拍摄的，因此也不知道该付钱给谁。

第十一单元　知识产权 Intellectual Property Rights

07:24—07:57

As the Consul General mentioned the Copyright Hub earlier, which is a very important piece of work that rights holders in the United Kingdom are working on. One important facet of that is programming a work to stop the metadata being stripped out to ensure that whenever a work is on the Internet, especially but not only images, that the ownership data stays with it, so that photographers don't find themselves seeing their works ever on the Internet, but never getting paid for what they have done.

总领事早些时候也提到了版权中心，这是英国版权持有人正在开展的一项非常重要的工作。其中一个重要方面是为作品编程，阻止元数据被剥离，确保以图像为主的作品上传到互联网时，数据的所有权都与原作品保持一致，这样摄影师就不会看到自己的作品出现在网上，却收不到一分钱。

07:59—08:41

We also work, again, with Google, which owns the service of YouTube, which is, I am sure you know, the large site which allows user generated contents but also the licensed work of the world's major films, studios and television companies. And YouTube has developed a system called contents ID, which means that any work that is on YouTube, they are able to identify. And If the rights holder wants it to be there, they can pay the rights holder. Or if the rights holder says no, that it shouldn't be up there, then YouTube will take it down. So again, using technology to protect revenues and still allows works to be developed.

我们还与谷歌合作，谷歌有 YouTube 的服务，相信大家都知道，YouTube 是一个允许用户创作内容的大型网站，也是一个获得世界主要电影公司、电影制片厂和电视公司许可的网站。YouTube 开发了一个名为内容身份识别代码的系统，也就是说 YouTube 上的任何作品都可以被识别。如果版权持有人希望它出现在那里，YouTube 可以付费给版权持有人。如果版权持有人认为自己的作品不应该出现在 YouTube，那么 YouTube 就会把它撤下来。正如之前所说的，利用技术来保护收入，也仍然保留作品的发展空间。

08:42—08:58

A few years ago, a lot of rights holders in United Kingdom saw YouTube as a big challenge. It was frequently infringing works. But today, because of content ID, everyone is very relaxed about YouTube and it is a great source of revenue.

几年前，英国的许多版权持有人将 YouTube 看作是一大挑战，认为 YouTube 上有很多侵权作品。但是今天，多亏了内容身份识别代码，大家对 YouTube 都非常放心，YouTube 成为一个很好的收入来源。

09:01—10:37

Once said that more about search, as I said earlier, we have developed the ability to find infringing works anywhere on the Internet using the same technology, the very same technology as the leading search engines. But it is not good enough to find the works, we also have to try to take them down. And in the Publishers Association, we have developed, with our members, a system called the Copyright Infringement Portal. This is a web-base system, which allows our publishers to upload a number of titles, which are then searched for across the web, internationally of course. When infringing copies of a work have found, a report is given to the publisher, and then we can send the notice to either the website or the server, or the Internet service provider, requesting that work, the URL that linked to the work is taken down. This is a system we have been operating for some three years. We have sent something like 260,000 notices in that time. And 80% of the time, the link is taken off the Internet and that infringing work is no longer there. And in this way, publishers, publishers of all disciplines, academic, education and consumer publishers are really managing to control a great deal of the on-line copyright infringement which is taking place.

正如我刚才说到的，关于搜索，我们已经有能力找到网上的侵权作品，采用的技术与各大搜索引擎的技术完全相同。但只找到作品还不够，我们还必须把它们撤下来。在出版商协会的资助下，我们与成员一起研发了一个名为版权侵权门户的系统。该系统基于网络，可以让出版商上传一些标题，再通过网络在全球范围进行搜索。如果发现侵权的复制品，它会向出版商发送报告，然后我们把通知发送给网站、服务器或互联网服务供应商，要求撤销该作品的网址链接。这个系统我们已经运行了3年，已经发送了大约26万份通知。80%的链接已都从互联网上删除，这样侵权的作品也就消除了。通过这种方式，各学科的出版商，包括学术出版商、教育出版商和畅销书出版商都在管控目前存在的大量在线版权侵权行为。

10:39—11:16

And the final way in which we are using technology to protect copyright on-line is through consumer education. Actually, I think, consumer education is the most important tool we have in combating copyright infringement. Because it is only, I think, when people really understand the importance of protecting copyright that they will tend not to infringe it. And this is as true of somebody uploading works to the Internet which they shouldn't do as it is of people making a photocopy of a book which they shouldn't do.

我们使用技术保护版权的最终方式是消费者教育。其实，我认为消费者教育是我们打击版权侵权的最重要工具。因为只有当人们真正认识到保护版权的重要性时，他们才不会去侵犯版权。正如人们明白不应该未经许可将作品上传到互联网，或者对书进行影印是一样的道理。

11:17—11:48
And all the consumer research certainly in the UK we have seen, is that actually when you explain to people how important copyright is, and explain to people how important it is that authors get paid, and explain to people that infringing copyright doesn't just take money from big companies and big studios and big publishers, but actually takes money from the authors' pocket. Very many people would stop infringing. At least they say they will stop infringing.

我们所看到的英国消费者研究都表明，您向人们解释版权有多重要，解释作者获得报酬有多重要，解释侵犯版权不仅是从大公司、大制片厂和大出版商处拿走了钱，实际上也从作者口袋里掏钱，虽然侵权人会口头声称不再侵权，但实际上效果不大。

11:49—12:47
So we are working together with Internet service providers to find the way of directly communicating with people who infringe copyright on-line. This is a conversation we have been having for about three years in the UK. And I hope in the next few months we will now have the system in place, so that when an individual user uploads a work at home, we are able to detect that infringement, and we are then able to ask their Internet service providers to send a message to them, perhaps on their screen, to say, you have infringed copyright. Here is why you shouldn't do it. And the aim is that they will stop. So again, using that technology against the infringer, but not in the way that admonishes them, not in the way that sends them many penalty, but just a way of educating them.

因此，我们正联手互联网服务提供商，想办法直接与在线侵权的人进行沟通。在英国，这种沟通对话已经持续了约3年时间。我希望在接下来的几个月内，我们可以建立一个系统，这样用户在家上传作品时，我们可以检测到侵权行为，然后要求他们的互联网服务供应商向侵权者发送信息，比如在他们的屏幕上显示：您已经侵犯了版权，这是您不应该侵权的原因。建立系统的初衷是侵权者会停止侵权。所以再说明一下，使用这种技术不是要以劝告或者严惩的方式来对付他们，而是要教育他们。

12:49—13:22
So I hope I have succeeded in providing you with an overview of the British

market, some perspectives as how digital technology works for everyone and how the tenets of copyrights and technology combined to drive growth and protect revenue. Thank you for your attention. Thank you to the interpreters for allowing me to be understood. And I am very happy to take any questions you may have. Thank you!

我今天介绍了英国市场的总体状况,对于如何利用数字技术造福人类、如何将版权和技术原理结合起来,推动增长,保护版权收入,我分享了我的一些看法。谢谢大家!感谢翻译,让大家知道我在说什么。我很乐意解答任何问题。谢谢!

第十二单元　人工智能
Artificial Intelligence

I. 实战练习一

1. 演讲背景

日本发明家、机器人大师高桥智隆应邀出席主题为"人工智能"的"腾讯智慧峰会"并发表主旨演讲。他在演讲中介绍了他和其他公司共同研发的人形机器人，分别是机器人宇航员 KIROBO、松下电池促销机器人 EVOLTA、参加机器人世界杯比赛的机器人、可以作为爱好收藏的人形机器人 Robi、机器人智能手机 RoBoHoN。他还一边介绍一边和机器人互动，让它们唱歌、跳舞、拍照等。

2. 预习词汇

Tomotaka Takahashi 高桥智隆（日本嘉宾名字）
Foxconn 富士康
Ghibli Anime 吉卜力动画
Hon Hai 鸿海精密集团
HTV 日本 HTV 货运飞船
interface 交互界面
Jiminy Cricket 蟋蟀吉明尼（出自动画《木偶奇遇记》）
Le Mans 勒芒
physical robot 实体机器人
Pinocchio 匹诺曹
Robi 日本的一款小型家居机器人
RoboCup 机器人世界杯
RoBoHoN 一款机器人人形手机
Sharp 夏普

3. 演讲文本

00:00—01:00

Good morning, everybody. My name is Tomotaka Takahashi. I'm creating robot.

And today I'm so impressed by other experts' speech. And you see there are so many AI and robots already inside of our life. But actually, we don't see physical robot. You know, none of you are actually robot. So what I'm creating is actual physical robot. I'm creating small humanoid robot like him. He is the first robot astronaut, named KIROBO. I developed him with TOYOTA and Tansu. It's a Japanese act agency.

大家早上好，我叫高桥智隆。我制作机器人。今天，各位专家的演讲让我印象深刻。同时，大家可以看到，在我们生活中，出现了很多人工智能和机器人。但是实际上，我们没看到过实体机器人长什么样，因为我们都不是机器人。而我正在制作的是一种实体机器人。我正在制作像他那样的小型人形机器人。他是第一个机器人宇航员，名为KIROBO。我携手丰田和日本一家代理机构Tansu公司一起合作研发这个机器人。

01:00—01:11
Japanese video
日语视频

01:11—01:46
Actually this is the first word spoken by robot in space. It's the inside of the international space station. And photos were taken by astronauts. And you can see blue earth behind the robot. And you see pictures are too beautiful and they look like just fake one but actually it's a real photo. And we sent him to the space station by Japanese rocket.

实际上这是机器人在太空中说过的第一个词。这是在国际太空站里面。这些照片是宇航员拍摄的。同时，您可以看到机器人身后的蔚蓝色的地球。看着这些漂亮的照片，你们甚至会怀疑这些照片是不是假的，但确实是真实的照片。我们用日本的火箭把这个机器人发送到了太空站上。

01:46—01:51
Video: And lift off. Lift off the HTV on a journey to the international space station.
视频：火箭发射。日本HTV货运飞船发射升空，飞往国际空间站。

01:51—05:29
And we sent him to the space station for communication experiment with Japanese astronaut. And I'll show you another of my work. This is EVOLTA robot for Panasonic battery promotion. It's a quite simple robot with just 2 double A batteries. And we went

to Grand Canyon to go up to the cliff, from bottom to the top, which is 530 meters in height. And this is, the robot is so small. It took a long time. Actually weather in Grand Canyon is so hard and it's windy, sometimes raining hard and lots of rocks and scorpions and snakes. But he spent 6 hours and 46 minutes to get to the top. After that, we found that there was still battery power left. So we went to Le Mans in France to do 24 hours tricycle riding without changing batteries. And every time Panasonic spent a million US dollars for this experiment. And I got a heavy pressure on me. And I set up two batteries in his shoulder. And the robot has infrared sensor to follow bike, human riding bike. That's how he, you know, trying to, go around the circuit. And once we turn him on, nobody can touch him. So we are just watching and waiting, and sometimes sleeping. Anyway, robot can be running, and even in a morning, he was still running. And then it was almost 24 hours. So this is just a tiny simple robot but the people somehow attached to his appeal. And then it was really well at the promotion. Now we can make any kind of geographics. We actually create physical robot and share fun with robot.

我们把机器人发射到空间站上,是为了和日本宇航员进行沟通、交流实验。我再给大家展示我的另一个作品。这款 EVOLTA 机器人使用松下的促销电池,这款机器人非常简单,动力只需两枚 5 号电池。我们还去了大峡谷,沿着峡谷底部一路登顶,那里的悬崖峭壁高达 530 米。大家可以看到,由于机器人很小,所以花了很长时间才登顶。实际上,大峡谷的天气状况十分恶劣,风非常大,有时还下暴雨,此外还有岩石、蝎子和蛇。但是这个机器人花了 6 小时 46 分钟就成功登顶。登顶之后,我们发现电池还有剩余电量。于是我们就去了法国的勒芒,在没有更换电池的情况下,让机器人进行 24 小时的三轮车骑行实验。松下每次都花上百万美元去做这些实验。因此,我压力很大。我在机器人的肩上装了两枚电池。机器人配备了红外线感应器,以追踪自行车,追踪人类骑行自行车。他得竭尽全力跑完整个跑道。一旦我们启动了机器人,任何人都不能触碰他。因此我们只能旁观静待,甚至有时候睡觉休息。无论发生什么事,这个机器人一直在跑,到了早上还在跑。整个过程持续了差不多 24 小时。这就是一个普通的小型机器人,但人们却在一定程度上为之着迷。之后,这种产品在促销中表现不俗。现在我们可以设置各种地形。实际上我们可以创造实体机器人,与机器人分享乐趣。

05:29—06:56

And that's one of our creation. And there's another one. It's for RoboCup. RoboCup is the world's biggest robot competition, doing soccer game. And then Louis Vuitton trophy is prepared for winner. And this is actual RoboCup. Actually robots are fully autonomist. He is onboard and nobody controls robot. Nobody remote controls robot. And bigger robots are from Germany and the smaller, smarter robots are from us.

And the German team is so strong. But our goal keeper is better than theirs. And the German team's strategy was really aggressive and offensive. So in RoboCup, two robots were coming towards a ball. And because of that, no one was saving the ball at the goal area. Anyway, we won RoboCup five times and we have developed these autonomist robots too.

这只是我们的一个作品。这是另外一个。这个作品是为机器人世界杯制作的。机器人世界杯是世界上最大的机器人足球竞赛，优胜者可以获得路易威登奖杯。这就是机器人世界杯的真实情况。实际上，这些机器人实现了完全自主行动。这是一种随车携带、无人控制的机器人，没有人遥控这个机器人。大一点儿的机器人来自德国，小型的智能机器人则是我们生产的。德国队实力非常强。但是我队的守门员比对方的更优秀。德国队的进攻来势汹汹。所以，在比赛的时候，他们的两个机器人经常追着球，这样他们的球门区就无人把守。反正我们赢了 5 次 ROBOCUP，我们还研发过这种自主机器人。

07:00—08:08

OK. And there's another one which is named Robi. Robi is a most successful humanoid robot as a business. It's a kid. I work with company DeAGOSTINI. And DeAGOSTINI is an Italian publisher. And they sell magazine with parts. And the customer has to assemble their own robot little by little. So it's a weekly magazine and every week customer got new parts and add to their own robot by one screwdriver. And little by little, customer can create own robot. This is an event done by hundred robots. Hundred robots dance and sing. And today I have Robi with me. And I will show it to you.

这个是我们的另一个作品，叫 Robi。从商业的角度看，Robi 是最成功的人形机器人，它就像一个孩子。我和意大利的一家出版公司 DeAGOSTINI 合作共同研发 Robi。他们出售的杂志里附送机器人的零部件，顾客要一点点地把零件拼起来。这是一本周刊，顾客每周都可以拿到新的零件，然后用螺丝刀把新零件装到他们的机器人上。就这样一点儿一点儿地拼起来，顾客就可以拼出自己的机器人。这是一次有上百个机器人参加的盛会，他们又唱又跳。今天，我把 Robi 带过来了，给大家看看。

08:08—08:39

So this is an actual robot. There are 20 motors inside. And also he has sensors and also voice recognition. And I turn him on. Robi, come here. Robi, come here.

这是一个真实的机器人，内置 20 个发动机，它还配有传感器及声音识别功能。我现在启动它：Robi，过来！Robi，过来！

08:54—08:55
Introduce yourself.
介绍一下你自己。

08:55—09:07
Robi：我叫Robi。我是由许多许多的零件组成的。我不但会说话，还会做很多事哦。
My name is Robi with many parts inside of me. I can not only speak but also finish many tasks.

09:07—09:24
Actually this robot is purchased in Shanghai and also some other Asian countries, Hong Kong (China), Taiwan (China), Singapore and also in Japan. And I'll ask him something. Come on. Let's dance.
事实上，在上海以及其他亚洲国家和地区，如中国香港、中国台湾、新加坡、日本都可以买到这个机器人。我现在让他做事：过来，我们跳支舞吧。

09:24—09:28
Robi：开始放音乐吧。
Music!

09:28—09:52
Music!
播放音乐。

09:52—09:55
Robi：唉，我累了。
Oh, I am tired.

09:56—10:18
So actually it's for hobby purpose. It's not practical at all. But the customer came, you know, experience of future, future which I've been talking with robot and actually robot can control some of the vacant devices in your house. And I'll ask one more thing for him. Do push-ups.
所以，这只是作为爱好收藏，不是实用型机器人。但是顾客来这儿体验未来，体验生活，与机器人聊天。而且，机器人可以操控您的房子中某些闲置设备。我再让他给大家表演一个，Robi，做俯卧撑。

10:18—10:46
Robi：我们一起做吧。开始咯。一，二，三，四，五，六。
Let's do it together. Ready? Go! One! Two! Three! Four! Five! Six!

10:46—11:37
So until now, you have to go to, for example, Samsung, to purchase robot like this. And then there are several robot shops. But the robot shop is one of my favorite place. But it's such a geeky place and I just can't go to robot shop with my girlfriend. So nobody, actually for ordinary people, it's too hard to purchase robot. And also robot is too expensive but when it comes a kit as a magazine, you can purchase one in the book store and each issue are quite cheap so that's why customer can try several issues and if it's too difficult, or too boring and then you can stop it. So that's why Robi becomes so successful.

直到现在，大家还要跑到三星一类的商店才能买到这种机器人。当然，也可以到其他机器人商店去购买。那是我最喜欢去的地方。但是，我没办法带上我女朋友一起去极客聚集的地方。所以普通人很难买到机器人。而且机器人卖的也很贵。但是如果把机器人的部件作为杂志的附赠品，大家就可以直接在书店购买，算起来每一个部件就非常便宜，这样顾客可以试着拼几个，如果顾客觉得太难或者太无聊的话，可以停下来不做。这就是Robi如此成功的原因。

11:37—12:24
Anyway, I get to move to next slide. So what is the role for humanoid robot? You know, human shape is not good at any physical task, unfortunately. So for cleaning up the floor, we are running that car type robot. They can do cleaning much better, compared to humanoid robot using human vacuum cleaner. But I think humanoid robots have human shape for communication and like this. So all the other physical tasks are done by other machines.

看看下一张幻灯片。那么人形机器人扮演着怎样的角色呢？很不幸的是人形机器人并不擅长任何体力工作。所以，我们采用车型机器人来完成像清洗地板这一类的工作。与使用日常吸尘器的人形机器人相比，车型机器人清洁工作做得更好。但我认为，人形机器人兼具人形，是为了进行沟通和其他类似功能。所以其他的体力活可以由其他机器去代劳。

12:24—14:36

But actually, we already have smartphones. You know, smartphone, you can do everything. You can control your TV set. You can control your home security device. And you can communicate with your friends. And you can control your, you know, home cleaning, floor cleaning robots. So that means there's no reason to have communication humanoid robot. But actually, smartphone itself is going down. And that's the biggest problem. You know, today, we have lots of great fixtures, but for most of ideas, interface is smartphone. But the smartphone is going down. Even you know, Samsung is losing money. And Apple, iPhone is not as, you know, innovative as it was before. So, what's the problem of smartphone? The smartphone is so successful because of touch screens and motion sensors. And also, they have one more thing, voice recognition. You know, voice recognition, for example, Siri, is now so smart. But we don't use Siri in our daily life. Why? You don't want to talk to your smartphone, but you can talk to your pet. Your dog can understand some words but, for example, your turtle or rabbit, or fish or even Teddy Bear, they can not understand any words. But still, we wanna talk to them. What's the difference? We don't wanna talk to square box like smartphone, but we can talk to other dumb creatures, which is we just can not feel any life inside of smartphone. So the square shape is a problem.

诚然，我们已经有了智能手机。大家都知道智能手机几乎无所不能。智能手机可以控制电视、家中的安全设备，还能和朋友联系。除此之外，还可以遥控机器人清洁家居和地板。这就意味着交际用的人形机器人没有存在的必要。但实际上，现在最大的问题是智能手机本身正在走下坡路。现在我们有很多出色的固定装置，然而大多数的理念都是基于智能手机的交互界面设计的。但智能手机却正在走下坡路，哪怕是三星公司也正在亏损，苹果公司的 iPhone 在创意方面也大不如从前。那么智能手机的问题在哪里呢？凭借着触屏和运动传感器，智能手机大获成功。除此之外，智能手机还有一道杀手锏——语音识别。Siri 就是智能语音识别的佼佼者。但我们在日常生活中不会使用 Siri，为什么呢？大家都不想和自己的智能手机聊天，但却愿意跟自己的宠物说话。您的宠物狗或许还可以听懂只言片语，但是像海龟、兔子、鱼甚至泰迪熊，它们根本听不懂您在说什么。尽管如此，我们还是愿意跟他们说话。那么跟宠物说话和跟手机说话有何不同呢？我们之所以不想跟智能手机这样的方正物体说话，却愿意跟其他同样不会说话的物体聊天，是因为智能手机没能让我们感觉在和生命体沟通。所以，方形的外形是个问题。

14:36—16:15

So, if we can use voice recognition much more, then the device can gather a lot more user data. And then the data can be used for service. And then when we got good service, we rely on the device. And then, we talk more, even more. So it's a good circle. So, that's why we have to combine smartphone and robot like Robi and become small enough to fit in your pocket, which is just like small little buddy. They can, you know, Jiminy Cricket, is helping Pinocchio in the story. Pinocchio is not smart, so Jiminy leaves him. You know, he helps Pinocchio find information. Jiminy Cricket itself is small and weak but he knows a lot more. He helps Pinocchio find information and similar story that is written in some Ghibli Anime and all the other different type of story from the ancient fairy tale to latest Japanese animation.

所以如果我们可以更广泛地应用语音识别技术，设备就可以收集到更多用户数据，然后这些数据就能用于服务。我们在享受更好的服务的同时也依赖于这种服务。这样一来我们和设备沟通的次数就会越来越多，这就形成一个良性循环。因此我们要把智能手机和 Robi 这样的机器人结合起来，机器人的体积还要小到可以装进大家的口袋，就像小伙伴那样。大家可以想象这种机器人就像《木偶奇遇记》里帮助匹诺曹的那只会说话的蟋蟀杰明尼那样。匹诺曹本身不够聪明，所以蟋蟀离开了他。杰明尼帮助匹诺曹寻找信息。虽然它很弱小，但学识渊博。它帮助匹诺曹寻找信息以及类似的故事还被写进了吉卜力动画，从古代童话到日本最新的动漫等各种故事。

16:15—17:55

So we somehow want to have a little buddy. And actually we have created a little buddy named RoBoHoN, the world's first robot smartphone. And he's in my bag. This is RoBoHoN. And behind there is a touch screen. It's actually Android-based smartphone. And it can be used as a, of course, telephone. You can put sim card in him. And he is small enough to fit in my pocket like Jiminy Cricket and (ringtone), I've got phone call. OK. Properly you can not understand how I can use it as a phone. This way. Hello. It looks a little bit strange but it's OK because I can not see myself. Anyway, come here.

所以我们也希望有这样的一个小伙伴。实际上我们已经创造了一个叫 RoBoHoN 的小伙伴，它是世界上第一款机器人智能手机。就在我包里。它就是 RoBoHonN，背后有一个触摸屏。它实际上是安卓系统的手机。只要您给他装上 sim 卡，他当然可以用来打电话。它小巧的身形就像匹诺曹的杰明尼蟋蟀，完全可以装进我的口袋。(铃声) 有电话进来。您可能不知道它怎么当手机用。是这样用的。您好！看起来有点奇怪，但确实可以用。我看不到我自己。RoBoHonN，先到这里来。

第十二单元 人工智能 Artificial Intelligence

18:12—18:13
Introduce yourself.
自我介绍一下。

18:15—18:24
RoBoHoN: Hi. I'm RoBoHoN. I know I don't look like one but I'm actually a mobile phone.
大家好,我是 RoBoHoN。我知道,我长得不像手机,但我的确是手机。

18:24—18:25
What can you do?
你可以做什么?

18:25—18:32
RoBoHoN: I'm small so you can carry me with you in your pocket or bag.
我小巧玲珑,方便大家随身携带。

18:33—18:35
Let's dance.
我们一起跳舞吧。

18:35—18:42
RoBoHoN: OK. Watch me dance. Look how good I am.
好,看我跳舞吧。看我跳得有多好。

18:42—19:00
Music
音乐声

19:00—19:56
So he is a smartphone but at the same time robot. And now we already have apps for calling taxi and restaurant recommendation, and the cooking tutor, and there are so many apps. So we want him to be the next generation platform. And he already knows my name, my face, my voice and where I live, where is my office, and my food preference and also my favorite actress. And also he has one of the key technologies on our smartphone is camera. And of course he has camera on his forehead. Take photo.

249

所以它既是手机，又是机器人。我们现在已经有各种叫车、推荐餐厅和教做菜的手机应用软件。我想要把它打造成下一代的平台。它知道我的名字、记住我的脸和声音、我的住址和办公地点。此外，它还了解我的饮食偏好还有我最喜欢的女演员，而且还具备我们智能手机其中一项关键技术，摄像头的功能。它的额头上就装有摄像头。RoBoHoN，给大家拍个照吧。

20:00—20:05
RoBoHoN: OK. Three, two, one, smile.
好的，三、二、一，茄子。

20:05—20:15
And now he took photo of me and you. And, projector.
刚刚它拍了一张我跟大家的合照。好，投影仪功能。

20:15—20:22
RoBoHoN: OK. I'm starting a projector. Please wait a moment.
好，正在打开投影仪，请大家耐心等待。

20:22—21:39
Actually he has projector on his forehead. Of course you can enjoy pictures on his small screen. But he can expand pictures, and for example, you know, he has a laser projector on his forehead. And in darker room, you can enjoy movie with your robot. So its focus is brilliant. I can even put on my shirt, you know. Anyway, so this is actually already a product in Japan. And he can be next communication platform. So there are three features of RoBoHoN. So RoBoHoN is small, and kind of slow so he just can't do any physical task, but it's OK. There are other services, other machines can work instead of him.

它的额头上还装有投影仪。当然，大家也可以在它的小屏幕上欣赏图片。其实它还可以放大照片，它额头上装有激光投影仪。您还可以和您的机器人一起在光线较暗的房间里看电影。这个机器人的拍照聚焦功能非常好，它甚至可以拍摄我穿衬衫的照片。这种产品已经在日本发售。它将成为下一代的沟通平台。RoBoHoN机器人有三大特性：体积小，动作慢，做不了体力活。但是这都不是事。其他的机器能够替它完成。

21:39—23:10
And secondly, he's a personal device. You might see lots of communication homes

robots. But they are staying in your home and sharing with your family members. Think about 20 years ago, in my family, we have desktop computer and I have had to share that one computer with my family members like my mom. Or we have big telephone, home telephone. And then we had to share one telephone with family members. So when I got phone call from my girlfriend, it's really, you know, annoying thing. Anyway, so we don't wanna go back to that age. We need our own robot, not sharing with our family members. So since RoBoHoN is a personal device, I can say anything. I can say even my private things. And also, as I mentioned, nobody wanna go to robot shop but you can purchase one in phone store and pay as a phone, and use it as a phone. And I hope people gradually understand the unique feature to be a robot. And that's a really important thing.

其次，它是您的个人设备。大家可能见过很多沟通型家用机器人，但这类机器人是"住"在您家里并且供一家人一起使用。大家可以回想一下 20 年前。我家里有一台台式电脑，我不得不和妈妈或其他人共用这台电脑。又比如说家里的固定电话也是要和家人共用。所以，我接到女朋友的电话时就非常麻烦。所以，我们都不想倒退回那个时代。我们需要属于自己的机器人，而不是和家里人共用一台。既然 RoBoHoN 是一台个人设备，我就可以畅所欲言，我甚至可以和它分享我的隐私。正如我前面提到的，没有人想去机器人商店，但大家可以通过手机商城来购买一台机器人，然后把它当手机一样支付和使用。我希望大家可以慢慢了解到机器人与众不同的特性，这一点非常重要。

23:10—25:39

So over 10 years ago, we are happy to have our cellphone, like Nokia phone. But suddenly, first generation iPhone came into our life. But actually first generation iPhone was not good enough. So we have to have both, Nokia and the first generation of iPhone, both. And then iPhone is gradually getting better and better, and then, we quit using Nokia and use only iPhone. That's where we are right now. So in probably next year, I believe RoBoHoN will be available in China too. And then you can purchase RoBoHoN with your smartphone. Unfortunately, RoBoHoN is not as sophisticated as your smartphone. So you have to carry both for a while. But then RoBoHoN becomes better and better, little by little, and then someday, you can quit using your smartphone. So I believe hardware platform is so important. There are so many smart AIs and so many great robots working in virtual world. But now we can have a hardware, a physical interface such as RoBoHoN. And I developed RoBoHoN with Sharp. And now Sharp is one of the group company of Hon Hai, Foxconn. And that's why I have lots of stronger connection with Chinese company and also Chinese consumers. And I wish in the near future, probably next year, RoBoHoN will be in your pocket, and RoBoHoN will be your important and friendly buddy. Thank you very much!

10年前，我们很高兴能有自己的手机，比如诺基亚手机。第一代苹果手机突然就进入了我们的生活。但实际上，第一代iPhone还有很多改进的空间。所以我们还不能完全摆脱诺基亚手机，我们既有诺基亚，又有第一代iPhone。之后iPhone变得越来越好，我们就不再使用诺基亚，只用iPhone。这也是我们的现状。也许明年RoBoHoN就能够在中国出售，你们在手机上就可以购买。遗憾的是，RoBoHoN目前功能还没有大家的手机完善，因此大家可能要暂时把两者混合使用。但是随着RoBoHoN功能不断完善，发展得越来越好，以后大家就可以把智能手机放在一边。所以，我认为硬件平台非常重要。很多人工智能和先进的机器人在虚拟的世界中发挥作用。现在我们有了像RoBOHoN这样的硬件和实体交互界面。我之前和夏普一起研发RoBoHoN，夏普公司现在是富士康集团旗下鸿海精密集团的一份子。因此，我和中国公司、中国消费者有着千丝万缕的联系。我希望在将来，也许是明年，RoBoHoN可以被大家放在口袋里随身携带。成为大家重要的好伙伴，谢谢大家！

II. 实战练习二

1. 演讲背景

尼尔森公司的代表应邀出席主题为"人工智能"的"腾讯智慧峰会"并发表主旨演讲。他在演讲中分享了尼尔森如何利用人工智能帮助营销人员提高营销效率。他认为营销人员的角色将逐渐变为消费者研究员，更加关注程序和灵活性，和实时数据的支持。尼尔森推出了市场营销云——快速集成应用程序，帮助营销人员规划、收集、分析数据，从而整体把握消费者行为，最后他还分享了营销云应用的两个具体例子，说明其可以帮助营销人员提高销售额。

2. 预习词汇

Tencent 腾讯
marketer 营销人员
AI/Artificial Intelligence 人工智能
Nielsen 尼尔森公司
real-time data 实时数据
platforming-gnostic 平台化的
share-gnostic 分享化的
content-gnostic 内容化的
linear sequential step 线性连续步骤

maze 迷宫
data set 数据集
consolidation 整合
application 应用程序
cloud 云
audience segment 细分受众群
resonance 反响
streamline 简化
big data 大数据
knowledge economy 知识经济
CPG/consumer packaged goods 快销品
variable 变量
return on investment 投资回报
ad exposure 广告曝光率

3. 演讲文本

00:00—00:27

Good afternoon. It's a real pleasure to be here. Thank you, Tencent, for inviting. Within the next ten to fifteen minutes, I'm going to lay the context for our final discussion, at the same time sharing with you unique approach to use AI-powered tools to help marketers become more effective at marketing.

下午好！很高兴来到这里。谢谢腾讯的邀请。在接下来的10～15分钟，我将为我们最后的讨论环节抛砖引玉，同时与大家分享使用人工智能驱动工具的独特方法，以帮助营销人员提高营销效率。

00:27—01:41

But before I do that, I come from Nielsen. And true to the nature of our business, we like to measure things. So let's do a quiz first. Please raise your hand if you think and if you are convinced, after a lot of presentations today, that the world of marketing has become more complex. Raise your hand if you think the world of marketing has become more complex. Raise your hand if you feel the world of marketing has become more complex. All right. So good job. You know, from all the presenters who did it today, most of you believe that. We at Nielsen believe that marketing today is at a critical stage in terms of where it is and where the world is. We believe that the role of marketers is going to evolve into becoming a consumer scientist, focused on procedure, activation and backed by real-time data insights.

在此之前，告诉大家我来自尼尔森。因为业务的性质，我们喜欢评估。所以我们先做一个测试。通过今天这些展示，如果您认为并且相信营销界变得更加复杂的请举手。好的，不错。您看，听了今天所有演讲嘉宾的展示之后，在座大多数人都相信这一点。我们尼尔森认为，现在的营销就其自身和世界而言，正处于一个关键阶段。我们相信营销人员的角色将逐渐变为消费者研究员，更加关注程序和灵活性，得到实时数据的支持。

01:41—03:03

There are a number of things that are happening in the marketing world that adding to this complexity. Let's take the consumer angle first. If you look at the two big trends in the consumer world, first, consumers today are platforming-gnostic, share-gnostic, content-gnostic, when it comes to consuming media. And the same consumers actually are buying in different ways. It causes different challenges. Talk of this. Sometime back, this is how the consumer purchase journey look like—a linear sequential steps starting from when a consumer becomes aware of a certain need, got exposed to an ad, and then ended up buying the product or buying more of the product. Fast forward today this is how it looks like, loops, complex interactions. I call it a crisscross maze of interactions and touch points. And what it does is a true challenge to marketers, where and how to influence consumers on this purchase journey, more importantly, which touch points are more important and which ones need to be focused more often.

营销界发生的很多事情都增加了这种复杂性。我们先来看看消费者的角度。看看消费者世界中的两大趋势，首先，在涉及到媒体消费时，当今的消费者是平台化、分享化和内容化的。同样的消费者实际上以不同的方式在消费。这会带来不同的挑战。说到这个，有时候这就是消费者购买过程——从消费者意识到某种需求开始，到接触到广告，到最终购买产品或购买更多产品，这是一个线性连续步骤。今天看起来它就像一个圈，是复杂的交互过程。我把它称为互动和接触点的交叉迷宫。而且对营销人员来说，如何影响消费者的消费，哪些接触点更重要，哪些接触点需要更频繁的关注，这是一大挑战。

03:03—04:37

And this is not the end of complexity. What brings it more complexity is that these interactions or these touch points are generating more data about consumers. Data, that means to be leveraged more effectively. And then this was not enough. We have further complexity in terms of marketers now facing the whole lot of solutions to manage their marketing data and processes. The whole technology world suddenly started focusing on marketing. And marketing is now, you know, embracing a lot of technology solutions.

Most of these solutions are based on targeting, or primarily centered on targeting. But majority of them are point solutions, which by definition means that they don't have the capability to give you a holistic view of a consumer's journey. So at Nielsen, we believe this whole complexity in terms of new data sets, changing consumer behavior, as well as marketing colliding with technology, has to lead to some form of consolidation. And we believe there is going to be an emerging set of integrated applications that are required that will be the holistic view of the consumers right from the time when they were exposed to their eye, to the time that they actually ended up buying the product.

而这并不是复杂性的终结。更复杂的是，这些互动或接触点正在产生更多关于消费者的数据。数据需要更有效的利用。这还不够。市场营销人员在管理营销数据和流程上面临众多解决方案，这样就更加复杂。整个技术世界突然开始关注营销。现在，市场营销正在采用许多技术解决方案。这些解决方案中的大多数都基于定位，或者主要集中在定位上。但其中大多数是点解决方案，意思就是无法让您全面了解消费者购买过程。因此，我们尼尔森认为，从新数据集，消费者行为改变以及市场与技术碰撞来看，整体复杂性会导致某种形式的整合。我们认为还会出现一套综合应用程序，这些应用程序将在消费者看到实际购买产品的过程中成为消费者的整体观点。

04:37—05:56

And to realize this vision, we recently launched Nielsen marketing cloud, which is a swift integrated application that come together and help marketers to plan, buy and analyze media, using different data sets, both Nielsen and outside. Essentially, this marketing cloud focus on three things. First plan, build detailed audience segments, create media plans targeted toward these audience segments, and then activated leveraging different market applications, using programmatic and other approaches across platforms. Evaluate, activating them, start analyzing them on a real-time basis. And evaluate the resonance and just streamline and become better at marketing. The goal here is to bring clients closer to consumers, to bring consumers, marketers and media all together, to assess what consumers bought, what they watched, how they interacted with, how they acted, how they reacted to a particular stimulus.

为了实现这一愿景，我们最近推出了尼尔森市场营销云，这是一个快速集成应用程序，它们汇集在一起，使用尼尔森或者是外部的不同数据集来帮助营销人员做计划，购买和分析媒体。本质上来说，这个营销云主要关注三件事情。第一，制定计划时建立详细的细分受众群，针对这些细分受众群创建媒体计划，然后激活不同的市场应用程序，利用的是跨平台的编程和其他方法。评估、激活，开始实时分析。对反响进行评估、简化流程，并在市场营销方面做得更好，目的是让客户更贴近消费者，将消费者、营销人员和媒体集中在一起，评估消费者购买的东西、关注的东西，评估他们在遇到特定刺激物时是怎样互动的，做了什么，有什么样的反应。

05:56—07:29

All of this, leveraging big data infrastructure. Here is our hoop. And the goal at the foundation of this marketing cloud is a number of data sets. We at Nielsen believe data is the new fuel of the knowledge economy. Data that is proprietary Nielsen data, other data that is owned by clients, data that is per body data. All these data comes together in a care-free, creative way and goes to the big data infrastructure. And then, clients start using different applications and start activating across channels, across platforms. And while they're activating it, there is a lot of data that has been collected at the activation points, which have got in-built in-flight analytics to measure what's the impact and then take active actions and calibrate. So think about the continuous flow of information going up, and then at the same time, real-time data flowing down, and then you're collecting and further collecting and becoming better and better. The beauty of this whole cloud is for every cycle, it becomes smarter, and it evolves; it becomes smarter, it evolves; becomes smarter, evolves; thereby providing marketers a holistic view of how they should plan in marketing efforts.

所有这些都利用了大数据基础架构。这是我们的环。这个营销云基础的目标是一些数据集。尼尔森认为数据是知识经济的新动力。数据是尼尔森专有的数据，客户拥有的其他数据，每个主体的数据。所有这些数据以自由、创造性的方式汇集在一起，并转向大数据基础架构。然后，客户开始使用不同的应用程序，并开始跨平台、跨渠道进行激活。在激活的同时，激活点收集了大量数据，数据点进行实时分析，评估影响，然后采取主动行动和校准。因此，信息持续向上流动，同时实时数据向下流动，您不断收集、持续收集，变得越来越好。整个云的美妙之处在于它的每一个周期都变得更加智能，不断进化，越来越智能，从而为营销人员提供整体性观点，指导他们规划营销工作。

07:29—08:41

Let me give you a couple of examples of marketing cloud in action. So here is the CPG haircare client. What we did, we listed different data sets in our marketing cloud and created a specific audience-based profile, focusing on key differentiating variables. Then we use the segment profile and leverage some of the applications in the marketing cloud to identify what specific channels, what specific areas deliver a better return on investment. And then based on that, we have the client to activate their media plan in terms of different channels and different platforms across mobile, display and video. And as a result of that, not only we became efficient in marketing spend, but also the clients got new insights into the shopper behavior that actually change the whole promotional strategy on shoppers. Further, they actually built new prospect target list and acquired samplers at scale and data, so cross channel, cross platform.

举几个营销云实例。假如说有一个快销品护发产品的客户。我们做的事情就是在营销云中列出了不同的数据集,并创建了一个特定的基于受众的配置文件,侧重于区分变量。然后我们使用细分市场资料和市场营销云中的一些应用程序来确定特定的渠道,确定哪些特定领域可以带来更好的投资回报。然后在此基础上,我们让客户激活他们的媒体计划,利用不同的渠道和移动、展示、视频等平台。这样我们不仅在营销支出方面变得高效,而且客户对顾客行为也有了新的见解。这实际上改变了整个促销策略。此外,他们还建立了真正的新的前景目标表,并且获取了相当规模的样本以及跨渠道、跨平台的数据。

08:41—09:33

Then we give another example from the automobile world. The challenge we got was how do you bring in and prove that there are some forms of action that have been done online and those campaign tactics actually drive offline sales. So leveraging by using marketing cloud, we collected in-market consideration data and then matched with the ad exposure, and then bring in a lot of creative versioning to help clients become better in terms of the creative version that they will show, and where they will show it and who they will show it to. And next, the result. Nine campaign tactics optimized in-flight. And see the results: best tactic is 2.9X, while the worst is 0.5X in terms of sales lift. Again, cross channel, cross platform.

再举一个汽车领域的例子。我们所面临的挑战是:开展多种线上活动能促进线下销售,我们如何引入这一策略?又如何证明?通过使用营销云,我们收集了市场内的对价数据,然后与广告曝光率进行匹配,进而引入大量的创意版本,以帮助客户在创意版本展示方式、展示地点以及展示受众方面做得更好。接下来就是结果。9种优化了的活动策略。看一下结果:最好的策略把销售额提升了2.9倍,最差的也有0.5倍。这些也都是跨渠道、跨平台的。

09:33—10:47

So at Nielsen, we believe that AI today and in the future, as it develops further, is going to further enhance and bring the swift applications in a much more creative way for marketers. We believe industry is going to some forms of consolidation and eventually you will have players who offer applications, applications that combine consumer data with media data, applications that provide a holistic view of consumers' journey right from the time when they got exposed to an ad to the time when they actually ended up buying the product or maybe even after that, and applications that constantly optimize your marketing effort to give you a better return on investment. All these applications will be leveraged by marketers to start doing one thing, that is connecting the dots, and actually start focusing on making decisions that directly impact the bottom line, so in other words, market more effectively.

因此,我们尼尔森认为,随着人工智能的进一步发展,它将进一步提升并为营销人员提供更具创造性的快速应用。我们相信行业正在进行某种形式的整合,最终会有提供应用程序的公司,这些应用程序将消费者数据与媒体数据结合在一起,从广告曝光到他们实际购买产品或者购买产品之后起,这些应用程序就可以全面了解消费者的购买过程,不断优化您的营销工作,使您获得更高的投资回报。所有这些应用程序都将被营销人员用来做一件事,那就是把各个点连接起来,并且专注于做出直接影响盈亏总额的决策,换句话说,就是更有效地进行市场营销。

10:47—11:11

There is an old saying in the market world, "What you can measure, you can manage." And ladies and gentleman, what I just shared is a way to effectively measure, manage and market effectively across channels, across platforms. Thank you very much! I'll be happy to take questions offline.

市场上有句老话:"您可以管理您可以评估的东西。"女士们,先生们,我刚刚分享的是如何进行跨平台、跨渠道地有效评估、管理和营销。谢谢大家!我很乐意在现场回答大家的问题。

参考文献

雷天放，陈菁. 口译教程［M］. 上海：上海外语教育出版社，2013.
任文. 英汉口译教程［M］. 北京：外语教学与研究出版社，2011.
王艳. 英语口译实务：二级［M］. 北京：外文出版社，2009.